Praise for *Death Is Our Business*

"Extraordinary. From civil wars in the Central African Republic to the battlefields of eastern Ukraine, *Death Is Our Business* provides a deeply researched account of how Yevgeny Prigozhin's Wagner mercenaries wreaked havoc on multiple continents, accumulating such influence—and such firepower—that they even threatened Vladimir Putin's hold on power. Essential reading for understanding Russia and modern warfare." —**Chris Miller,** *New York Times* **bestselling author of** *Chip War* **and** *Putinomics*

"John Lechner is an amazingly bold reporter who has been to the key places where the Wagner Group fought, interviewing members, veterans, and victims to deliver a shrewd, granular sense of how Russian mercenary forces operate." —**Adam Hochschild, bestselling author of** *King Leopold's Ghost*

"A meticulously researched account of Russia's arrival and expansion in Africa through the use of private mercenaries. A detailed and thorough study for any reader seeking to learn more about the recent history of operations and outlook for the future." —**Jessica Donati, author of** *Eagle Down*

"Unearths the brutal truths of the Wagner Group with unparalleled access and precision, exposing the shadowy fusion of profit, power, and violence driving Russia's global ambitions. A riveting and essential read." —**Eliot Higgins, founder of Bellingcat and author of** *We Are Bellingcat*

"Terrific! Taking us through a decade of the world's most intractable conflicts, *Death Is Our Business* is a front-row seat to the Kremlin's war against the West and an essential first look at the future of Great Power Competition." —**Admiral James Stavridis (ret.), PhD, former Supreme Allied Commander at NATO and coauthor of** *2034*

"In his gripping and fast-paced narrative, John Lechner traces the rise of the Wagner mercenary group and its mercurial leader, Yevgeny Prigozhin, whose private military company has extended Russia's reach into the far corners of the African continent. Prigozhin's attempted coup led to his demise, but Wagner lives on. A must-read for anyone seeking to understand the new realities of Russian warfare and the Kremlin's growing global influence." —Angela Stent, author *Putin's World*

"Lechner is one of the foremost experts on Russian warlord Yevgeny Prigozhin's goon army. It's no surprise then that his book gives us the best account yet of its rise and fall. It's a chilling dive into the future of conflict and a vital read for anyone wanting to understand Russia's brutal war strategy." —Christopher Miller, *Financial Times* chief Ukraine correspondent, author of *The War Came to Us*

"A gripping, unflinching, and deeply researched book. Lechner busts myths and exposes the even more incredible truths of the Wagner story." —Jade McGlynn, author of *Memory Makers*

"Whether chatting with Russian gunmen in dusty African warzones or decoding the splenetic social media posts of its founder, John Lechner has been tracking the Wagner mercenary army with daring and determination for years, and this excellent book is both first-rate journalism and a penetrating analysis of the Kremlin's use of deniable military force." —Mark Galeotti, author of *Forged in War*

"Wagner was an important part of Russia's military strategy in Ukraine, and foreign policy in the Middle East and Africa. *Death Is Our Business* is crucial to understanding Wagner's role, and how the Russian state uses these kinds of organizations." —Michael Kofman, Senior Fellow, Russia and Eurasia Program, Carnegie Endowment for International Peace

DEATH IS OUR BUSINESS

DEATH IS OUR BUSINESS

RUSSIAN MERCENARIES AND THE NEW ERA OF PRIVATE WARFARE

JOHN LECHNER

BLOOMSBURY PUBLISHING

NEW YORK · LONDON · OXFORD · NEW DELHI · SYDNEY

BLOOMSBURY PUBLISHING
Bloomsbury Publishing Inc.
1385 Broadway, New York, NY 10018, USA
50 Bedford Square, London, WC1B 3DP, UK
Bloomsbury Publishing Ireland Limited,
29 Earlsfort Terrace, Dublin 2, D02 AY28, Ireland

BLOOMSBURY, BLOOMSBURY PUBLISHING, and the Diana logo
are trademarks of Bloomsbury Publishing Plc

First published in the United States 2025

Maps by Gary Antonetti

Bloomsbury Publishing Plc does not have any control over, or responsibility for, any third-
party websites referred to or in this book. All internet addresses given in this book were
correct at the time of going to press. The author and publisher regret any inconvenience
caused if addresses have changed or sites have ceased to exist, but can accept no
responsibility for any such changes.

ISBN: HB: 978-1-63973-336-1; EBOOK: 978-1-63973-337-8

LIBRARY OF CONGRESS CATALOGING-IN-PUBLICATION DATA IS AVAILABLE

2 4 6 8 10 9 7 5 3 1

Typeset by Westchester Publishing Services
Printed and bound in the U.S.A.

To find out more about our authors and books visit www.bloomsbury.com
and sign up for our newsletters.

Bloomsbury books may be purchased for business or promotional use. For information on
bulk purchases please contact Macmillan Corporate and Premium Sales Department at
specialmarkets@macmillan.com.

For product safety–related questions contact productsafety@bloomsbury.com.

For Sothir

AUTHOR'S NOTE

Given the nature of events described in this book, a significant number of the people who shared their stories and experiences with the author have been anonymized. Anonymous sources will be introduced by one name in quotation marks (e.g., "Boyar"). Often, personal details have been changed to further protect their identity. Non-anonymous sources will be introduced by their first and last names without quotation.

In some instances, sources asked to write only their first name, callsign, or nickname. In these cases, they are introduced with one name not in quotations.

TABLE OF CONTENTS

INTRODUCTION

WACHTMEISTER: Das ist nur der Schein.
Die Truppen, die aus fremden Landen
Sich hier vor Pilsen zusammenfanden,
Die sollen wir gleich an uns locken
Mit gutem Schluck and guten Brocken,
Damit sie sich gleich zufrieden finden,
Und fester sich mit uns verbinden.

—FRIEDRICH SCHILLER, *WALLENSTEINS LAGER* (1798)

SERGEANT-MAJOR: That's just for show.
All these troops from foreign lands,
That have gathered here where Pilsen stands,
We have to win over behind our lines
With tasty titbits and tasty wines,
So that they think it was worth the journey
And pledge themselves to us more firmly.

—FRIEDRICH SCHILLER, *WALLENSTEIN'S CAMP* (1798)
(TRANSLATED BY F. J. LAMPORT)

Bogdan, like millions of Ukrainians, left his country years ago to find work. In early 2022, he was home visiting his wife and child, planning to fly back to Estonia on February 24. When the day arrived, the airport was closed. Russia's full-scale invasion of Ukraine had begun. Almost immediately, Bogdan's village, just outside of Konotop in Ukraine's northeastern Sumy province, was under occupation.

I met Bogdan about a year later, on a bench outside a cancer treatment facility in Kyiv. Spring was giving way to summer, when the scent of overgrown grass and hot pavement blend in the late afternoon. Bogdan is tall and lanky, the result of weight loss that renders his deep voice unexpected. His Slobozhan speech is an expressive mix of Ukrainian dialect and southern Russian. He hops from one to the other, fiddling with a metal brace screwed to his leg.

"The Russians came through—thousands of vehicles, even tanks," he told me, heaving the brace onto the bench. "But they didn't touch us. They just wanted to get to Konotop."

Once the Ukrainians liberated the village, Bogdan volunteered to fight. After training in western Ukraine, he was sent to Konstiantynivka, a small town just outside Bakhmut. The first battles were terrifying, cowering in some shallow hole, shooting in the enemy's direction until ordered otherwise. On October 23, Bogdan's platoon captured a field. The fighting was fierce, and ten of the platoon's fifteen soldiers were wounded.

"We were lying in the mud, cutoff for twenty-four hours. For people like me, shot in the legs, we tied tourniquets. For the ones hit in the neck." He paused. "Well, that was it."

A voice crackled over his radio: *We'll be there as soon as possible.* Shouts . . . direction unclear. Chaos.

When Bogdan got his bearings, he was sitting in a parking lot next to a crumbling gas station. A man walked up.

"Do you know where you are?"

"No," he said, eyes on the ground.

The man placed a finger under Bogdan's chin and lifted his head. "PMC Wagner."

They took him to the basement of an old furniture factory behind the Russian line. They'd set up a makeshift hospital, where, it turns out, the painkillers were pretty good. Too good. After two jabs, Bogdan didn't feel the beatings.

"They asked about positions, tanks. But I'm just an ordinary soldier. They didn't care and kept hitting me. And I didn't care because I was high. Sometimes they'd press a finger into my wounds, and I'd jump off the chair and belt out the national anthem."

When they were done, the men led him deeper into the basement. Peeking from under the blindfold, Bogdan saw hundreds of computers—a command center. They threw him in an empty room.

At some point another guy, real professional-looking, entered. He took off the blindfold.

"His eyes," Bogdan recalled. "Dark, pitch-black. I think I'll never forget them."

"You're getting a tattoo," the man said.

"How about a portrait of Putin?" a sidekick mused.

"Screw that," replied another, turning to Bogdan. "We don't think Putin's some great leader. At least not good enough for a tattoo."

They chose "I love PMC Wagner" instead, inking it in large letters across Bogdan's chest.

"You know, it's funny," Bogdan told me, his face losing contour in the fading light. "One would insult you, another come by just to chat."

Some Wagner mercenaries told Bogdan they don't fight for anything, just each other. Another, a nationalist, said he was from Kievan Rus (Kyivan Rus in Ukrainian), a medieval East Slavic polity claimed by Ukrainians and Russians. Yet another said he was pissed when Ukrainians knocked down statues of Lenin, the Soviet leader Russian nationalists blame for what they believe to be the two countries' artificial division. All the while, Bogdan nodded his head, hoping he would live.

Other Wagnerites bragged that Ukrainian volunteers like him were no problem. "We're mercenaries, not *zeky*," they said, referring to the thousands of convicts Wagner recruited to the front lines.

After the tattoo, Bogdan spent months in the hospital waiting for a prisoner exchange. One day, two burly, bearded men tossed fatigues onto his bed. He couldn't walk, so they loaded him into a truck. On the bumpy road to Bakhmut, one Wagnerite stared at Bogdan.

"You know, we'd never be taken alive. I'd pull a grenade before they could get me."

"OK."

Bogdan and I made our way inside, where the vernal hum of mosquitoes dissolved into the creaky rhythm of crutches on loose tile. We wound our way through corridors until we found his room, coated in warm pink.

"I know I only fought six months. But I think I can say I was in the war."

"I think you can say that."

Crawling into one of the beds, he recalled: "They'd ask all the time: Do you know who we are? We're Wagner. For them, it's something godlike. Something divine."

★ ★ ★

After a brief two-hundred-year hiatus, private warfare is back, albeit in new ways. The return comes, in part, because nation-states and their public standing armies are relatively new in the *longue durée*. This is not to detract from the nation-state's impact. The past two centuries witnessed its values and attributes permeate all aspects of society, such that it is taken for granted worldwide that states, not individuals, *should* field armies. For most of history, however, private armies and mercenaries were the norm—"an honest, albeit bloody trade." Such was mercenaries' ubiquity that toward the end of the seventeenth century's Thirty Years' War, European powers faced a mercenary crisis. The Swedes, wrote C. V. Wedgwood, "had to demobilize nearly a hundred thousand men, of whom the most part were Germans without other hope for the future save that which the career of a soldier had offered them." The Peace of Westphalia eventually ended the Thirty Years' War and introduced norms still held dear in international relations: State borders should, theoretically at least, be inviolable. Nor should states interfere in each other's domestic affairs. In the slow march to the nation-state that followed, European rulers came to see advantage in recruiting public standing armies from within their borders. A century and a half later, when Friedrich Schiller finished *Wallenstein*, his trilogy of plays on the Thirty Years' War, mercenaries had become more a subject of fascination than terror.

States with capitalist, commercial cities and access to rural populations were best positioned to field standing armies. Rulers seized "the means of war from others who held the essential resources—men, arms, supplies, or money to buy them—and who were reluctant to surrender them," leading to a centralization that differed from empires, pirate leagues, warrior bands, federations of city-states, and other early state-like structures. "War made the state, and the state made war," wrote Charles Tilly in his famous study on the development of European nation-states.

By the nineteenth century, the nation-state was largely responsible for the prosecution of warfare on the continent. But private warfare hardly disappeared. It thrived, in fact, when European powers competed to carve up the world. In practice, colonial empires were brutal engines for extraction. Empire, however, was always framed in humanitarian, civilizing terms, which meant Europe's own poor and middle-class citizens could be quite sensitive to government expenditure on far-flung regions. Development had to pay for itself. To help manage costs, colonial powers at different points in time outsourced much of the administration and exploitation of their colonies to private European companies. Once in Africa, these private companies, in turn, outsourced the collection of taxes, the capture of men for forced labor, and security to local power brokers. Such structures of governance—centralized bureaucratic administrations in the capital that periodically, though often violently, enforced their rule in the countryside—endured after independence. Local power brokers continued to leverage former colonial powers to serve their interests, and vice versa.

During the Cold War, leaders of postcolonial states became experts in pitting America and the USSR against each other to attract concessions and resources. Governments in what was then called the "Third

World" nimbly navigated a constrained environment by framing their struggles in capitalist versus communist terms. One could say the Cold War itself was a product of decolonization.

The late 1980s saw a sharp decline in financial and military support from both superpowers. The Soviet Union turned to internal reform, while Cold War leaders like U.S. president Ronald Reagan and British prime minister Margaret Thatcher proselytized small government as the path to global prosperity. Reagan and Thatcher's teleological narrative of progress found its footing in the "Washington Consensus": deregulation and privatization. The Washington Consensus became doctrine among donors like the World Bank and the International Monetary Fund (IMF), which imposed austerity measures in response to debt crises in the developing world. African governments reined in public spending and, in some instances, outsourced security to nonstate actors in ways that benefited their regimes. In one such case, Sudan's leader, Brigadier General Omar al-Bashir, "privatized much of the state, selling it off on the cheap to his cronies in the security organs, while withdrawing services from the country's peripheries." Bashir privatized Sudan's civil war too, hiring ethnic militias to do the fighting for the government. These forces secured control of Sudan's oil fields for the state and enriched themselves through the proceeds of predation, dispossession, and looting.

Other African governments outsourced security to humanitarian interventions—United Nations peacekeeping missions in particular—and began hiring private military companies, or PMCs, too. The South African Eeben Barlow was the first to recognize this opportunity and founded Executive Outcomes in 1989. For Barlow, the emerging demand for security coincided perfectly with a surge of retired, experienced, white South African soldiers. Barlow offered to do what "blue helmets," or United Nations peacekeepers, could not. Executive Outcomes found success on the battlefields of Angola and Sierra Leone, but their product was too early to market. Journalists and advocates were uncomfortable with Barlow's ties to mining companies looking to exploit liberated territory and his PMC's links to the apartheid government.

Discomfort with PMCs wouldn't last long. The September 11, 2001, attacks on the World Trade Center and resulting War on Terror thrust America's privatization of warfare into overdrive. The new enemy, according to Defense Secretary Donald Rumsfeld, would require a small footprint. "We must promote a more entrepreneurial approach," Rumsfeld wrote in 2002. "One that encourages people to be proactive, not reactive, and to behave less like bureaucrats and more like venture capitalists." The neoliberal doctrine and the Washington Consensus reached its zenith: By 2010, private contractors exceeded U.S. troops in Iraq and Afghanistan. And the most famous firm to emerge from Bush-era privatization was Blackwater.

Erik Prince's enterprise started out as a security firm providing space for military and law enforcement to train, then went into protection services for American occupation officials in Iraq. Like Executive Outcomes before it, Blackwater largely recruited veterans from the military, including special forces, though they also recruited soldiers from Latin America. At the executive level, the firm hired top government officials to leverage their networks for future contracts, and the company always framed its services as part of the U.S. military's "Total Force." Without hundreds of thousands of private contractors employed by firms like Blackwater, the War on Terror, as it had been fought and planned, would have required a civilian draft. To detractors, private contractors made it far easier for U.S. administrations to go to war without the "sufficient backing and involvement of the nation." The U.S. military is not obligated to report deaths of contractors; in Afghanistan, where more civilian contractors were killed than U.S. troops, the political costs of war were kept, for a long time, artificially low.

In his 2014 book *The Modern Mercenary*, Sean McFate divided PMCs into two types: mercenary companies and military enterprisers. Mercenary companies, like Executive Outcomes, are private armies that "conduct autonomous military campaigns." Military enterprisers, such as Blackwater, "augment a powerful state's" regular armed forces and embed with one government. McFate believed these two PMC types could merge into a new category, and PMCs would have to differentiate themselves by offering "combat-oriented services" and paying less attention to human rights. As it turned out, that same year one man would play an immeasurable role in creating this novel PMC.

Yevgeny Viktorovich Prigozhin's facial features rested in a natural scowl. He had, by all accounts, a penetrating gaze. "I felt," said one woman who worked for him, "that he could see right through me." His aura, she believed, was that of a living historical figure, someone who pulsated some grand, obscure fate. A polished dome complimented Yevgeny Viktorovich's sharp visage, evoking a Bond villain. And like any good antihero, his origins, and his path to success and fame, were anything but ordinary.

In his youth, Prigozhin spent nine years in prison for robbery and fraud. After his release, he claimed he sold hot dogs until he had enough money and connections to enter the restaurant business. In 1997, he and a partner opened a restaurant in St. Petersburg that one client in particular, Vladimir Putin, came to enjoy. That special relationship launched the restaurateur into the lucrative world of government contracting. Prigozhin's companies provided Russian schools and the army with meals, earning him the nickname "Putin's Chef."

In 2014, Prigozhin became a purveyor of both meals and men. On the heels of Moscow's invasion of Crimea, the Ministry of Defense (MoD) was sponsoring small bands of mercenaries and volunteers to fight in eastern Ukraine on behalf of the Luhansk People's Republic (LNR), which had declared itself independent. Prigozhin wanted in and linked up with Dmitry Utkin, a career soldier with the call sign "Wagner," a name that would eventually become a catchall term for the companies and entities connected to both men. To insiders, Wagner Group was simply "the Company."

Prigozhin's men proved themselves an effective fighting force on the front, and brutal enforcers in the rear. The Company grew with Russia's increasing assertiveness abroad and Prigozhin's constant lobbying. Starting in 2015, contractors worked closely with the Ministry of Defense in

Syria. Wagner forces helped take Palmyra from the Islamic State, only for the generals in the MoD to claim credit for the victory and unceremoniously pull them out of the campaign. A year later, Wagner-affiliated mining companies and "security types" were arriving in Africa, a continent largely free from the bitter infighting and rivalry inherent to Russia's competing security institutions.

It was only in 2018, however, that Prigozhin started making a name for himself. "Putin's Chef" was known back home mostly for poisoning school children and soldiers with his food. His infamy went international when he took on the world's sole superpower on multiple fronts. In February, Prigozhin ordered his mercenaries to attack the Conoco gas plant in Khasham, where U.S. special forces and their Syrian partners were embedded. A four-hour battle ensued between Russian and American citizens that, at its worst, could have "plunge[d] both countries into bloody conflict."

After that it seemed like Wagner was everywhere. Prigozhin's political operatives were found funding candidates in Madagascar's presidential election, while Wagner soldiers were fighting a jihadist insurgency in northern Mozambique. Journalists began searching for signs of shadowy Russian "influence" in Africa and even Latin America. U.S. and European governments took notice. A new Cold War was emerging, and Wagner was the tip of Russia's spear. The U.S. Department of State called the mercenary group a state-backed organization that "exploits insecurity to expand its presence in Africa, threatening stability, good governance, and respect for human rights." The former commander of U.S. Special Operations Command Africa, Major General Marcus Hicks declared, "Like it or not, a twenty-first century 'scramble for Africa' is underway."

In 2021, the Malian military carried out its second coup in as many years, and tensions erupted between the West African regime and France, whose forces were on the ground as part of a counterterrorism operation. The French government threatened to depart and Prigozhin's men stepped in, offering not only to defeat the jihadists but to free Mali and the rest of Africa from the grip of Western neocolonialism. Amid his troop's withdrawal, French president Emmanuel Macron accused Wagner of "taking resources that should belong to [the people]" and of "awful abuses against the civilian population." A month after his condemnation, Wagner operatives crossed, again, into Ukrainian territory.

By late March 2022, the Russian military had failed to make significant headway in Ukraine. Russian military planners were one month into what they assumed would be a three-day special operation to topple the government in Kyiv. The Ministry of Defense needed Wagner's experienced fighters, and they needed Wagner's brand to recruit more men. Billboards popped up in Russian cities; "The 'W' Orchestra Awaits You" signs read, tapping into masculine ideals and mercenary tropes. Meanwhile, on the front lines, the fighting was fierce. Prigozhin lost some of his best men in Popasna, but he delivered Putin a victory and more territory. By early August 2022, Wagner reached the outskirts of Bakhmut. Prigozhin, now a "Hero of Russia," vowed to take it. Convicts he'd recruited, illegally, from Russian prisons flooded the front lines, and Bakhmut became the barometer for either country's success, or failure, in the war.

The world's attention, combined with an already-fiery ego, proved an unstable, explosive mix for Wagner's boss. Wagner had begun as a state project, yet over time Prigozhin forged his own path, especially in Africa. That freedom, though, was also the product of Africa's relative lack of importance to the Kremlin. When he returned to Ukraine years later, things were different. Here, Putin's inner circle was in charge. And they were no fans of the Bakhmut celebrity, especially the populist, tell-it-like-it-is personality he cultivated on social media. So Prigozhin set his sights on them. Baptized in blood, his men resurfaced as the true patriots of Russia, ready to cleanse the Kremlin of its lecherous bureaucrats.

On Saturday, June 24, 2023, the world's most famous mercenary force mutinied—speeding toward the capital unimpeded. Authorities declared a counterterror regime, roadworkers tore up Moscow's main highways. The elite in Moscow scurried from view, while images of an unfazed

babushka, stubbornly sweeping the sidewalk around tense, armed mutineers, went viral on social media.

Bogdan was home in Ukraine at the time, watching on Facebook as
the Wagner column advanced on Moscow.

"Honestly, I wanted them to get to Moscow," he told me over the
phone. "The more they fight with each other, the better for us."

For a brief twenty-four hours, the world watched as a convoy of mercenaries, long assumed to be the shadowy arm of a global nuclear force,
seemed poised to overthrow it.

Experts have scoured history to find precedents—from Frederick the
Great's eighteenth-century Freikorps to the ronin of feudal Japan—to
explain how Wagner Group burst onto the world stage. Most analyze
the history of Wagner through a "statist" lens, which suggests that
Prigozhin's band of mercenaries was simply an arm of the Kremlin, a
tool for expanding Russian influence abroad. Under this logic, the Kremlin's decision to employ private actors in the pursuit of "national interests" was risky. Did Machiavelli not write five hundred years earlier that
"mercenaries and auxiliaries are useless and dangerous. If a prince bases
the defense of his state on mercenaries he will never achieve stability and
security"? A quick perusal of European history would show Wagner's
mutiny perhaps inevitable, the result of the state's inability, as Schiller
wrote, to provide enough tasty titbits and wines for its mercenaries.

In most of the world, however, the relationship between states and
corporations is more fluid than meets the eye. America's national security relies on private enterprise. Many companies solely contract with
the U.S. government, and their employees spend parts of their careers in
both the public and private sectors: what many disparagingly call the
"revolving door." Public-private boundaries are perhaps even more
blurred, in practice, in the former Soviet Union. In the delirium of Soviet
collapse, wrote Georgi M. Derluguian, "actors could no longer securely
predict the consequences of their own decisions." While employees of
the state and corporations undoubtedly perceive themselves as belong-

ing to discreet categories, Douglas Rogers adds that "shifting networks, connections, teams, alliances, clans, friendships, [. . .] and more [lie] just beneath the abstracted labels of 'corporation' and 'state.'" In other words, in navigating the renegotiation of the entire socialist system, Russian businessmen and government employees leveraged personal relationships that frequently crossed private and public spheres.

Prigozhin was a natural networker. But his road to success was very different from Russia's richest men, who became billionaires through the privatization of state assets. They belonged to a group of elite that political analyst Tatiana Stanovaya calls "Putin's Friends and Associates," men who were by Putin's side from the beginning. They hold a different position to the "political technocrats," who earned Putin's trust though effective management, and distinct from regime "protectors," like former FSB* head Nikolai Patrushev, who manage the state's repressive intelligence agencies. Prigozhin had risen into yet another category: the "implementers," who "do not hold any particular personal value for Putin," yet their "position is fairly secure as long as they do not make big mistakes." These men, with assets mostly concentrated in Russia, do not have the same international exposure as energy barons. They can gain the Kremlin's favor through patriotic projects while staying relatively insulated from Western sanctions. And while they were not always profitable, such projects could ensure the continued flow of government contracts.

In the Putin system, Russian elite enjoy outsized freedom to lobby for and pursue lucrative policies they can frame within Russia's "national interests." Prigozhin had a unique talent for selling what Russia's national interests were, and how Wagner fit in.

It is important, then, to view Wagner as a unique sociological phenomenon, that could manifest only at a particular time and place. The

---

* The Federal Security Service (FSB) is Russia's primary successor to the Soviet Union's KGB. The FSB's responsibilities include domestic surveillance, counterintelligence, counterterrorism, border security, among others.

PMC's adventures abroad were, in many respects, a by-product of one man's tireless drive to overcome his station in Putin's Russia. Prigozhin enjoyed riches far beyond those of an ordinary Russian, but Putin's inner circle was far richer and rarely had to answer for their mistakes. They had little interest in admitting an uncouth ex-convict into their club.

But Wagner and its new manifestations are the product, too, of structural forces shaping our violent century. Domestic struggles over power, resources, and identity tend to spark conflict. Yet as countries descend into war, belligerents advertise their cause within larger threat narratives to attract political, financial, and material support from outside powers. Great and regional powers reify these narratives when they back local actors with aligned ambitions. During the War on Terror, for example, many autocratic governments positioned themselves as "bulwarks" against radical Islam and received from the West weapons, equipment, and a reprieve from criticism on human rights issues. Their behavior differed little from militantly anti-communist autocrats (or Soviet-backed communist regimes) a few decades prior. Today, we are in a new Cold War, taking the form of "Great Power Competition," and countries are repositioning themselves yet again to balance, and profit from, tensions among the U.S., Russia, and China.

Prigozhin was only one of many to make riches from our more dangerous, polarized world. As colleagues would attest, Wagner's boss was rarely the smartest guy in the room. What he was good at was recognizing opportunity in instability and bringing a team together to take advantage.

The more I traveled the world covering Prigozhin's operations and the more I spoke with those involved, the degree to which Wagner achieved its goals felt increasingly irrelevant. More important than Wagner's wins on the ground was the perception of its success. The dozens of Wagner mercenaries and associates I spoke with firmly believe they increased their country's stake in the world order. And with a little help from Wagner, the West, too, convinced itself that Russia was back, a great power ready to take on U.S. hegemony. The U.S., in turn, benefited from a revitalized rival, requiring a more aggressive foreign policy to protect its interests and values. Prigozhin met his end, but Wagner Group lives on in official and semi-official operations, showing the strength of its product-market fit. Entrepreneurs the world over have taken note, crafting new services they can sell to states looking for a toehold in geopolitical hot spots.

Wagner's rise was the symptom, not the cause, of a world increasingly at war, in which over one hundred million people are now displaced. Still, the PMC helped usher us into the seventeenth century with twenty-first-century technology—onto a battlefield in which the distinction between soldier and mercenary is close to immaterial. This is the dark underbelly of globalization: The planes, ports, and supply chains that deliver packages to us the same day also make it possible, and cheap, to ship unemployed young men, who have only seen war and whose only skill is to bear arms, from one hell to another. The supply, and the demand, only grow.

I

Soldiers

Ті, хто бачив хоч раз нашу країну, кажуть, що хотіли б жити й
померти на її чудових полях.

—Тарас Шевченко (1844)

And those who have seen our country just once say they'd like to live and die
in her lovely fields.

—Taras Shevchenko (1844)

On July 14, 2006, Air Force One, carrying President George W. Bush and First Lady Laura Bush, touched down in St. Petersburg, Russia. President Bush was there to attend the Group of Eight (G8) summit, a forum for the eight "highly industrialized nations"—France, Germany, Italy, the United Kingdom, Japan, the United States, Canada, and Russia—to foster consensus on global issues. Russia was the latest country to join the forum, becoming a member in 1998 under Russian president Boris Yeltsin. Eight years later, his successor, President Vladimir Putin, was about to host the summit for the first time.

After disembarking, the two Bushes followed a Russian honor guard to lay a wreath at the Monument to the Heroic Defenders of Leningrad. The 160-foot-tall ruddy obelisk on Victory Square was dedicated to the residents of St. Petersburg, then Leningrad, who had survived and repelled Nazi Germany's nine-hundred-day siege of the city. The German blockade killed nearly 650,000 of Leningrad's citizens, mostly from disease and starvation, including Putin's older brother Viktor. At the conclusion of the brief ceremony—a tribute to the Soviet Union and America's previous alliance against Nazi Germany in World War II, and Soviet sacrifice in what they called the "Great Patriotic War"—the couple split: the First Lady to visit a pediatric center for HIV/AIDS; the president to meet with members of Russian civil society. They met again in the early evening to join President Putin and his then-wife, Lyudmila, for a social dinner at the Konstantinovsky Palace.

St. Petersburg is famous for its summer "white nights," when the sun never truly sets below the horizon and instead coats the city's canals and bridges in a patina of dusk. Putin showed Bush his first ever car, a white Zaporozhets, and after sufficient admiration, the presidents and their respective wives sat down for dinner in the palace. Both men stuck to button-downs. Their casual style and the sleek, modernist decor of the room clashed with that of their attendants, who fluttered around them in comically oversized, light blue three-piece suits, matching bow ties, and white gloves, lending an air of prom night to the head-of-state affair. Leading the troupe, and serving Bush personally, was an attentive bald man in a jet-black suit and silver tie. The menu he crafted for the evening featured Astrakhan tomatoes in balsamic vinegar, crayfish with gooseberry marmalade, and fried smelt with turnips and baby zucchini. Bush ordered a steak.

If the president were paying closer attention to his server, he may have recognized Yevgeny Prigozhin from four years earlier, when he had dined with the Russian president on St. Petersburg's Neva River. Then, too, the menu catered more to the palate of Russia's nouveaux riches, not Texas cowboys: there were pricey morsels like duck liver pâté and gingerbread, served with prunes and aged-port caramel; black caviar on ice; fried fillet of beef with black truffles, accompanied by fresh morels and baby carrots boiled in a rowan broth; and a raspberry mille-feuille for dessert. Whether Bush tried all four courses in 2002, or just the steak, remains a mystery. Regardless, there were more important issues on the president's plate that evening.

In the last gasp of the Soviet era, NATO* member West Germany made Mikhail Gorbachev an offer he couldn't refuse: extensive financial packages in exchange for reunification with East Germany. Both President George H. W. Bush and German chancellor Helmut Kohl presciently believed it was critical to lock in Cold War victories before a potential Soviet hard-liner coup. When the putsch did come in August 1991 it was, to the relief of both leaders, half-hearted and disorganized. The plotters managed to detain Gorbachev in Crimea, but they failed to capture Boris Yeltsin, a populist politician willing to hasten the Soviet Union's collapse to break out from under his former ally's thumb. In December 1991, Yeltsin, together with the leaders of Ukraine and Belarus, signed the Belovezha Accords, dissolving the Soviet Union.

Like his predecessor, Yeltsin relied on Europe and the U.S. for political legitimacy and financial assistance while his team implemented "shock therapy" to transition to a market economy. The administration of President Bill Clinton and Chancellor Kohl, who continued to provide vast sums to facilitate the withdrawal of troops from the east, backed Yeltsin in 1993 when he dissolved, then had tanks fire on, the Russian parliament. Western leaders were willing to stomach such moves: They feared popular nationalist and communist opposition to Yeltsin's rule and needed the Russian president's support on combating nuclear proliferation. The violent dissolution of socialist Yugoslavia in 1991 and the conflict that

---

* The North Atlantic Treaty Organization (NATO) was founded in 1949 as an alliance between the United States and eleven other countries. Its purpose was to counter Soviet expansion in Europe and prevent the revival of nationalist militarism on the continent. In 1955, after West Germany joined NATO, the Soviet Union and its satellite states, including East Germany, formed the Warsaw Pact.

followed led to fears that wars between former Soviet states over new international borders might go nuclear.

Yeltsin's ill-fated, brutal invasion of separatist Chechnya seemed to confirm his country's willingness to fight over borders. Understandably wary former Warsaw Pact states, especially Poland, Hungary, and the Czech Republic, pushed to join NATO. Their lobbying efforts, Clinton's need for American voters of Eastern European descent in midterm elections, and strong backing for NATO expansion from powerful individuals in the State Department and National Security Council all shaped the discourse over NATO enlargement, which shifted from a question of whether to "when."

Still, Clinton knew NATO expansion would weaken Yeltsin's standing and fan the flames of opposition to the Russian's presidency. To shore up Yeltsin's chances of reelection in 1996, Clinton pressured the International Monetary Fund to loan the Russian government billions of dollars and held off any announcement regarding NATO enlargement. Yeltsin's victory over his communist opponent in presidential elections cleared the way for Poland, Hungary, and the Czech Republic to join NATO.

As a consolation, Yeltsin was invited to join the G8 and sign a carefully noncommittal "Founding Act on Mutual Relations, Cooperation and Security between NATO and the Russian Federation." But NATO left the door open to the accession of more states as well, including former Soviet republics.

To stave off claims of weakness, Yeltsin sought to flex Russia's diplomatic muscles in Europe's other tumultuous region: the Balkans. The war in Bosnia between Serbian, Croatian, and Muslim forces "prompted fervent debate [in Russia] about the country's path after the collapse of empire, its relationship with the West and its place in the post–Cold War order." Yeltsin was no fan of the Serbian leader Slobodan Milošević's jingoistic ethnonationalism, but Belgrade had found allies among Russian nationalists, who believed in Russian-Serbian mutual aid grounded in Orthodoxy, and communists, who sympathized with

socialist Yugoslavia's disintegration. Prominent figures began paying
highly publicized visits to the region. In one instance, author and leader
of the National Bolsheviks, Eduard Limonov, was filmed firing on a
besieged Sarajevo. Yeltsin's team had to walk a tight rope between these
groups and allies abroad. They opted to emphasize that Russia is a great
power that should be included in any resolution to the conflict, positioning Moscow as a bridge between the West and Serbia.

War in the Balkans also helped solve a major existential crisis for
NATO. Soviet collapse, the end of the Warsaw Pact, and a Western-
leaning man in the Kremlin all called into question the alliance's
future purpose. Many in Europe called for NATO's disbandment.
For the United States, disbandment meant removing military bases
and nuclear weapons from Western Europe. In Bosnia, however,
NATO could pivot from a defensive alliance to a force for humanitarian intervention.

Rump Russia was hardly able to compete with the alliance of Cold
War victors. Yeltsin's limited influence over Milošević and Bosnian Serbs
only further exposed Moscow's weakness on the world stage. Nonetheless,
diplomats did manage to attain co-leadership of the peacekeeping Implementation Force (IFOR) following the Dayton Peace Accords in 1995.
IFOR was a surprising example of Russian-NATO cooperation on the
ground, but the Russians were still clearly the junior partner.

Relations worsened when the Albanian Kosovo Liberation Army
(KLA) launched a military campaign for an independent Kosovo. Despite
its Albanian majority, Serbs considered Kosovo the cultural heart of
Serbdom. Milošević sent Serbian military and paramilitary forces to put
down the KLA, resulting in widespread human rights abuses. Clinton
concluded that Milošević needed to be punished for his "systematic
campaign of violence." When Milošević refused to back down, NATO
launched a bombing campaign without United Nations Security Council
(i.e., Russian) approval.

Moscow's security elites began to wonder: If the West was using force
to prevent Milošević from retaining Serbia's inextricable, albeit volatile,

cultural heartland, what would stop it from supporting Russia's own separatist movements like Chechnya in the future? Moreover, Russia would once again be a junior partner in a future peace agreement on Kosovo. As a show of force, a contingent of Russians sprinted from Bosnia to Kosovo's capital, Pristina, to seize the airport and ensure a stake in the negotiations.

Six months later, Yeltsin resigned and handed the reins of power to the relatively unknown Vladimir Putin.

Putin gave Western leaders the impression that he was "genuinely interested in developing a more productive relationship [. . .] after the 1999 Kosovo campaign." The Russian president even raised the possibility, like his predecessor, of joining NATO. There still were optimists in both the U.S. government and NATO who believed that Russian membership was possible. In June 2001, Bush told reporters he had looked Putin in the eye and gotten a "sense of his soul." Three months after that famous line, Osama bin Laden's al-Qaeda network attacked the World Trade Center and the Pentagon. President Putin was the first world leader to call Bush to offer his condolences. He followed up with assistance for the U.S. campaign in Afghanistan and "acquiesced" to U.S. military bases in Central Asia.

In the lead-up to the 2003 U.S. invasion of Iraq, the Bush administration thought, wrongly, that Russia was on its side, that any objections to overthrowing Saddam Hussein were simply economic. Russia, the historian Angela Stent noted, indeed had a "deep and complex" relationship with Iraq that included oil and arms deals. But weeks before the war, Putin sent Alexander Voloshin, head of the presidential administration, to Washington to explain Russia was more worried that the invasion "could fuel extremism and terrorism." The United States nonetheless launched its invasion, under the auspice of promoting democracy, without the consent of the UN Security Council.

That same year, a Western-leaning politician from the Republic of Georgia, Mikheil Saakashvili, came to power in the Rose Revolution. The revolution reflected Georgians' desire for less corruption, economic well-being, and choice of leadership. But the Bush administration's embrace of Saakashvili created discomfort among many Russian officials, who feared a thin line between America's military effort to promote democracy in Iraq and the support of democracy in Russia's "near abroad."

Putin's foreign policy suffered further in 2004, when Ukrainian president Leonid Kuchma tried and failed to hand his office over to his ally and Moscow's preferred candidate, Viktor Yanukovych, the governor of Donetsk Oblast. Weeks before the election, Yanukovych's popular rival, Viktor Yushchenko, almost died, very conveniently, from a poisoning attempt. Yushchenko miraculously recovered and when initial results declared Yanukovych the victor, Ukrainians flooded the streets wearing orange—the color of Yushchenko's campaign—to protest the results. People power worked, and Yanukovych and Yushchenko agreed to a runoff, which Yushchenko won. Putin was forced to begrudgingly accept the outcome of the Orange Revolution. In the years following, Yushchenko tried to break out of Moscow's orbit and push for NATO membership. Moscow, meanwhile, kept up the political pressure on Kyiv through the price of natural gas. In January 2006, Moscow turned the gas off and sent a chill through homes across Ukraine.

As the 2006 G8 summit neared, both Congress and members of Bush's administration pressured the president to take Putin to task. In a speech given in Vilnius, the capital of Lithuania, Dick Cheney condemned the "gas wars" and accused Russia of democratic backsliding. Arizona senator John McCain called on Bush to "get tough with Putin," or boycott the summit altogether.

Bush, however, opted for a more conciliatory tone at the summit. The president felt he needed Russian cooperation on preventing nuclear proliferation to countries like Iran and North Korea. But more importantly, Russia's economic and political status was changing, thanks to rising oil prices. James Goldgeier, a senior fellow at the Council on Foreign Relations, wrote at the time: "It is a lot easier for the Russians to say [. . . ,] 'Hey, we don't need to listen to you guys' [. . .] in a way that was not true 10 years ago when Boris Yeltsin was looking for assistance from the [IMF]."

In the press conference that followed their meetings, Bush and Putin were both keen to highlight good relations. Bush noted he had a "great dinner," the night before. "And I talked about my desire to promote institutional change in parts of the world like Iraq," the president added, "where there's a free press and free religion, and I told him that a lot of people in our country would hope that Russia would do the same thing."

"We certainly would not want to have the same kind of democracy as they have in Iraq, I will tell you quite honestly," Putin quipped to laughter.

For Prigozhin, the dinner might have been a thrilling moment: to stand in a private room behind two men discussing events of a world they could destroy several times over. And yet, obsessed with power and all its intrigue, the difference between serving and sitting at the table must have been painfully evident.

The bonhomie Putin and Bush forged over Prigozhin's "great dinner" would soon falter. In February 2008, Kosovo declared its independence from Serbia, which the U.S. recognized the next day. "Kosovo cannot be seen as a precedent for any other situation in the world today," Secretary of State Condoleezza Rice wrote. Speaking on television, Putin disagreed: "The Kosovo precedent is a terrifying precedent [. . .] In the end, this is a stick with two ends and that other end will come back to knock them on the head someday."

A few weeks later, Putin's handpicked successor, Prime Minister Dmitry Medvedev, won presidential elections. The West saw Medvedev as more liberal-minded than Putin, but the relationship was challenged yet again when the West's darling in Georgia, Mikheil Saakashvili— goaded by Russia and expecting Western support (which never came)— sought to reestablish Georgia's control over Russia-backed separatists in

South Ossetia. The short Russo-Georgia war ensued, leaving hundreds dead and thousands displaced. A few days after the ceasefire, in a speech that referred to Kosovo, Medvedev announced Russia's recognition of South Ossetia and Abkhazia—Georgia's other separatist republic—as independent.

Two years later, events in the Middle East quashed a final attempt to "reset" Russo-American relations under U.S. president Barack Obama and Russian president Dmitry Medvedev. In 2010, the Arab Spring brought the overthrow of both Tunisia's and Egypt's autocrats. Protests spread to Yemen, and, on February 15, 2011, demonstrations erupted in the Libyan city of Benghazi. Libya's longtime ruler, Muammar Gaddafi, met the protests with violence and threatened to exterminate the protestors like rats. The United Nations established a no-fly zone—an operation designed to ground Gaddafi's air force—over Libya and authorized the use of force to protect civilians. The no-fly zone became a NATO air campaign to remove Gaddafi, who was eventually dragged out of hiding and executed.

The events in Libya shocked Putin. NATO had overthrown yet another government, and Medvedev had done nothing to intervene. He could no longer be trusted with a second term. But when Putin announced his return, Russians themselves took to the streets. First the "color revolutions" in Ukraine and Georgia, then the "Arab Spring," and now protests in Russia. All proof, in Putin's eyes, of Western machinations to weaken his country and, potentially, overthrow its leader. Worse, trouble was brewing in "brotherly" Ukraine.

Once president, Yushchenko failed to implement many of the promises he made during the Orange Revolution, which paved the way for the election of his old rival, Viktor Yanukovych, in 2010. Yanukovych promptly abandoned his predecessor's NATO ambitions but many Ukrainians, especially in the west and center of the country, remained hopeful that his government would continue to pursue integration with the European Union (EU). In November 2013, however,

Yanukovych decided to ditch a summit where he was expected to sign an association agreement. The Ukrainian president had caved to Putin, who was in the process of creating his own EU rival: the Eurasian Economic Union. In exchange for turning down the agreement, Putin offered Yanukovych's government a $15 billion loan and discounts on natural gas. By December 1, over half a million protestors were on Kyiv's Maidan square.

Marian was born in western Ukraine's Carpathian Mountains. He was proud of his Ukrainian language and identity but ashamed of his country's corruption and dependence on Russia. Wanting an escape, he chose college in Poland. When Yanukovych announced his decision to abandon the EU agreement, Marian, along with another thousand Ukrainians, protested in front of the embassy in Warsaw.

On November 30, Yanukovych's government was the first to escalate when Berkut riot police violently dispersed demonstrators in Kyiv. Had Yanukovych not chosen violence, the protests would have likely lost steam. Instead, watching Berkut chase and beat up women on YouTube had a catalyzing effect. Marian returned to Kyiv, where he joined thousands of protestors gathering on the Maidan. As the pro-Maidan movement grew, a minority of far-right activists and street fighters from a confederation of right-wing organizations, "Right Sector," or Pravy Sektor, began to engage in violence on the side of the protestors. While the majority of those on the Maidan disavowed Pravy Sektor's views, the violence was useful in accelerating events. Pro-Yanukovych and Russian media quickly latched on to the role of far-right actors as evidence that the entire Maidan movement was a fascist, Western-backed provocation.

On February 18, 2014, protestors, Berkut, and pro-government hooligans clashed in front of Ukraine's parliament. Protestors set fire to the headquarters of Yanukovych's political party, the Party of Regions. A police counteroffensive on Maidan followed in which twenty-seven people, including nine policemen, were killed.

Marian and his friends went to a clinic, hoping to protect those inside. The doctors shooed them away, saying they would be kidnapped or killed when Berkut arrived. There were rumors they were checking hospitals for those with gunshot wounds. It was a terrifying environment, one that began to feel like a war. Marian remembers seeing more arms among the protestors, though the Berkut still had overwhelming firepower.

On February 20, protestors killed two Berkut. Police snipers then unloaded on unarmed, advancing protestors, killing thirty-nine in one hour. The Thursday massacre destroyed any legitimacy Yanukovych had left, even within his own Party of Regions.

With his support melting away, Yanukovych agreed, under Western mediation, to protestors' demands to reinstate the 2004 constitution, granting more power to parliament. Yanukovych would be allowed to stay in power until December. When the agreement was announced, however, Yanukovych's security services evaporated. Yanukovych, too, was soon on the run. The Ukrainian parliament, or Rada, voted in the constitution and nominated politician Oleksandr Turchynov as interim president. On February 23, the Rada voted to repeal a Yanukovych-era language law that gave Russian the status of an official language.

The Revolution of Dignity, or Maidan Revolution, like many revolutions, overturned the balance of power between regional identities; in this case, power in Ukraine shifted from the east back to the west. U.S. and European rhetorical support for protestors infuriated Putin and his most trusted advisor at the time, Security Council secretary and former head of the FSB Nikolai Patrushev. They were convinced that America and its European proxies were behind the Maidan Revolution, which meant Russia's Black Sea Fleet was under threat. In mid-February, Putin's inner circle made the decision to seize Crimea. The final meeting included the Russian president, Nikolai Patrushev, FSB Director Alexander Bortnikov, head of the Presidential Administration Sergei Ivanov, and Defense Minister Sergei Shoigu. Only Shoigu reportedly expressed reservations. On February 27, a group of unidentified, clearly professional men, claiming to be an "armed self-defense force," seized the Crimean parliament and raised the Russian flag.

★ ★ ★

Moscow's successful, nearly bloodless, seizure of Crimea left Western analysts scrambling to understand Russia's "new military." A little-known article penned a year earlier by the chief of the General Staff of the Russian Federation Armed Forces, General Valery Gerasimov, suddenly became quite important. In the West, Gerasimov contended, military measures to achieve political outcomes had given way to informational, humanitarian, and other nonmilitary means. To overthrow Gaddafi in Libya, for example, "a no-fly zone was created, a sea blockade imposed, and private military contractors were widely used in close interaction with army formations of the opposition." To combat this new form of Western warfare, Russia, Gerasimov believed, should avoid aping the West and instead outpace it. Gerasimov was outlining what he believed to be Western strategies of subversion. Western journalists and pundits, however, posited Gerasimov was describing Russia's own tactics. It was a form of mirroring; two foes were convinced the other was engaged in "hybrid warfare."

Over the years, the annexation of Crimea has gained the reputation of a clean, well-planned operation—the paragon of "hybrid warfare." Yet the relative lack of physical violence associated with the "little green men," largely unidentified Russian soldiers without patches or insignia, who took over Crimea's administrations and institutions masked significant confusion on the ground. Independent and semi-independent actors from Russia also flooded the peninsula. Crimea was an opportunity for these volunteers to advance their own projects.

Alexander Kravchenko was born in a Cossack village, in what is now Kazakhstan. The Cossacks—descendants of escaped serfs who settled in the Russian Empire's southern borders—believe, Kravchenko informed me, in three things: "Orthodoxy, military service, and loyalty to one's ancestors." Repressed during Soviet rule, Russian Cossacks,* along with other communities, rediscovered, or in many cases re-created, their heritage during the late Soviet nationalist revivals. To this day, Kravchenko and his fellow Cossacks never miss an opportunity to wear the *cherkeska*: a version of Caucasian highlanders' traditional coat that sports, across each side of the chest, a row of thin, rectangular pockets for storing musket bullets. One can replace the *cherkeska* with army fatigues retaining, of course, a sheepskin *papakha* cap.

In 1992, Kravchenko left the army and was living in St. Petersburg. There he joined a local Cossack organization, Nevskaya Stanitsa, and was engaged in "what you Americans call *business.*" Another member of Nevskaya Stanitsa had just returned from the war in Transnistria, a heavily Sovietized, Russian-speaking territory that fought a brief war with the Republic of Moldova. The veteran told the Cossacks about an opportunity to fight with Serbs in disintegrating Yugoslavia. Kravchenko leaped at the chance and traveled to Višegrad, in eastern Bosnia. There he befriended another Russian volunteer, Igor Girkin.

When Kravchenko met him in 1992, Girkin had been fighting in Bosnia for some time. He had graduated from Moscow's Historical and Archival Institute and his favorite topic, Kravchenko remembered, was Russian imperial history. He practiced that love through reenactments of historic battles. "He was not your typical war reenactor however," Kravchenko added, "in that he also wanted to participate in real battles. The fall of the Soviet Union gave him the opportunity."

Girkin fought in Transnistria then Bosnia, where he joined the Second Russian Volunteer Detachment, or the "Czar's Wolves." When Kravchenko arrived with his small batch of volunteers a few months

---

* Cossack communities are present in both Russia and Ukraine, but the history of Cossack identity diverged following Soviet collapse. In Russia, Cossack identity was more exclusive, state-funded, and militarized. In Ukraine, Cossack communities rarely received state funding. Cossack identity in Ukraine became more inclusive as Ukrainians sought to differentiate themselves from Russians after 2014.

later, they were directed to headquarters in an abandoned school. As they lay down to sleep, Kravchenko noticed Girkin "down on his knees" in prayer. It was a shock to the Cossack. He had only seen his grandmother pray in such a way. After fighting for two months, Kravchenko was nearly blinded. He stayed in Serbia until 2000, then moved back to Russia.

In 2014, now sturdier, with a grizzly beard, mustache, and poor eyesight, Kravchenko joined his fellow Cossacks in Crimea to provide what they considered security and protection to the local population opposing Ukraine's Maidan movement. During the days of empire, many Cossacks were engaged as a frontier force for the Russian Tsars. In exchange for military service, they were exempt from serfdom and received plots of land. For post-Soviet Cossack organizations, Crimea was a chance to reenact and reestablish these relationships with the state, providing muscle on Russia's borders in exchange for cultural rights, land, and preferential privileges. Kravchenko's goals on the peninsula, however, were humbler. "I was curious to see what was going on, and I wanted to provide moral support to local volunteers," he told me.

One of Kravchenko's contacts from Serbia, Hadži Bratislav Živković, found his way to Crimea as well. Živković's long black beard and his *subara* cap tassel caught the attention of many journalists covering events on the peninsula. And the self-styled Chetnik leader was happy to oblige with interviews. He had fought in Croatia and Bosnia in the early 1990s, then Kosovo in 1998. After the NATO bombing campaign, Živković became, in his own words, head of the revitalized Chetnik nationalist movement to protect the Serbs in the north of Kosovo. "At the time, I thought if we went to Crimea, the Russians would help us in Serbia," he said. Živković's Serbs were tasked with guarding Sevastopol, where they set up a checkpoint on the road to the city's northeast entrance.

Kravchenko's friend from Bosnia, Igor Girkin, now under the nom de guerre "Strelkov," also arrived in Crimea. By this time, Girkin, or "Strelkov," had worn many hats. He fought in Chechnya, became an

FSB officer, and even spent a stint as a journalist. All in addition to his passion for war reenacting. He had also made a powerful friend in Konstantin Malofeev, a conservative oligarch who had a history funding nationalist causes. Together with Malofeev, his former PR consultant Alexander Borodai, and several Cossacks, Girkin began raising a militia structured on his experience in the FSB (likely with Moscow's help). He then set about "persuading" Crimean parliamentarians to vote Sergei Aksyonov, a man with ties to local organized crime, as prime minister. Once elected, Aksyonov proposed a date for a referendum on Crimea's status as a Ukrainian territory. Two days after the highly disputed vote, Russia officially annexed Crimea.

In a revolutionary environment, or in any country in conflict, it is nearly impossible to analyze events in isolation. Those on the ground, even the insiders making decisions, usually operate on partial information at best. Fear of the unknown breeds misunderstanding and miscalculation, and what feels like chance in the moment gains, in hindsight, the impression of inevitability. The period between November 2013, when the Maidan protests first began, and the start of the war in Donbas was one such environment.

In Crimea, the Kremlin mobilized various current or former ultranationalist security service members like Girkin and volunteers to facilitate the annexation. After its success, Putin's inner circle thought those Russian patriots were no longer needed. Russian nationalists had long called for Crimea's return, citing the 1954 Soviet transfer of the peninsula from Russia to Ukraine as unjust. The greater Russian public remembered Crimea's warm beaches and the Black Sea Fleet. There is no evidence that the Kremlin, hopeful that the annexation had sufficiently satisfied the nationalist base Putin was cultivating back home, desired annexing territory outside Crimea.

But Russia's actions in Crimea led anti-Maidan protestors and political entrepreneurs to believe the Russian military would come to their aid in Ukraine's eastern region as well. The anti-Maidan movement began drawing nationalist volunteers from Crimea to Donbas.

In March 2014, Stanislav Vorobyev, the founder of the Russian Imperial Movement (RIM) was in Crimea. Vorobyev founded RIM in 2002, which at the time was a "small, monarchist, and ultra-Orthodox movement offering paramilitary and martial arts training in a basement of a suburban building in St. Petersburg." Vorobyev marched against Putin in 2012. Only two years later he was pressing authorities to give his three hundred men arms and equipment to take the southern Ukrainian city of Kherson. The authorities refused. "We don't need Kherson," they told Vorobyev. "Our task is Crimea." When the Russian Federation formally annexed the peninsula in March, Vorobyev and his men left. Back in St. Petersburg, they were detained by the FSB and questioned, confirming, in Vorobyev's eyes, the cynicism of Putin's nationalist gambit in Crimea.

Whereas the decision to annex Crimea came from the top, events in eastern Ukraine, as journalist Anna Arutunyan has shown, were in many respects initially driven from below. On April 7, 2014, pro-Russian separatists stormed the headquarters of the Donetsk regional government and declared the Donetsk People's Republic (DNR). Their actions started to attract volunteers like Vorobyev. The Kremlin was losing control, just as the Ukrainian government was in the throes of a post-revolutionary handover of power.

Five days later, one man would change the course of all events to come. On April 12, Igor "Strelkov" Girkin, a friend of Kravchenko's and later of Vorobyev, led a group of fifty-two men—part of the militia he had raised in Crimea—into eastern Ukrainian territory where they met a representative of the new, self-declared DNR, Governor Pavel Gubarev. The group initially planned to seize the town of Shakhtarsk, but Girkin changed his mind and chose the city of Slovyansk instead. His decision to invade Ukrainian territory, Arutunyan posits, went against the advice of his handler Borodai, his benefactor Malofeev, and likely the FSB. Vorobyev agrees, "I'm 90 percent sure he acted against orders. In Crimea, Strelkov was working for the Kremlin. In eastern Ukraine, he was on his own."

"I was the one who pulled the trigger of this war," Girkin later told a Russian imperialist newspaper. "If our unit hadn't crossed the border, everything would have fizzled out."

Whether Girkin acted on his own, or on orders, is the subject of intense debate. The Ukrainian government's position was, and remains, that Girkin represented the Russian state in Slovyansk. Maidan activists like Marian point to Girkin's January 2014 visit to Kyiv to protect Orthodox relics as evidence of long-standing plans. What is undebatable, however, is the success of Girkin's accelerationism. Following his commandos' seizure of Slovyansk, anti-Maidan protestors began capturing more administrative buildings in towns across Donbas, convinced Russian military support wasn't far behind. Kyiv's interim government was likewise convinced Russia had invaded again, and it was not prepared to lose more territory. On April 16, Interim President Oleksandr Turchynov announced an "anti-terror operation" against insurgents.

On April 29, in neighboring Luhansk, another group of protestors seized regional headquarters. They declared independence as the Luhansk People's Republic (LNR) two weeks later. Like in Donetsk and Slovyansk, the citizens of Luhansk had a range of nuanced attitudes toward the Maidan Revolution in Kyiv. "We didn't particularly like Yanukovych, either," one resident who helped organize the vote for LNR independence admitted to me. Anti-Maidan sentiment did not necessarily presuppose pro-Russian sentiment. "We just wanted the country to wait for new elections," referring to the agreement allowing Yanukovych to stay in power until December, "not an overthrow of the government." But rising violence, fear, and confusion were creating binaries, forcing residents to choose one side or the other for protection. Events in western Ukraine, in Odesa, heightened this sense of threat.

On May 2, anti-Maidan forces barricaded themselves in Odesa's Trade Unions House. Pro-Maidan forces sought to storm the building. The Trade Unions House caught fire, killing forty-two pro-Russian Ukrainians. For many Luhansk residents, the deaths of pro-Russian activists in

Odesa were proof the people of Donbas were not welcome in post-Maidan Ukraine. New identities crystallized, with thousands of pro-Maidan Donbas residents leaving places like Donetsk and Luhansk for Kyiv-controlled territory.

The deaths in Odesa were blared across Russian-state television and a surge of Russian volunteers poured into eastern Ukraine for the "Russian Spring."

After the Crimean referendum, Živković decided to follow the action to Luhansk. He brought his Serbian volunteers and stationed them in Slavyanoserbsk, a town founded in 1754 by Serb settlers. He named the battalion after General Jovan Šević, who, with the blessing of Catherine the Great, established the colony of Slavo-Serbia in 1753.

In July, Vorobyev and his associates began sending fighters to the DNR through an agreement with a local separatist leader, Aleksei Mozgovoi (commander of the Prizrak Brigade), allowing him to avoid cooperating with Russian authorities. Neo-Nazis Aleksei Milchakov and Yan Petrovsky, who had received training from Vorobyev's RIM, created the Rusich battalion. Cossacks arrived with their own units, like Pavel Dremov's First Cossack Regiment. Local separatist leaders like Alexander "Batman" Bednov (Batman Battalion) shored up their ranks with volunteers from Russia.

A large portion of the volunteers who drifted into Donbas came alone. Often, they were motivated by the cause, or by a chance to improve their lot in life. "Boyar" worked as a technician on household appliances. In August, he crossed into Donbas and joined Oplot (Bulwark) Brigade under Alexander Zakharchenko—one of the local leaders who seized Donetsk regional headquarters that April. "I went to Donbas for an idea. At the time, there was a lot of news in Russia about how the Ukrainians were destroying innocent people." Boyar also had what he called "his own ideology": that the Russian people and the Russian government were the strongest in the world, and that the Ukrainian nation was a weak branch of the greater Slavic ethnos.

"Arkady" had studied to be a journalist. He never served in the military but decided to go to Ukraine—or *Novorossiya* ("New Russia") in his words—for religious reasons. Two times he tried to cross the border through the Interbrigade, a volunteer movement tied to Eduard Limonov, the author and dissident who was filmed firing on Bosnia's besieged Sarajevo. The group was stopped and turned back by Russian border officials. The second time, he crossed alone, looking for Slovyansk, where everyone was gravitating to Igor Girkin. Arkady, armed with a sharp pen but no guns or gear, fell upon a band of Cossacks and local militiamen.

What united such disparate individuals was a narrative that denied Ukrainian identity. Each, to one degree or another, traced Russian claims on Ukraine to Catherine the Great's *Novorossiya* and blamed Soviet founder Vladimir Lenin for the artificial designation of Ukraine and Belarus. Of course, there were also motives far more banal. "I was also there for adventure," Boyar conceded.

Those first volunteers coming from Russia were altruists and patriots, Arkady fondly remembered, but as the summer progressed "things went in the wrong direction. Guys were arriving who just wanted to run away from their wives, kids, from the law or creditors. There were still the idealists, but they became a minority."

When the DNR and LNR declared independence, Interim President Turchynov had few troops who were combat ready. Kyiv had to send its own volunteers, forces like the nascent far-right group Azov Brigade, to Donbas. Many members of these pro-Maidan paramilitary forces were, in fact, native Russian-speakers from recently separatist regions. In June, businessman and staunch pro-Maidan supporter Petro Poroshenko entered office vowing to retake Crimea. Ukrainian forces reorganized and began logging victories against the local separatists and Russian volunteers. In the face of the counteroffensive, Arkady, gathering that he needed to be in a disciplined regiment with hierarchy and training, fell in with Vorobyev's unit, the Imperial Legion.

Kyiv's military response to separatism in Donbas presented the Kremlin with a problem. Putin could leverage Crimea's prior status as part of the Russian Soviet Republic and Russians' fondness for the peninsula as a vacation destination to justify his actions there. In his annexation speech, the Russian president couched the operation in the language of human rights and international law: "Crimean authorities referred to the well-known Kosovo precedent—a precedent our Western colleagues created with their own hands in a very similar situation, when they agreed that the unilateral separation of Kosovo from Serbia, exactly what Crimea is doing now, was legitimate and did not require any permission from the country's central authorities." Putin, in his mind, was simply shifting borders as Russia saw right or fit, just like the West in Kosovo.

In Crimea, local elites had quickly signaled their willingness to engage in sedition. In Donbas, however, former officials from Yanukovych's Party of Regions did not side with the separatists. The separatists emerged from the margins of society, making the conflict far messier. Russian security forces knew people in the Party of Regions, but they didn't know these local mechanics or coal miners. To boot, an overt Russian intervention would risk full-scale war with Ukraine and more sanctions from the West.

But the separatists and volunteers could not hold off an increasingly confident Ukrainian military. Leaving pro-Russian militias to their fate would spark the ire of the nationalist circles Putin had recently begun to cultivate. Winning over Vorobyev's RIM was perhaps a lost cause, but the average nationalist supporting Crimea's annexation from their couch was more important.

Caught between expensive sanctions and international isolation on one side and the ire of newly won audiences on the other, the Kremlin's response to fast-moving events in Ukraine was ad hoc. What the West came to see as a well-established doctrine for "hybrid warfare" was more, to borrow a phrase from Charles Tilly, a by-product of efforts to carry out more immediate tasks. One ad hoc initiative, the employment of mercenaries, would have consequences far beyond what Russian officers could imagine at the time.

★ ★ ★

A document detailing the internal history of Wagner, part of a set of leaks given to the Dossier Center, provides some detail on the formation of what we now call the private military company (PMC) Wagner Group. "On May 1, 2014, in the village of Veseloye in Rostov Oblast', territory was allocated for a field camp dedicated to the training of the personnel of the 'Wagner' combat unit. This is where the first people (around 10 persons) arrived from Leningrad Oblast, who formed the organizational core of the unit." The date matches that of another curious document leaked in 2023, which claims to be the founding charter for Wagner. The agreement was a simple piece of paper, framed, typed-out, and edited in pen. Allegedly signed by Yevgeny Prigozhin and Dmitry Utkin, it outlined the agreed upon terms and conditions for a "director" and "commander."

> In connection with the difficult situation in Ukraine and the necessity of defending Donbass (the heart of Russia) we, the undersigned, pledge ourselves to observe the following obligations.

The director would provide weapons, financing, consistent employment, and protection from Article 359 laws against mercenarism. The director promised to resolve all questions collegially, to take personal part in the operations, and not to go against the Russian people. The requirements of the commander included selecting a team, training them, preventing desertion, prohibiting the use of alcohol and drugs, and finishing tasks to completion. The commander, Dmitry Utkin, promised to never go against Vladimir Putin, and to tell things how they are.

There are few details on the life of media-shy Dmitry Utkin. We know he was born in Sverdlovsk in 1970, then moved with his family to the Soviet Ukrainian village of Smoline. In the 1990s, Utkin joined the special forces of Russian military's intelligence unit, the GRU. Like the U.S. Green Berets, one of the GRU's historic responsibilities is to train and equip insurgents and proxy forces. He fought in Chechnya where his wife at the time—he had many—Elena Scherbinina, says he won his first medals. After the Chechen campaign, Utkin and Scherbinina moved to Pechory, close to Russia's border with Estonia. Yet the military man had trouble adjusting to life off the battlefield. "He was always worried that he wasn't fighting," Elena told journalists. "He wanted the career of a military officer." Utkin commanded the GRU's Seven Hundredth Special Detachment of the Second Special Brigade in Pechory until 2013. He then left the service and signed a contract with the PMC Moran Group. Utkin may have had one or two maritime missions under his belt before he commanded a group of mercenaries working for Slavonic Corps LLC, a Moran-affiliated company. Slavonic Corps' mission, to guard oil facilities in Syria, ended in disaster when Utkin's unit was ambushed by the Islamic State and his bosses were charged with violating laws against mercenarism. The director's protection from Article 359, therefore, was a particularly valuable deal point.

According to one theory, it was Russia's Ministry of Defense that connected the "commander," Dmitry Utkin, to the "director," Yevgeny Prigozhin. While preparing mercenaries and proxies to support militias in breakaway Donetsk and Luhansk, the Russian military, an MoD source believes, invited Utkin to the southern Russian city of Rostov, close to the border with Ukraine. Even though Slavonic Corps' mission ended in disaster, Russian security forces would have noted Utkin's willingness to fight under company contract. If the date of the founding is accurate, Utkin may have been in Rostov as early as April 2014, when Igor Girkin invaded Slovyansk.

Utkin's unit was one of many proxies forming at the time, a source in the MoD emphasizes. "It was not expected that Utkin would eventually become the commander of a few thousand men, and in 2022, of tens of thousands of men. At first Utkin's group composed no more than two hundred, not a particularly important role."

The majority of these two hundred men Utkin recruited from his old Slavonic Corps unit. Recruitment was by word of mouth. "I remember the guys were talking about an opportunity to join [him]," said "Andrei," who fought with Slavonic Corps in Syria.

A fellow Moran Group contractor, Alexander Kuznetsov, "Ratibor," joined the growing force. Ratibor was a former *spetsnats* officer, considered the most talented and knowledgeable commander. Of medium height, stocky build, and sociable, Ratibor could find common interest with most of the men he met, though he sometimes, a colleague noted, tended toward lordly manners. "With men of equal status, he was always friendly, no matter his mood. With his subordinates he could be harsh." In 2008, Ratibor was arrested for kidnapping and theft. He joined Moran Group after his release in 2013. He went to Donbas a year later, commanding the Rusich battalion for a brief period. The choice of Rusich reflected, perhaps, his soft spot for neo-pagan beliefs. There was also Sergei Chupov, "Chup," who served in Afghanistan with the Soviet Airborne Forces (VDV), then Chechnya with the Ministry of Internal Affairs. Each man was given a number preceded by "M," the lower the number, the earlier a mercenary joined "the Company." Ratibor's identification number, for example, is M-0271.

For Yevgeny Prigozhin, to be given such a task as "director" of a military operation was no small feat. Born in Soviet Leningrad in 1961, Prigozhin found himself on the other side of the law at a young age. At eighteen years old, he had the nickname "Jacquot" and led a team of burglars. His job was to choose the houses and targets to rob. One of his accomplices later recalled to *Proekt Media*: "Jaquot tried to choose dwellings familiar to him, for example, those that his girl-friends invited him to." In the spring of 1980, after midnight, Prigozhin and his small gang stumbled out of the Okean restaurant in St. Petersburg, when Jacquot spotted a woman passing by. The group followed her home. When the woman reached her building, an accomplice asked to bum a cigarette. While she rummaged through her purse, Prigozhin jumped from behind and strangled her unconscious. The gang then robbed her. Caught in 1981, "Jacquot" was sentenced to thirteen years.

Nine years later, Prigozhin walked out of prison—allegedly with a few extra tattoos—and returned to Leningrad, which became St. Petersburg a year later. Amid Gorbachev's collapsing Soviet Union, the ex-con traded cars at an infamous auto market on Energetikov Avenue. The stint, according to *Proekt Media*, didn't last long. A former classmate, Boris Spektor, brought Prigozhin into his business empire with Mikhael Mirilashvili, a Jewish-Georgian gangster and owner of several casinos. Spektor backed Prigozhin's management of a grocery chain before both he and Mirilashvili invested in his first restaurant, the Old Customs House. Prigozhin hired a Brit, Anthony Gere, to manage it. The Old Customs House met with little success when it first opened in 1995, though Gere and Prigozhin eventually attracted St. Petersburg's elite with caviar, champagne, and other high-end luxuries. Success at the Old Customs House allowed Prigozhin to open a second restaurant, a renovated pleasure boat floating on the Neva: New Island.

Those who worked with Prigozhin during his restaurant days described him as aggressive, manipulative, and violent. "He always looked for people higher up to befriend. And he was good at it," one businessman told the *Guardian*. Prigozhin, the businessman remembered, could please anyone if he needed something from them. For those he considered subordinates, his temper could be terrifying. The construction of Prigozhin's St. Petersburg mansion, "Northern Versailles," near Olgino, for example, ran into a number of issues that infuriated the owner. The window installation, for one, was of poor quality, so Prigozhin refused to pay. When the installers visited his office, "Prigozhin received them and listened to them carefully," a person familiar with the investigation remembered. "He then called security to beat the shit out of them. Then they were dragged out of the office and into the basement where they fucked them up one more time."

Prigozhin's capacity for charm and violence made him a powerful force. He had, one businessman noted, "no off switch." It wasn't money or power that motivated Prigozhin, it was the thrill of the chase.

According to most reports, Anatoly Sobchak, then mayor of St. Petersburg, and his protégé Vladimir Putin first met Prigozhin at the Old Customs House, though Putin may have met Prigozhin a few years earlier supervising St. Petersburg's gambling industry. But New Island was where the restaurateur really ingratiated himself with Russia's emerging elite. When Vladimir Putin became president, he began taking foreign dignitaries to the swanky river restaurant in his hometown. The Russian president took a liking to the hardworking restaurateur: "Putin saw that I wasn't above bringing the plates myself," Prigozhin later told journalists. Soon he was catering state dinners and parties held by Putin's inner circle. Prigozhin often lost money catering those affairs, but the connections were invaluable.

Ironically, only Prigozhin claimed he sold hot dogs in the early 1990s. In an interview, he said he and his mother, Violetta Prigozhina, mixed mustard in the family kitchen. "We made $1,000 a month, which in ruble notes was a mountain; my mum could hardly count it all." Russian journalists have been unable to confirm the hot dog tale, but the timing of Prigozhin's rags-to-riches narrative is interesting. The interview, held in 2011, was one of the few Prigozhin gave to outside media and came after public interest in his factory to produce ready-made meals for state institutions. Prigozhin had pitched the plan a year prior to the deputy head of the Presidential Administration Alexander Beglov, who passed the idea to Dmitry Medvedev, who passed it to Putin. Putin personally visited the site and told Moscow mayor Sergei Sobyanin and Minister of Defense Anatoly Serdyukov to order meals for the schools and military.

Defense Minister Serdyukov did not have a lot of friends at the time. He was an outsider—not a military man, but a bureaucrat and finance guy—whom Putin placed in the Ministry of Defense to push through reforms. The 2008 war with Georgia revealed many Russian military weaknesses. Equipment broke down, conscripts were poorly trained, and there were tremendous coordination issues. In some instances, commanders were communicating with each other on cell phones. Russia needed a leaner, more flexible, better equipped military for the battles to come.

In Russia, it is mandatory for men to serve two years in the army. Conscription allowed for a large military, but one constantly plagued by issues of quality. A culture of brutal hazing and low wages made it difficult to keep men in uniform. Serdyukov wanted to lower the military's reliance on mandatory service and transition to a professional force, akin to Russia's competitors in the West. The problem for Serdyukov, however, was that conscripts often took care of daily chores. A military people signed up for would require outsourcing what keeps it running—cooking, cleaning, logistics—to the private sector.

Prigozhin registered his company Concord in the 1990s, but when he entered the world of government contracting, the number of companies and offshore filings linked to him ballooned. There are well over one thousand companies and other accounts affiliated with Prigozhin, many of which were registered under his mother, Violetta, his wife, Lyubov, his daughter, Polina, his son Pavel, and any number of business associates. In 2011, for example, Prigozhin's mother, Violetta, was the 100 percent owner of "Concord Management and Consulting," itself a 10 percent owner of "Concord M" (Prigozhin owned the other 90 percent). Concord Management and Consulting and Concord M were each 50 percent owners of "Concord Food Combine."

The complexity of Prigozhin's network served many purposes. The first goal was to obscure the money he was earning from government contracts. In 2013, a company "Obschepit" won eighteen military contracts worth 233 million rubles (roughly $10,000,000 at the time). The owner of "Obschepit" was Pavel Arnold, an affiliate of Prigozhin. "Obschepit" bought a helicopter that Yevgeny used to commute from Northern Versailles to properties outside St. Petersburg. Hiding wealth was important, even before U.S. sanctions took a bite down the road, but the complex holding companies and offshore accounts also allowed Prigozhin to bid on the same contract through different front companies. Who you know, however, is more important than how many front companies you have. To maintain preferential access to tenders, Prigozhin had to fight to retain Putin's gaze and the attention of other powerful people around him. The information space was an excellent path to grace and would allow the ever-obsessive Prigozhin a chance to control his own image along the way.

In 2013, a young journalist at the independent Russian media outlet *Novaya Gazeta*, Alexandra Garmazhapova, and a colleague saw an advertisement on social media.

> Internet operators needed! Work in a glamorous office in OLGINO!!! (metro station Staraya Derevnya), 25,960 RUB per month. The job: placing comments on internet sites; writing thematic posts, blogs, social media.

So, on a bright summer day in St. Petersburg, Alexandra and her friend walked into an office that, with floor-to-ceiling pane glass and acute, white gables had the feel of an oversized ski lodge. Greeting them inside the Internet Research Agency (IRA) was Aleksei Soskovets, a young man active in St. Petersburg's political scene and the pro-Putin youth organization, Nashi. Soskovets demanded Alexandra's passport for a quick background check. The next day, when she and her friend returned to the office, they were hired. Soskovets led them through the IRA's hallways, past various offices with signs posted to the doors: "Blogger and Commentary Management," "Rapid Response Department," "Commentary Department," "Department of Social Media Specialists," "CEO."

Once at their desks, Soskovets explained how the job worked. "Our job is to raise visits to a website. You can [leave comments by] robots, but they work mechanically, and sometimes the websites ban them. So, it was decided to do this with people. You write comments yourself on the topics we tell you. For example, on the G-20 Summit you can write that it's a great honor for Russia to host it, but that the traffic makes it difficult to get home." The IRA would provide the articles that required comments from the "internet operators," and it was expected that Alexandra and her colleagues would write around one hundred comments per day. Previous trolls had saved screenshots to document their work. They were mostly comments on the social media site LiveJournal, and they mostly made fun of America or Russian opposition politician Aleksei Navalny. Correlation and causation were not a priority. "They say it's so crowded in the States because of the skyscrapers," a previous internet operator curiously wrote in one post.

"There are always two types of propaganda in Russia," Alexandra explained to me later. "There's the Kremlin propaganda on the national level, then local propaganda." Once local officials recognized the power of social media in the 2000s, they began hiring young people and students to shape narratives online. Prigozhin's troll factory was simply the first that had been infiltrated by journalists.

When Alexandra "worked" for the IRA, it was dedicated to influencing Russian speakers in Russia, mostly seeking to shape their opinion of the Russian opposition. Prigozhin almost certainly recognized the importance of such a patriotic initiative, given how sensitive the regime was to the mass demonstrations of 2012. He even financed a "documentary film," *Anatomy of a Protest*, that vilified the protestors. Some journalists trace Prigozhin's troll farm to efforts to provide positive coverage of his companies and projects. An insider, on the other hand, alleges that the troll farm came out of a conversation between Prigozhin and the First Deputy Head of the Presidential Administration Vyacheslav Volodin, a regime "protector."

"Volodin complained to the Chief that the bloggers were fucking him over," the source divulged. "So, the Chief told Volodin—I'll make my own network of bloggers, everything will work fucking great."

The war in Donbas was yet another chance to showcase one's patriotism.

In many respects, Prigozhin and Utkin were an unlikely pair. Like his old business partners, Mirilashvili and Spektor, Prigozhin was Jewish. Utkin, on the other hand, was an open neo-Nazi, a pagan with "SS" tattooed on his neck. His call sign, "Wagner," was an homage to one of the Nazis' favorite composers, Richard Wagner.

By 2014, Prigozhin's contracts with the Russian military placed the businessman close to decision-makers in the Ministry of Defense. And after long years of serving President Putin and honored guests like President Bush, Prigozhin had a degree of access to Putin himself. Some members of Wagner believe that thanks to these relationships, Prigozhin was invited, along with others, to act as a *kurator*, a "manager" or "handler," for the various mercenary groups in Donbas. Others believe that Prigozhin, sensing an opportunity in Ukraine, struck a deal directly with Putin or a member of the presidential administration, then contacted various mercenary networks to set up his own small force for Donbas. The head of Concord had plenty of connections in St. Petersburg who could introduce him to Utkin.

While we don't know when and how Prigozhin and Utkin first met, we do know that they were cementing their relationship just as Ukrainian forces were closing in on separatists and Russian volunteers in Luhansk. According to one internal document, Utkin's unit, consisting of three hundred men, reached Luhansk in late May or early June 2014. By the document's own admission, they bolstered the city's defense by shooting down a Ukrainian IL-76 plane that tried to land at Luhansk airport on June 10. The IL-76 was trying to resupply a small Ukrainian brigade based at the airport. Utkin's strike killed forty paratroopers and nine crew, a shocking figure at that point in the war.

On August 10, according to Russian accounts, LNR militias retook the border town of Ivarino, which opened a corridor for Russian mercenaries, volunteers, and likely Russian military personnel to pour into the regional capital. Ukrainian forces then launched an assault on Khryashuvati and Novosvitlivka, two villages in between Luhansk and the Russian border, to cut off further supply routes to Russia. Utkin's men were already positioned in the villages. Together with local LNR militias they launched a counterattack ten days later. Utkin's unit seized all of Khryashuvati within a week. By Russian accounts, Ukrainian forces lost thirty soldiers and three tanks. The next move for separatist forces was the airport. But Utkin, according to Wagner Group's telling, ran into a problem. The local militias didn't want to participate in the operation, leaving the task to Wagner and his "forty men."

In one almost certainly exaggerated telling, Utkin and his band of forty faced an enemy of four hundred at Luhansk airport. Most thought they were "going to their deaths." Utkin, however, chose a clever time to attack to beat the odds. His men stormed the airport after lunch, when most soldiers were full, playing on their phones, assuming war, at least for that day, was over. The attack caught the larger force off guard and forced panicking Ukrainians to retreat.

The Ukrainian forces' version of the events is decidedly less dramatic. Soldiers present at the time put Ukrainian numbers at closer to 150, not 400. Moreover, they attribute their ultimate retreat to intense shelling, almost certainly from the Russian military, which had, by August, covertly intervened in the conflict. The airport was destroyed, and there was not much to defend among ruins that left Ukrainian positions exposed.

Four days after the capture of Luhansk Airport, Ukraine and Russia-backed separatists signed a twelve-point ceasefire agreement, called the Minsk Protocol. The Russian military's covert intervention was more influential in bringing Ukrainian president Petro Poroshenko to the table than Utkin's victory at Luhansk Airport. Nonetheless, the battle became a part of Wagner's founding mythology.

While Utkin and his men were in Luhansk, Prigozhin was upholding his end of the agreement by securing financing and logistics. That summer, he met with defense officials in Moscow, where he demanded a parcel of land to train his "volunteers." The officials didn't have much choice: "The orders come from Papa," Prigozhin told them, referring to Putin.

After handing over Luhansk Airport on September 1, Utkin brought his men to the company's new training facility in southern Russia, Molkino. They shared the base with the GRU's Tenth Special Forces Brigade. That a Russian mercenary unit would share a base with the GRU reflected a shift in the Kremlin's policy on eastern Ukraine. It was now taking ownership over the DNR and LNR. Local separatist leaders, plucked from provincial obscurity to lordship over vague fiefs, unwittingly entered their third act.

★ ★ ★

"Branko" was a member of Serbian special forces who had fought in Bosnia and Kosovo. In 2014, he arrived in Luhansk, on the invitation of his friend Radomir Počuča, a commander in the Serbian police. When Branko saw that the twenty-five men before him had just three rifles, he left for another group, which brought him to a hostel in Luhansk.

His new unit was not the only one in the hostel. Going out each day, Branko peeked into a few rooms along the corridor, where serious-looking men pored over maps. He had no clue who those men were, of course, but they would nod and great each other cordially in the hallway.

On a mission in November 2014, Branko was on the front when an ordinance exploded nearby. He was transported to the hospital in Luhansk where one afternoon, to his surprise, a man walked up to his bed. The fifty-two-year-old retired colonel, with gray bangs combed straight down his forehead, typical Russian style, introduced himself as "Andrei Nikolaevich."

"We heard you're good," Andrei Nikolaevich told Branko. "And that you need some money."

"That's true," said Branko.

He handed him $450, then scribbled something on a piece of paper. "Go to this address in Russia and tell them that Andrei Nikolaevich sent you."

After Branko was released from the hospital, he prepared to go to Molkino. Another friend from the special forces, "Lucky," had been invited too, along with one other Serb, Davor Savičić. Savičić, a Bosnian Serb, claimed to be a paramilitary veteran. Before popping up in Luhansk, he had been on the run from Montenegrin police after someone owing him 15,000 euros died mysteriously in a bomb blast. Živković recruited him to Luhansk where Savičić proved he could burn bridges as easily as cars. After he drunkenly fell out of a truck, Živković kicked him out of his brigade. (Others say Savičić left after a fight over who would command the unit.) Savičić wandered Luhansk looking for a contract, and eventually stumbled upon Andrei Nikolaevich in the same unassuming way Branko did.

Savičić wanted to join Branko and Lucky. But Branko felt his story didn't add up. He put a gun to Savičić's head. "Davor began crying saying he wasn't a spy, that he really was in the military and so on. And Lucky defended him too, saying he was a good guy."

Branko put his gun away, and the three headed to Molkino. When they arrived at the base, Branko told the guards he was sent by Andrei Nikolaevich. As he found out later, "Andrei Nikolaevich" was Andrei Nikolaevich Troshev, call sign "Sedoi," or "Gray Hair." Troshev was the managing director of Prigozhin and Utkin's organization, or as insiders only called it: "the Company."

After spending time training and shooting, Branko was sent back to Luhansk. Once there, he was shocked how much money was flying around. "Troshev, Utkin, even Ratibor; everyone was lining their pockets."

The most common scheme was to over-invoice the Russian military. Commanders told the MoD they had 200 men on the payroll. Really they had 150 men and pocketed the extra salaries. Commanders over-invoiced for equipment as well. "It was too much money," Branko felt. "Wagner could have been a great thing, if there wasn't so much money flying around."

Utkin and Prigozhin's team weren't the only ones making money in Donbas. Local militia commanders also turned to racketeering. The war was becoming one large asset grab.

On January 1, 2015, local separatist commander Alexander "Batman" Bednov was ambushed outside Luhansk by men with automatic weapons and grenade launchers. The commander, along with six of his men, was killed. The story was that Ukrainians had carried out an assassination deep in enemy territory, but few citizens believed it. The Minsk peace process was well underway, and Batman was a popular figure who had made his opposition to Minsk very apparent. Rumors spread that the leader of the LNR, Igor Plotnitsky, had given the order to liquidate independent commanders.

A few months after Batman's car was sprayed with bullets, a vehicle carrying the commander Aleksei Mozgovoi, Vorobyev's local partner, blew up. Then, local Cossack commander Pavel Dryomov, who was critical of LNR leadership, died when his car exploded on the way to his own wedding. By this point, Igor "Strelkov" Girkin had resigned from his post, a move likely demanded by Moscow given his role in the death of 298 civilians on Malaysian Airlines Flight 17. Whether it was LNR authorities or the Russian military, it seemed there was an effort to bring the separatist militias into one, centralized structure.

Russian officials wanted to stabilize the war in Donbas. While the first Minsk agreement never held, intense diplomatic negotiations were taking place for a second, and the Russian military began deploying more unmarked troops, or "little green men," to seize territory before the front line froze. Debaltseve, wedged between the borders of the DNR and LNR with railroad lines that connected the two, was an important pocket of Ukrainian resistance. Separatist militias, volunteers, and mercenaries converged on the town in what would become the last major battle in the war.

Jan's Ukrainian unit had already been in Debaltseve for months. He felt the Ukrainians' hands were tied. "Thanks to the first Minsk agreement, we weren't allowed to go on offense. We weren't allowed to open fire," he fumed. Meanwhile, his unit was coming under constant shelling. The Ukrainians could sense they were fighting more than local militias. "It's very simple. The accuracy of the enemy's artillery, the accuracy of their shooting, how they moved, it all showed these guys weren't coal miners."

Utkin's unit deployed to Debaltseve around January 22. It was one of many; Arkady's Imperial Legion also went to Debaltseve, where they took a village to the west of town without a fight. On February 3, separatists and Russian forces north of Arkady cut off the highway leading from Debaltseve to Bakhmut. Two days later, under the cover of tank fire, the fighters for the Imperial Legion crawled through vegetation to within fifty meters of the Ukrainians. "The first tank did its job covering our advance, the second, too. But the third tank's commander was drunk and didn't move into position. And so, we were left relatively exposed and had to retreat with injuries." The second day was a repeat of the first. Arkady's men advanced on the block post behind the cover of a tank and a BMP (infantry fighting vehicle), but again the vehicles' drivers took off leaving the men exposed. Five were killed that day, which the Imperial Legion celebrates as "the greatest sacrifice we made for the Russian lands."

Utkin's men were also taking heavy losses. In an intercepted phone call with Managing Director Troshev, Utkin complained: "Yea, for now I'm just standing, standing, standing. Because, well, to be honest, I'm fucked out here, Nikolaevich. I already haven't fucking slept for several days; I'm starting to lose it [. . .] You gotta pull me out of here. My own fucking guys are going to shoot me soon." The analyst Jack Margolin estimates that Utkin's unit had upward of eighty casualties, a high figure. Utkin would later earn another nickname among his men, "the butcher."

On February 18, 2015, Ukrainian president Petro Poroshenko issued orders for an "organized" retreat from Debaltseve that was anything but. Ukrainian soldiers slogged through fields and backroads under heavy fire, forced to leave wounded behind. For Jan, the retreat wasn't neces-sary. "We could have kept going," he believed. "But we pulled back for political reasons."

Boyar was farther south, on the Mariupol front. Separatists held the city center for a few months in 2014, before the far-right Azov group and other Ukrainian forces pushed them out. During the battle for Debaltseve, Russian-backed separatists launched an offensive to retake Mariupol. Boyar thought the fighting was "interesting," even fun. "But then one day the Russian feds said: 'Boys, time to stop.'" Disappointed, Boyar left for Russia, then joined the French Foreign Legion.

Once Arkady and other patriotic "idealists" realized the Minsk II ceasefire was serious, they also quit Ukraine. "We went to the DNR first because there was freedom, there were no laws repressing us," Arkady's supervisor, Stanislav Vorobyev, told me. But the ultranationalists were disappointed to see Putin's government co-opt their movement. They wanted a greater Russia, based on the borders of 1917. Despite Putin's nationalist rhetoric, he and his circle, according to Vorobyev, derived their legitimacy from the Russian Federation, which, like Ukraine and Belarus, was an artificial state, the product of the Soviet Union's divisive policies. Worse for the ultranationalists, a chief Kremlin ideologist, Vladislav Surkov, was tasked with managing the two statelets' institu-tions. "We wanted Great Russia. And Surkov's protégés wanted to build the Russian Federation. I wasn't going to fight for that shit," Arkady told me. After Surkov took over, the Imperial Legion was kicked out of Donbas.

Marat Gabidullin arrived in Luhansk in July 2015, five months after Minsk II. The opportunity to join Utkin's men was a chance to change a life that was moving sideways. Marat was a born soldier. He joined the military during the height of perestroika's optimism in the Soviet Union. Five years later, he was stationed in Russian Siberia and salaries were irregular. Marat handed in his resignation the moment he was nominated for subcommander of an intelligence unit. It was a decision he regretted immediately but couldn't overturn. As a civilian, Marat first did whatever he could to make money, sometimes transporting goods or providing protection. At one point, these odd jobs resulted in a conflict with a "criminal authority." Marat shot him. After his release, Marat began providing protection for businessmen, and a life of petty crime, troubles with alcohol, and family strife followed.

Then one day, Marat was talking to his buddy at the gym, "Samurai." Unlike Marat, Samurai had stayed in the military and fought in the two Chechen campaigns. After retirement, he joined the PMC Moran Group, protecting ships in the Gulf of Aden. Samurai told Marat about a company recruiting mercenaries in southern Russia. Marat had never heard of Prigozhin, or Utkin, let alone Utkin's call sign, "Wagner." After a chat with his family, he packed up his car and drove to Molkino.

Marat has a passion for fitness and mixed martial arts. He has a wiry frame and hollow cheeks that he keeps clean shaved. A rectangular, well-trimmed mustache and beard outline a thin mouth. He passed the physical exams with ease. In the early days, passing the tests gave a recruit permission to find a vacancy under Wagner's commanders. Marat had to seek one out and confirm his willingness to take him on. The Bosnian Serb Davor Savičić, now going by the call sign "Volk" (Wolf), had an open spot.

When Marat joined, the Company had five hundred to seven hundred men. His assault company, the main military unit in those early days, was an international force. Another company was led by Ratibor, the special forces veteran. Ratibor went to the front line, while Savičić's stayed behind in Luhansk to provide security. The city was becoming less safe, Marat later wrote in his memoir, as the number of incidents involving alcohol and firearms increased. When Marat visited Luhansk's hospital, a doctor explained most of beds were occupied by women, victims of domestic violence.

Relations between the mercenaries and local militia were, by this point, exceedingly poor. Rumors had circulated that Marat's group was responsible for the deaths of local leaders. Branko, who was a part of Marat's unit, was convinced that Wagner had indeed killed Batman. "Batman and others were refusing to share a slice of their racket with the GRU and FSB," he believes, so the GRU sent Wagner to deal with it.

And while neither Marat nor Branko knew this at the time, internal Wagner documents admit to "liquidating" Batman and bringing the various Cossack formations "into line." A February 2015 call, intercepted by the Ukrainian Security Service, between Utkin and a senior GRU officer, Oleg Ivannikov, offers further proof of the plan. "The process of negotiations," Utkin said, referring to the Minsk II ceasefire, "as I understand, has stalled due to the fact that our motherfuckers continue to pepper them with fire."

"Well, I hope it's not ours out there," Ivannikov responded. "These Cossacks are uncontrollable. I think we'll sort it out now."

Toward the end of their stint in Luhansk, after Minsk II was signed, Savičić's platoon set out to the contact line, the front separating Ukrainian and pro-Russian separatists. There Marat realized his Serbian commander had no clue how to fight. Savičić insisted on setting camp in an exposed house close to the line of contact. If the platoon, he reasoned, was so close to the front, they could save time marching. The one "reconnaissance mission" ended with Savičić's men lost, using their smartphones' GPS to find their way back.

The front line was starting to freeze. Russian authorities turned their focus to managing the new statelets on their border. There was still little interest in annexing the "independent" DNR and LNR, to the frustration of many pro-Russian residents. Thousands of pro-Ukraine residents in Donbas had fled across the contact line, leaving behind those who believed in the cause or were too vulnerable to escape it. In Kyiv, politics and more pressing issues began to take precedence over the "manage-able" conflict in Donbas. Front line communities would soon feel forgotten by both Ukraine and Russia.

Morale in Marat's platoon was low, and he was grateful to leave Luhansk. Luckily for him, the director was cooking up a new deploy-ment to the Middle East.

II

Oil Men

Palmyra, urbs nobilis situ, divitiis soli et aquis amoenis, vasto undique ambitu harenis includit agros ac, velut terris exempta a rerum natura, privata sorte inter duo imperia summa Romanorum Parthorumque est prima in Discordia semper utrimque cura.

"Palmyra is a city renowned for its location, the richness of its soil, and its pleasant waters. Its fields are surrounded on every side by a vast circle of sands, and it is, as it were, cut off from the rest of the world by nature. Since it maintains its independence, though situated between the two mighty empires of Rome and Parthia, at the first moment of any conflict between them, it is a source of concern for both."

—PLINY, NATURAL HISTORY, 5.88 (TRANSLATED BY ELLISTON BISSELL)

Following the battle for Debaltseve and the signing of the Minsk II agreement, the demand for mercenaries, and Prigozhin and Utkin's services in Donbas, decreased. Units disbanded. Fighters like Arkady and Boyar went home, then on to other endeavors. "The Company," or what we now call "Wagner Group," could have easily disappeared as well. Prigozhin, however, was different from other

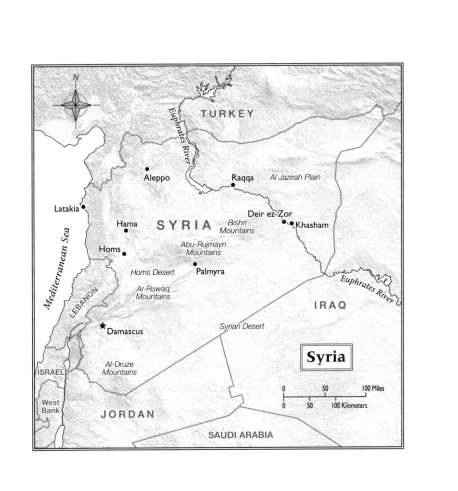

managers and sponsors. The entrepreneur was looking to build a PMC like the U.S.'s Blackwater, which had received top contracts for its role in America's War on Terror. Now with a small military force under his control, he began looking for new ways to profit from it. Luckily for him, Russia was about to intervene in Syria.

When the Arab Spring reached Syria in early March 2011, Bashar al-Assad's regime, like the regime of Muammar Gaddafi in Libya, met protests with shocking brutality. The violence, endemic to the political system the Assads and a few loyal families built, only fueled further protest and forced the opposition to take up arms. Still, the rebels were under-equipped, short of cash, and often split along community lines.

The Assad family is known for being interested only in its own power. Both Bashar and his father, Hafez al-Assad, deftly balanced outside powers to extract concessions from America and the West; the Soviet Union and its successor, Russia; the Gulf States; and Iran. As protests morphed into civil war, however, Russia and the West were keen to wait on the sidelines. Moscow maintained dialogue with Syrian opposition despite Putin's fury at NATO's intervention in Libya, a historic relationship between the Assads and the Soviet Union, and Russia's small naval base at Tartus. Across the Atlantic, President Barack Obama's administration was horrified at the violence Assad employed, but the U.S. did not intervene, either. Instead, the Obama administration continually warned Assad that any use of chemical weapons against rebel-held areas would lead to consequences.

By the summer, hundreds of thousands of Syrians were gathering in the center of Hama. Hamwis finally had a chance to express their hatred for the regime thirty years after the troops of Bashar's father massacred up to ten thousand civilians in the city. Hafez al-Assad framed the bloodshed as an operation to stamp out Islamist "terrorists." Bashar and the hard-liners in his family planned to do the same in response to the Arab Spring. The regime intentionally released several known al-Qaeda operatives from prison, many of whom, as hoped, joined the protests in Hama and encouraged citizens to take up arms.

In July, the French and American ambassadors to Syria visited the rebellious city and met with protestors and activists. A Syrian oligarch named Mohammed Jaber, who was working for Bashar's brother Maher al-Assad, sent buses packed with regime loyalists to storm the embassies in revenge. Jaber also organized pro-regime thugs, or *shabiha*, into "Popular Resistance Committees."

Mohammed and his brother, Ayman, had a long history of working for the Assads. The brothers were "part of the clientelist circle of businessmen that rendered handy services to the [Assad] regime and provided it with revenues while turning a tidy profit for themselves." In this respect, the Jabers were not too different from "implementers" like Prigozhin within the Russian system. Ayman Jaber married into Assad's family, which opened the door to kickbacks in Syria's energy, iron, and steel industry, while Mohammed, a former general in the Syrian Arab Army (SAA), had important defense and national security contacts. Like the Assad family, and many of the regime's elite, the Jabers were Alawites, a religious minority distinct from, yet often associated with, Shi'ism.

At the end of July 2011, Bashar sent the Syrian army to crush the uprising in Hama, killing hundreds of civilians. But Assad's brutality and deliberate policies of sectarianism led to desertions, especially of officers and soldiers from Syria's Sunni majority. To shore up Assad's ranks, Iran—particularly through Hezbollah in Lebanon—started sending men to support the Syrian Arab Army. Meanwhile, Gulf States like Qatar and the UAE—in competition with each other—began quietly intervening on behalf of the rebels.

Assad lost significant territory to rebels. In August 2013, the regime issued a decree enabling oil companies and other businesses to hire mercenaries for the protection of state assets. The new law presented the Jaber brothers with an opportunity, one it appears they were aware of prior to legislation's approval. Already in 2012, they were in talks with the Russian private military company (PMC) Moran Group.

"Mercenarism," and therefore private military companies (PMCs), are illegal in Russia according to Article 359 of the 1996 Criminal Code. But the War on Terror had been a boon for the security industry, allowing Russian contractors to work for Western companies guarding facilities and convoys in Iraq and Afghanistan. The piracy crisis off the coast of Somalia further opened the industry to Russian entrepreneurs. Large firms hired Moran Group, as well as companies like RSB Group and Vega, to guard their ships and train their crews. Moran Group worked around Article 359 by registering outside the country and routing contractors, bound for the Middle East or Africa, through European cities under the guise of tourism. As is the case with Prigozhin and Utkin in Donbas, we don't know who exactly connected Jaber with Moran Group. Russian journalists contend Syria's ambassador to Russia and the FSB brokered the deal. On the other hand, Moran Group's aptly surnamed head, Vyacheslav Kalashnikov, was a former FSB officer. Seeking guidance from old colleagues, insiders contend, would have been a natural move—not necessarily indicative of an FSB plot. Some believe Moran's deputy CEO, Vadim Gusev, signed the deal directly with Jaber; Gusev had been laying plans to diversify away from maritime security after the detention of several contractors in Nigeria. In 2012, Gusev registered a new entity, Slavonic Corps Limited, in Hong Kong.

When Assad signed the decree legalizing the use of mercenaries, the recruitment drive for Slavonic Corps was already underway. One of the men to sign up was "Andrei." After serving in the military, Andrei wanted to join one of the maritime security companies, protecting ships from pirates, but for whatever reason it hadn't worked out. Still, he spent time on internet forums, where veterans and fans of military affairs discussed PMCs and potential contracts. When he heard of a chance to guard gas facilities somewhere abroad, he signed right away. "It was a chance to see the world," he told me. And the money didn't seem bad, either.

In August, when Andrei prepared to deploy, the Assad regime launched a devastating sarin gas attack on a city district in Damascus, killing up to 1,400 people. The attack put the Obama administration's "red line" on the use of chemical weapons to the test. The president was loathe to engage in another Middle Eastern intervention. The U.S. had finally withdrawn from Iraq, and NATO's recent intervention in Libya only brought further instability. The administration wavered, and Russian diplomats—and perhaps Putin personally—jumped in. Moscow called for Assad to hand over his stocks of chemical weapons, thus relieving the U.S. of its need to act.

While Moscow collaborated with the U.S. within a UN framework on the handover of chemical weapons, Slavonic Corps touched down. Andrei joined the *muzhiky*, which consisted of fifty to sixty men, many prior Moran Group employees, and was led by Dmitry Utkin. Andrei remembered Utkin as a competent commander. "He knew how to act quickly and adapt to a new situation, and he respected his subordinates. He could joke on any topic but at the same time was strict and demanded discipline. Everything was built on this. Discipline and order. Nothing extra." Another unit consisted of around two hundred Kuban Cossacks.

The corps made their way to a base in Syria's temperate, coastal Latakia region. They relaxed on the beach posing with AK-47s. Sometimes they fired into the sand. The mood shifted, though, when Assad's military delivered heavy weapons for a trip to Deir ez-Zor, a city in the east's energy-rich, ISIS-held desert. Watching infantry fighting vehicles roll in, some of the mercenaries grew nervous and threatened to mutiny. The plan was to guard oil fields, they said, not capture them. But Gusev threatened to withhold $4,000 from any refusenik. More concerning than the presence of these vehicles was their terrible shape. The team decided to outfit Hyundai trucks and Jeeps with machine guns instead, and the convoy set off for the desert.

As the group turned northeast on the road to Deir ez-Zor, a Syrian pilot, seemingly trying to show off, flew his helicopter low to buzz the convoy and crashed. A dire omen. It was becoming clear the road was not safe. The Russians regrouped in Homs before giving the road another go. They drove straight into an ISIS ambush.

A Syrian unit was engaged first, Andrei remembered. The Cossacks fell in second when they tried to circumvent the ambush to the left of the road. Pinned down, they began returning fire. Andrei's company, which had trailed the convoy, took up positions along the road to prevent the insurgents from flanking them. Another group entrenched itself outside of Es-Sukhne. After eighteen hours of battle, insurgents kept coming, and Slavonic Corps risked encirclement. The number of fighters that ambushed the Russians on the outskirts of Es-Sukhne, like any good fishing story, varies by account—from one thousand to the highly unlikely six thousand.

"Utkin understood that with the weapons and men we had, there was no way we were going to break through. Help wasn't on the way."

A sandstorm, rare for that time of year, swept through the battle-field. Visibility dropped to zero, and Utkin told his men to hold hands and form a chain. He managed to lead them out, and the Cossacks followed suit. Six members of Slavonic Corps were wounded, two seriously. Had it not been for the sandstorm, the convoy may well have been destroyed.

The mercenaries limped back to Latakia. Mohammed Jaber was furious with the corps' performance. The mercenaries knew the Kremlin wouldn't be pleased, either. In September, Assad had agreed to hand over his stocks of chemical weapons, allowing Russia to position itself to the West as a responsible, neutral actor. Slavonic Corps' embarrassing mission, conducted alongside pro-Assad forces, suggested that Russia was secretly backing Assad. On October 28, two planes brought Slavonic Corps to Moscow, where they were met by the FSB. Everyone was interrogated then released, but in November, Gusev and another leader became the first citizens to be charged with Article 359 on mercenarism. They were sentenced to three years.

Coming down so hard on a mission that the FSB, MoD, or parts of either may have approved in the first place allowed the Kremlin to distance itself from the PMC. Had Slavonic Corps only conducted guard duty, making little noise, their mission could well have ended without arrests. It would be wrong, however, to call their Syrian adventure a failure: Despite being ambushed by an overwhelming force, thanks to Utkin and other commanders, no one was killed. The mission proved that, in the right context, with the right team and equipment, mercenaries could be useful for far more than guard duty. Those lessons would soon be put to the test in Donbas. "Once they saw how everything could work, what the results could be, and how to properly employ such companies, conclusions were made," Andrei believed.

The hand-wringing over Assad's use of chemical weapons soon gave way to a threat the West truly considered existential. In the summer of 2014, the U.S. and two international coalitions began bombing ISIS in Iraq and Syria. The administration announced a Department of Defense (DoD) program to arm moderate rebels to fight ISIS and entered into a partnership with the Kurdish People's Defense Units (YPG). As the actors in the Syrian conflict multiplied, Assad's grip on power weakened and his reliance on auxiliary forces grew.

In 2015, Russia formally intervened in Syria. Both Moscow and the Assad regime referred to a history of cooperation and friendship, and since the war had broken out, Russian diplomats had vetoed UN resolutions condemning the regime. But this narrative doesn't explain well the timing of Russia's intervention. Kirill Semenov, a Russian expert on the Middle East and North Africa, argues instead that Syria was a way for Russia to reopen diplomatic channels with the Americans following events in Ukraine. The West had hit Russia hard with sanctions after the annexation of Crimea and covert intervention in Donbas. Intervention in Syria would force the Americans to cooperate on an issue important to them: defeating ISIS.

The first group of Wagner fighters arrived in Syria in September. We don't know whose decision it was to send the Company there. A source in the Ministry of Defense believes Prigozhin took the initiative, securing approval from Putin himself, rather than leaders in the MoD. Wagner brought mostly instructors and tank specialists to repair Syrian equipment in Homs. Marat, together with other contractors, touched down later that month. The first mission, Marat remembers, was an effort to sell Wagner's services. "Not everyone in the MoD was aware of our activities in eastern Ukraine," Marat said. For around a month the

Company was involved in operations typical of the Green Berets. They trained the Desert Hawks and gathered intelligence. Then, the small Wagner forces started engaging the enemy in Latakia. But soon a guided shell hit the artillery tent of Marat's brigade, killing nine people. The MoD panicked; there was no plan yet how to hide casualties. That October, the generals told the Company to pack its bags. Utkin, Marat, and others flew home.

They were not in Russia for long. It seems that after October, Russian and Syrian military planners recognized Assad's ragtag army and militias—even with Russian air support—couldn't retake territory from more motivated rebels. The decision was made to consider Wagner a mercenary force and not include their casualties in official statistics. The Kremlin understood there was little appetite among the Russian public for sending Russian soldiers to distant Syria. The deaths of contractors would be far quieter, a lesson learned from America's wars in Iraq and Afghanistan. Outsourcing war to contractors lowered the political costs.

In January 2016, Marat and fellow mercenaries landed in the same province Slavonic Corps was based in three years earlier. He and three hundred other mercenaries were to embed with Ayman and Mohammed Jaber's PMC "Desert Hawks" and launch an offensive on rebel-held Latakia.

It seems an unlikely coincidence that first Slavonic Corps, then Prigozhin and Utkin's Company signed deals with the Jaber brothers. That the MoD forced the Company to leave Syria in the fall of 2015 suggests Prigozhin was looking for backdoor entries into the country, perhaps through a local intermediary. Utkin's role as a commander in Slavonic Corps placed him in a position to either know Mohammed Jaber personally or know of him, making it easy for the Company's number two to introduce Prigozhin to Jaber. Of course, there were certainly individuals in the FSB and GRU who could connect Prigozhin and Jaber as well. As with any complex project, the deal Prigozhin struck with the Jabers was likely contingent on initiatives and lobbying from all sides. Buy-in was needed from several institutions, including the Russian

Ministry of Defense, since at some point the operation would have requested equipment and ammunition. Wagner, Syrian forces, and Iranian militias all would report to Russian military headquarters, though Wagner and Desert Hawks commanders would have significant freedom to make tactical decisions on the ground.

Prigozhin's agreement with the MoD was informal, which left him vulnerable to the whims of competing Kremlin insiders. He needed more touchpoints in Syria; if the Company was indispensable to multiple decision-makers, within both the Russian and the Syrian government, they could lobby against any MoD change of heart. A local partner also provided a degree of legal cover for the Company's presence.

Since Utkin last saw the Jabers in 2013, the brothers had grown their PMC to an estimated five thousand men. Among the Syrian military, the Hawks had the reputation of an effective fighting force, especially since Mohammed Jaber drew top talent by offering higher salaries than the regular army. It was hardly a perfect partnership for Prigozhin, though: There were grumblings that the Jabers were looking to carve out their own fief in Latakia. Nor did the brothers necessarily have a positive view of Russian mercenaries after terminating their contract with Gusev, but, by this point, the rebel Free Syrian Army, al-Qaeda-affiliated al-Nusra, ISIS, and Kurdish rebel groups had taken vast swaths of the country. Delivering victories to Assad was existential. The Jabers would have been fools to turn down Russian cooperation.

Utkin deployed Ratibor's company and Marat's company to work with the Desert Hawks. Marat always considered Utkin a fascist "of the Italian variety," fascinated with empire. "Nationality did not matter to him, as long as you were a specialist in your field," Marat told me. "He appointed me, a Muslim Tatar, as a company commander. At the same time, he disbanded the platoon of Davor Savičić, a Slav, and deprived Orthodox Serbs of commanding positions."

Complicating the structure, Marat's reconnaissance company was divided into two groups that worked with units attached to different Jaber brothers. Other Wagner units stayed behind, at first, to conduct training and other tasks. Almost immediately, Wagner ran into issues with the Hawks. They may have been better than the regular Syrian Army but, in the Russians' eyes, the Hawks were poor soldiers. They frequently refused to carry out orders, were quick to retreat, and spent more time taking selfies than looking for the enemy. There was a sense among the Company's commanders that the Syrians were taking advantage of the Russians, forcing them to risk their lives on dangerous advances while the Hawks sat behind safely.

One morning in February 2016, when the Hawks and Wagner forces reached the outskirts of Kinsabba, a small town in northeast Latakia on Syria's border with Turkey, the *dukhi** attacked. It is difficult to know for sure the composition of rebels in and around Kinsabba at the time—it was even unclear to Wagner sources fighting them—though they likely included a mix of Free Syrian Army and the al-Qaeda-affiliated al-Nusra Front. The Hawks received the order to retreat, but Ratibor, fed up with the lack of progress, told his men they would defend their positions.

After the shelling and rocket attacks died down, Marat caught a few hours rest. The group knew another attack would come at dawn. Sure enough, Chup's voice crackled over the radio in the early morning—more movement from the *dukhi*. Worse, the Hawks who were supposed to support his platoon had disappeared. This wasn't an accident; Marat had noticed that there was a lot of tension within the Hawks' ranks as the Jaber brothers competed for Assad's favor. But it had a real effect on the Company's ability to fight. The next thing Marat heard on the radio was that Chup—a well-respected commander—had been killed. He had taken a direct hit from a mortar.

---

* The term *dukhi* comes from the Soviet Union's invasion of Afghanistan. Meaning "spirit" or "ghost" in Russian, it was a blanket term for the mujahideen and other insurgents fighting the Soviets. *Sadyk*, borrowed from the Arabic for "friend," was the Russian term for allied forces. Both terms followed Russian-speaking soldiers into Chechnya, Syria, Libya, and beyond.

A few days later, the Hawks and Wagner made their move on Kinsabba. On the first attempt, they sat exposed in a few abandoned buildings, waiting for their Syrian compatriots to begin the assault. The Syrians, however, started looting what little was left of the village, already ruined after rebels took the town. Realizing the Hawks wouldn't advance, a furious Ratibor ordered his men back to camp. On the second attempt, the platoon came under fire before finding shelter in woods to the east. After crawling along craggy rocks, they finally had Kinsabba in view. Looking through binoculars, Ratibor saw outfitted pickups at the town's entrance. He called over the radio. The Russian general overseeing the operation told him the *dukhi* had already left, the town was liberated. They forgot to inform the mercenaries.

Following the Latakia offensive, Syrian and Russian generals set their sights on Palmyra, in the middle of the country's oil- and gas-producing region. Famous throughout its four-thousand-year history, Palmyra is the "Pearl of the Desert." In 2015, ISIS captured the city and destroyed many of its ancient monuments. Recapturing it would be symbolic for the Assad regime.

Palmyra sits on an oasis, protected by mountains to the north and west, and desert to the east. In March 2016, the MoD tasked Wagner and the Hawks with taking the mountains first. Fighting ISIS, Marat remembered in his memoirs, was an entirely different beast. Unlike al-Qaeda's al-Nusra, or the Free Syrian Army, ISIS was "strong, disciplined, well-equipped, ruthless to the point of sadism, and held death in contempt." The Company's first assault on ISIS positions in the mountains was pushed back. They regrouped and began methodically capturing each summit in the mountain chain. For Utkin's men, it was a brutal slog through rocky, cold cliffs. But taking Palmyra would prove invaluable for the nascent PMC. Utkin pushed his commanders to make quick progress. The Company left the rear for the Desert Hawks to guard.

Finally, with Palmyra in sight, Utkin called company commanders—Ratibor, Nik, Marat, and the others—into a meeting. His plan was to descend into Palmyra and provide support for the Syrian army and Iran-backed Hezbollah forces pushing into the city. The next day, Utkin's men, with artillery and support from MoD helicopter fire, assaulted ISIS's positions along the west. Despite being well dug-in, the enemy was overwhelmed by Wagner's assault. In pursuit of the fleeing jihadists, Marat's unit fell into an ambush. He was hit by a grenade and evacuated to Russia. Assad's forces, with significant support from the Russian Air Force, fully captured Palmyra on March 27. The Company claims to have suffered around 160 casualties in the offensive, with 40 dead and 120 wounded.

A few months later, back in Moscow, the Mariinsky Theatre put on a heavily televised performance in Palmyra's ancient Roman amphitheater. Marat and others received their medals for bravery in a secret ceremony, but they were left with a sour taste in their mouth. "For an entire year, the Syrian army, its tanks, its air force, its artillery had not managed to advance a meter to conquer this ridge, but [Utkin's] mercenaries, in two days and without any loss, took the fortifications of the first line." The Russian military's top brass, however, took credit for the victory without acknowledging Wagner's contribution. For a second time, the MoD, flush with its victory in Palmyra, decided they no longer needed Prigozhin and Utkin's services. "The decision," Marat told me, "came from the highest levels." The MoD told the Company's men to hand in their weapons, and the mercenaries flew back to Moscow. If the Jabers protested against Wagner's departure—doubtful given tensions all around—their arguments failed to convince Assad and the Russian generals.

Prigozhin and Utkin's PMC was only two years old, but already fighters within Wagner had developed an esprit de corps. Yes, they were mercenaries, but they were also Russian patriots; men, in many respects, more willing to fight and die for the motherland than the regular Russian military. For Prigozhin as well, the MoD's decision must have been infuriating. The Company was a means for him to rise through the ranks of Putin's regime. That would be difficult if Putin didn't even know Wagner's contributions. To stay on Putin's radar, Prigozhin and the Company needed to find ways to start exerting a degree of independence from the MoD.

★ ★ ★

After they were pulled out of Syria, Utkin's men spent the next few months hanging around Molkino, their base shared with the GRU. Prigozhin stayed busy; he had no off switch. When he touched down in Syria, just like his restaurant days in St. Petersburg, he made every effort to ingratiate himself with Bashar al-Assad's inner circle. The Jaber brothers were always a stepping stone to greater things.

In December 2016, Prigozhin had a stroke of luck. ISIS went on a surprise offensive—the first in eighteen months—and recaptured Palmyra. The loss of Palmyra, Russian military expert Michael Kofman notes, was due in part to a disagreement over strategy between Moscow on one side and Assad and Iran on the other. The Russians wanted to push toward Deir ez-Zor to link up with the U.S. campaign against ISIS, while Assad and Iran saw rebel-held Aleppo as the main threat. The campaign to take Aleppo left Palmyra exposed.

It was a humiliating loss. Wagner was promptly needed back in Syria. This time, though, Prigozhin signed a deal directly with the Syrian government, bypassing the Jaber brothers. That would prove another lucky break. The Jabers had grown too powerful, prompting other Syrian oligarchs, even the Assad regime itself, to worry. "We could control over 60 percent of the country, if we were allowed to," Mohammed Jaber told a *Der Spiegel* journalist in 2017. Shortly thereafter, his men stopped Assad's presidential motorcade at gunpoint. That was the final straw. Assad put Ayman Jaber under house arrest, while Mohammed fled to Russia. The Desert Hawks were disbanded and incorporated into the Syrian Army.

The new agreement with the Syrian government allowed Prigozhin's company, "Evro-Polis," to recapture oil fields from "illegal armed groups" on behalf of Assad. In exchange, the regime would reimburse

Evro-Polis its costs, and the company would receive a 25 percent share of liberated oil fields' profit. Prigozhin had registered Evro-Polis the year prior, but around the time of the deal, the company's activities changed from "wholesale and retail trade" to oil, gas, coal production, and drilling. Valery Chekalov, known from other Prigozhin-linked companies like the Museum of Chocolate in St. Petersburg, was named Evro-Polis's general director.

The profit-sharing deal structure was not necessarily Prigozhin's idea. The Jaber brothers had also reportedly inked a similar deal with Assad in the Badia region. Nonetheless, the agreement provided legal cover for the redeployment of Prigozhin's PMC to Syria. Perhaps, Prigozhin and Utkin were thinking at the time, the deal with the Assads would hedge some of Wagner's financial reliance on the MoD. Independence, though, is a double-edged sword.

After his injuries in Palmyra, Marat was put on Wagner's reserve list and went home. There he received the news that his wife was diagnosed with cancer. Without a job, and medical bills about to add up, Marat called a friend in Wagner who handled the mercenaries' medical treatment. The friend got Marat a job working in Prigozhin's spacious headquarters in St. Petersburg—all Prigozhin's disparate businesses shared the same building—where he finally met "Number 1" for the first time. Number 1 greeted Marat and offered his hand. "I immediately noticed," Marat wrote in his second memoir, "his distinct manner of looking at his interlocutor from under his brow, slightly tilting his head forward, as if preparing for a fight." Number 1 told Marat he had heard of his wife's cancer, and that he shouldn't worry. He would pay for her operation and treatment in Germany.

A grateful Marat threw himself into mundane office work, reporting on movements in Syria and any mention of Prigozhin in the press. He noticed how tense employees became when Number 1 entered the office. Even the managing director Andrei "Sedoi" Troshev, "almost Prigozhin's equal in status," seemed to fear him. As Marat grew to know his boss, he noticed "a defining feature of Prigozhin was his unshakable belief that any decision he made in any situation was correct. Even when he encountered negative consequences of his actions, he managed to turn what happened into another victory, a result of carefully thought-out plans."

Leaks published by the Dossier Center provide critical insight into the structure of Prigozhin's PMC at that time. Evro-Polis sent its Syrian clients an organization chart that included a "director," presumably Yevgeny Prigozhin, and "commander," presumably Dmitry Utkin. Those titles remained from the Donbas days, while the rest of the Company's structure became much more complicated. The commander oversaw a staff office and a management team. The management team, consisting of about thirty individuals, ran eight assault detachments (*shturmovoi otryad'*), a tank company, artillery division, an engineer-sapper company, and several positions within "security services." A "protection company," designated for guarding oil wells, fell under the "Chief of Site Protection." Other key figures within the management team included a "Deputy Commander for Work with the Syrians," "Deputy Commander on the Rear," "Deputy Commander for Weapons and Equipment," "Chief of Artillery," "Translator," etc. The training center and base back in Molkino had a separate chain of command, with its own security service and group of instructors. It was this structure of Evro-Polis that would become known to the world as "Wagner Group."

As for the mercenaries, the Company drew a range of characters with varying ideologies and priorities. Dmitry Utkin often told his men they were fighting "for our Russian mother," and the Company attracted men with nationalist, often white supremacist, beliefs—a trend not unknown to Western PMCs and militaries. When a member of Vorobyev's Imperial Legion invited Arkady, the arch-Orthodox monar-chist, to join the Company in Syria, he felt an immediate connection to the mission: "Just imagine," Arkady told me. "A Russian expeditionary force marches through the desert along roads trekked by Roman legions, driving anti-Christian evil spirits straight to back to hell. The expedi-tion performs tasks the Ministry of Defense at that time couldn't handle . . . It was a Russian Crusade. Even if everyone didn't understand it that way." Indeed, Arkady conceded, the motivation for most Wagner mercenaries to fight abroad was less a crusade and more a complicated mix of patriotic beliefs, a love for martial life, an addiction to adrenaline, and the need for a paycheck.

When Arkady was in Ukraine, he was unaware of Utkin and his mercenary detachment fighting on the other side of Debaltseve. During the operation, however, he frequently ran into "specialists," men in plain uniform who spoke with a hard "g."* Arkady and fellow volunteers referred to these men as "subcontractors," assumed to be employed by Russia's Ministry of Defense. When he arrived in Syria, he was impressed by Wagner Group's army in miniature. "Compared to the chaos in [Ukraine], the Company was ordered and disciplined, without the army-like lethargy. It had its own artillery, its own heavy equipment. We had our own security service that monitored mercenaries' cell phones and conversations with home, so foolish people would not reveal unnecessary things."

In late January 2017, the Company launched operations to seize oil and gas fields from the Islamic State. While the exact figure is unknown, it is likely between one thousand and twelve hundred Wagner mercenaries participated in the successful operation to take the critical fields in Hayan and Jazel that February.

Another three hundred fighters helped recapture Palmyra. The mission was relatively quick. Syrian forces had the backing of not only Wagner, but Lebanon's Iran-backed Hezbollah militia as well. The Russian military provided air support, and while neither government would acknowledge any form of cooperation, the U.S. launched airstrikes on ISIS positions in Palmyra.

---

* Russian speakers identify southern dialect by the pronunciation of "g." Russian speakers in the south of Russia and regions of Ukraine, such as Donbas, are often known to pronounce "g" as an "h," e.g., *govorit'* versus *hovorit'* ("to speak").

After Palmyra, recruiting opened further. A dozen or more men from the Imperial Legion joined the Company's ranks, as did men from the neo-Nazi Rusich battalion, including leader Aleksei Milchakov. Milchakov was infamous for cutting the head off of and allegedly eating a puppy before posting the photos to social media, along with Nazi flags and other far-right paraphernalia. During the war in Donbas, Milchakov also bragged about personally photographing mutilated Ukrainian corpses. Despite their religious differences—conservative Orthodox versus pagan—Arkady was indifferent to the Rusich battalion's presence and ideology. "Rusich fight for Russia. They lose their soldiers and get wounded. What else needs to be said about them after this?"

Several local militiamen from the LNR also wanted to fight in Syria, and a few commanders petitioned Prigozhin to let them. But Utkin held Donbas locals in low esteem. Instead of incorporating these men in various assault detachments, the Commander created a special task force *Karpaty* (Carpathians), which would keep them all in one place. The detachment was essentially an assault force, cannon fodder for storming enemy positions.

As Wagner expanded its ranks, Prigozhin took care to protect his bottom line. He convinced the Syrian government to approve the formation of a local PMC, "ISIS Hunters," made up of Syrian mercenaries who were much cheaper to pay. Prigozhin placed a dual Syrian-Russian citizen as its head. As a requirement, ISIS Hunters also included an officer from Assad's feared domestic intelligence services, the *mukhabarat*.

In April 2017, Arkady, in a group of roughly 1,500 Wagner fighters, launched an attack to take the oil fields in Shair. The fighting was intense. The Islamic State's pickup trucks, outfitted with machine guns in the truck bed, or "technicals," were ideal for a desert environment. Suicide bombers drove cars packed with explosives into Wagner's lines. The mercenaries grew frustrated losing men due to poor kit: another attempt by Prigozhin to cut corners and save money. The Russian military, in contrast, had the country's most up-to-date technology at their disposal, but that stayed on base.

In September 2017, the Company took Es-Sukhne, the same town where Slavonic Corps fell into an ambush four years prior. They then grabbed Al-Shola from an Assad-allied oligarch whose militia refused to surrender. The Euphrates River came within their sights. On the island of Kati, Wagner captured two hundred to four hundred Islamic State fighters. As the Company advanced, small units stayed behind to guard liberated assets.

One of these units captured Hamdi Bouta, a Syrian construction worker conscripted into Assad's army while visiting his family from Lebanon. Around April, Bouta escaped into the desert and stumbled into the Shair gas fields where a group of Wagner fighters found him. The mercenaries executed Bouta with sledgehammers, recording the incident on video. After killing him, they cut up Bouta's corpse and burned the pieces. One of the executioners later identified in the video, Vladislav Apostol, was believed to have ties to Rusich. The depravity of the punishment—filmed on camera—was most certainly intended as a message. For whom and to what purpose isn't quite clear, though the goal may have been to prevent further Syrian desertions, a constant issue plaguing the Russians. It would be one of the first recorded instances of the Company's human rights abuses.

While Arkady and others rushed on to Deir ez-Zor, a city which had been under siege from rebels then ISIS for years, Prigozhin was growing anxious. Despite the PMC's victories, the Assad government had yet to pay the Company for its services. In a letter to the Syrian minister of presidential affairs, Evro-Polis stated it had extinguished five oil and gas wells—set on fire during the Islamic State's retreat—and ensured a daily production of up to two million cubic meters of gas and four thousand barrels of mineral oil, totaling $550,000 daily. Evro-Polis had invested in capital repairs and planned to double production by May. The company claimed to have invested $120 million into the project, with no cost sharing or response from the other side.

In short, Assad was slow rolling the Russian mercenaries, leveraging his regime's opaque bureaucracy. "There are no individuals capable of resolving the emerging issues," the Evro-Polis letter complained. "The Minister of Oil in the Syrian Arab Republic cannot make independent decisions, citing a lack of authority. There is a constant redirecting of issues from one official to another, and the actions of these officials do not imply that the issues will be resolved soon, jeopardizing the project's implementation." Evro-Polis's representatives had yet to hear back on any of their concerns. "We ask you, honorable Mansur Azzam, to imme- diately inform the President of the Syrian Arab Republic Bashar al-Assad on the contents of this letter."

The $120 million investment figure cited by Evro-Polis may well have been exaggerated, but Prigozhin's deal with the Syrian government was clearly not as lucrative as the director had imagined. The oil and gas fields Wagner liberated enroute to Deir ez-Zor were small. The assets were perhaps profitable as standalone entities. That didn't mean, however, that they could cover Evro-Polis's repairs, let alone the costs the Company incurred in deploying its mercenaries.

The largest oil and gas fields—95 percent of the country's energy resources—were on the other side of the Euphrates; that is, on the other side of the deconfliction line, where the predominantly Kurdish Syrian Defense Forces, also recognizing ISIS's imminent collapse, had turned away from Raqqa toward Deir ez-Zor in a race to capture, with U.S. support, as many of the oil and gas fields as possible.

A month after the U.S. and SDF took the Conoco gas fields—the most profitable in Syria—from the Islamic State, Russian mercenaries and pro-Assad forces captured Deir ez-Zor and the town of Khasham. The Conoco facilities lay only three and a half kilometers to the north.

Meanwhile, Marat's wife had recovered from a successful operation. Bored with office life, the husband requested a transfer to the field. Prigozhin granted his request, and Marat became an advisor to the ISIS Hunters. Before departing, Marat noticed Prigozhin had become obsessed with seizing Conoco. The facility could produce 450 million cubic feet of natural gas per day, equivalent to hundreds of millions of dollars in revenue per year. It was, perhaps, a chance to bring Wagner's Syria venture out of the red.

★ ★ ★

Throughout his life Prigozhin bullied his way ahead, always doubling down when others fold. After trying and failing to negotiate control of the Conoco facility with Kurdish leaders, he began laying plans to take it by force. He thought the Americans would want to avoid a "World War III scenario"; in other words, that they'd prefer to retreat rather than fire on Russian nationals and risk escalation with Moscow. The Americans, he perhaps calculated, had already blinked when Assad used chemical weapons. They also failed to support the Kurds when Turkey—a NATO ally—intervened in Syria. Why would they back the Kurds against Russia?

On February 6, Marat was called into a meeting where, to his surprise, Utkin was present. Utkin gave the floor to the chief of staff, who revealed Number 1's order. "The Americans won't interfere in our operation," the chief of staff added.

Utkin laid out a plan. The *Karpaty* assault force, which had several old tanks at its disposal, would storm the SDF and U.S. base. The Second Assault Detachment would take the road to the north of Conoco, before turning east to the Jafra gas facility, also controlled by the SDF and Americans. The Fifth Assault Detachment would follow in the rear. Marat's ISIS Hunters unit would attack on the left flank. The Russian military, Wagner leadership said, promised air cover.

At 3:00 p.m. on February 7, 2018, more than five hundred troops and twenty-seven vehicles had gathered around al-Khasham. American officers in the Middle East and Washington were glued to their screens watching footage beamed from Reaper drones flying high above the rising storm. By evening, the Americans prepared for the worst: Three massive Russian T-72M tanks rumbled to within a mile of their base.

Then, around 10:00 p.m., the sky lit up, the barrage of shells giving brief form to approaching shapes.

A convoy of armored vehicles carrying U.S. Special Forces pulled into the base just as the shells began landing. Wagner's *Karpaty* detachment advanced on foot.

Back at command, U.S. officials were urgently calling their Russian counterparts through their deconfliction line. Each time—reports vary, but there were perhaps three separate calls, and at least one call while Russian forces were still gathering—the Russian Ministry of Defense denied any knowledge of the operation.

That was little consolation to the American and SDF forces on the ground at Conoco. They were outgunned: their small arms no match for Russian artillery, tanks, and a ten-to-one ratio. Air support would be critical, but the Russian military had long-range air defense in Syria that could reach Conoco, making it dangerous for U.S. aircraft to get too close.

The Americans fired one warning shell in Marat's direction. But he and the ISIS Hunter division ignored it and kept pushing forward. Finally, after the Russian military denied any knowledge of the operation one last time, U.S. command gave the order to their men: "weapons free."

The first thing Marat remembers was a salvo of Hellfire missiles from the Reaper drones hanging in the pitch above. That shut down Wagner's surface-to-air system. A convoy of U.S. special forces arrived in five trucks loaded with .50-caliber machine guns on the roof. One of the men later told journalist Kevin Maurer:

> Josh's team in truck two tracked a small group of mercenaries about 1,000 meters from the trucks and closing. The gunner rotated the .50-caliber machine gun robotically stabilized on the roof. It could put thousands of rounds on target from more than 1,000 yards. Even on cyclic, where the gun doesn't stop shooting until it runs out of

bullets, it could maintain a grouping that fits on the hood of a small car. Josh zeroed in on the group of Russian and pro-Syrian fighters and fired. The .50-caliber machine gun on top of the truck roared and the white-hot silhouettes of men approaching the berm exploded into parts scattered across the black sand.

Soon the other .50-caliber guns joined in. The Americans' targeting was far more accurate. Wagner and the Syrians, it seemed, didn't have night vision.

As the *Karpaty* detachment was being cut down, the special forces caught sight of fifty-ton Russian tanks on the horizon. That was a problem. The Americans took aim and hit the tanks with quick bursts from the .50-calibers. The bullets simply bounced off.

Wagner's T-62 and T-72 tanks crawled forward, firing 125-mm cannons. Luckily for the Americans, the tanks were wide of their mark. Again, night vision, or the lack of it, saved them. But Wagner was still advancing, and Marat and his men found their way toward an SDF block post.

There was a moment where American forces thought they might have to retreat. Word had come from command that the Russians were scrambling Su-30SM multirole fighters. There was no way the small American team could withstand bombardment from the Russian Air Force. But the U.S. had also scrambled F-15E Strike Eagles. By the time the Su-30s were in the air, the American pilots had them painted. The air support promised by Russia's MoD never arrived.

Then came the distant thump of helicopters.

Two U.S. Apache attack helicopters unleashed chain guns on the mercenaries below. "They circled around those who were trying to move to the second line and simply rained down fire from guided and unguided weapons." Marat gave the order to retreat, and his men started breaking away from each other. Anyone standing close together was obliterated.

An F-15 fighter jet screamed past, hitting more Russian vehicles. Then came the "low rumble of turboprop engines." An AC-130, or "Spooky," the world's largest artillery gunship that can keep continual fire on a target while flying in wide circles above.

The Russians and Syrians jumped into nearby houses for cover that turned to dust. One mercenary summarized the onslaught: "Several Apaches circling like a carousel, the flying battery of an AC-130, a B-52 bomber coming out of Qatar [likely referring to B-1B bombers from Saudi Arabia], several Reaper drones, and all this other shit was enough to destroy the entirety of Syria."

Strikes continued through the early morning. Finally, the Russians called the Americans over the deconfliction line asking for a ceasefire on humanitarian grounds. The Russians were given two hours to collect their dead. Out of Marat's unit of roughly seventy-five soldiers, twenty-five were dead and another twenty-eight wounded. The *Karpaty* never recovered. The few survivors were folded into the Fifth Assault Detachment.

Years later, Prigozhin claimed that Minister of Defense Sergei Shoigu, and the Russian military command, had been negotiating with the Americans while Wagner units approached Conoco. When the Americans made it clear they would attack, the Russian Ministry of Defense, according to Prigozhin, deliberately did not pass the message to Wagner. Marat, on the other hand, thought the MoD didn't provide air cover for more mundane reasons.

Wagner attracted men who had an aversion to bureaucracy. Commanders like Ratibor were free to respond to events as they unfolded on the battlefield. The Russian military, on the other hand, was risk averse. Commanders were constantly on the line with their superiors, waiting on approval for decisions whose timing could mean the difference between life and death. Few took responsibility willingly.

The Russian command may well have given Prigozhin the green light to take Conoco, trusting his conviction in an easy victory. Yet when it was clear the Americans would fight back, the Russian officer on the other side of the deconfliction line would have done anything to avoid an escalation scenario, the same scenario Prigozhin was convinced the Americans would also seek to avoid. For some poor Russian officer suddenly facing "World War III," a first reaction to deny knowledge of the attackers makes sense. Once Russia's top brass understood what was happening, U.S. planes were in the air, and it was too late (it's unlikely they would have ordered the Russian Air Force to hit Americans anyway). When word reached Minister of Defense Sergei Shoigu in Moscow, the Russians requested a ceasefire.

Tensions between Prigozhin and Shoigu prior to Khasham almost certainly existed. Sergei Shoigu was the minister of defense and a master bureaucrat. Prigozhin's style was that of a bulldozer. Shoigu could hardly have enjoyed dealing with a man outside the MoD, technically subordinate to him, who nonetheless had the ear of Vladimir Putin. Both probably complained about each other to their boss. Sending Russian mercenaries to their death intentionally, however, would be an outsized response to internal bickering.

Whether Prigozhin and Wagner were punished for the events in Khasham is also uncertain. Few spoke of the battle after it happened, Marat noted, especially the commanders, though a few months after the disaster at Conoco Prigozhin was once again incensed. The Syrian government had awarded contracts to renovate two profitable enterprises—a fertilizer plant in Homs and a gas-processing facility in Twinan—to the Russian company Stroytransgaz, owned by billionaire businessman Gennady Timchenko.

While there is no evidence to suggest the Syrian government was responding to the events at Khasham, the handover of prized assets to Timchenko was a bitter pill to swallow. Prigozhin had been working nonstop to graduate from an "implementer" in Putin's regime to one of the president's "friends and associates." His mercenaries fought three years in Syria, only for one of Putin's oldest friends to reap the rewards.

It wasn't just the money; it was also proof that Prigozhin was still on the outside looking in.

Stroytransgaz's contract to renovate the plant and gas-processing facility included a revenue-share agreement that came at the expense of Syrian businessmen close to Assad. Timchenko worried about saboteurs. The gas-processing facility in Twinan was also along the Palmyra–Deir ez-Zor highway: ISIS territory. Timchenko's assets were in grave need of protection, but, given Prigozhin's temperament and reputation, he could not outsource security to Wagner. Aware of Syrian troops' poor reputation, the oligarch never considered hiring a local PMC. Instead, he met with the Russian military's General Staff, who worked with him on the creation of a new private military company, PMC Redut, which would be run by friends in the reserve: Konstantin Mirzayants, Sergei Salivanov, and Andrei Blokhin. Timchenko quickly ran into the same issues that had confronted Prigozhin and other Russian PMC entrepreneurs before him. Establishing a legal entity necessitated convoluted multilayered accounting for allocating funds and paying personnel. PMC Redut's needs were relatively modest for that much paperwork. Guarding the two facilities required fifty fighters each, not even enough to constitute a full Wagner detachment. PMC Redut's organizers, therefore, kept things simple. Payments were made in cash. No contracts. Like the Donbas agreement between Prigozhin and Utkin in 2014, terms were written down on a piece of paper without an emblem or stamp.

Thus, another Russian "PMC" was born, a paramilitary formation serving a single commercial project. PMC Redut even lured away several Wagner personnel, including Marat, who had become disillusioned with his employer after the Battle of Khasham. The willingness of Prigozhin and Utkin to sacrifice hundreds of men without thinking through risks clearly was too much.

Wagner never made another attempt to capture SDF-held assets. The following year President Trump announced a drawdown of forces in Syria, although a limited number would remain "where they have oil."

Behind the scenes, the U.S. government helped broker a deal between the SDF and an American firm, Delta Crescent Energy. Delta Crescent's founders were a former U.S. ambassador and an ex–Delta Force army officer who ran his own private security firm.

Only eight days after Wagner's defeat in the Battle of Khasham, a grand jury for the District of Columbia indicted thirteen Russian individuals, the Internet Research Agency (IRA), Concord Management and Consulting LLC, Concord Catering, and a host of other shell companies for their role in interfering in the 2016 U.S. presidential elections. Special Counsel Robert Mueller and his team assembled the case and found that as early as 2014, employees of the IRA created groups and pages on social media that "addressed divisive U.S. political and social issues." IRA employees wrote derogatory posts about presidential candidates with the aim of "sowing discord." Prigozhin's employees posed online as real Americans and organized at a grassroots level. They planned in-person rallies, rather unsuccessfully, and communicated with unwitting persons affiliated with the Trump campaign.

Prigozhin's disinformation campaign was only part of a larger investigation into Russia's interference in U.S. elections. The "Mueller Report," released in March 2019, assessed the multiple prongs of that interference, from the IRA's work on social media, to the GRU's hacking and dumping of Clinton campaign emails, to Russian government links to the Trump campaign. Those hoping to find definitive collusion between Putin and Prigozhin's disinformation campaign were disappointed, though the Kremlin could easily have funded the IRA's activities through Concord. The company already received state contracts. But it is also possible that Prigozhin personally financed U.S. election interference.

Prigozhin had other media assets besides the IRA. RIA FAN news agency is one example. RIA FAN had no business model; there was no attempt to generate advertising revenue. Its existence, some Russian journalists posit, was more a function of Prigozhin's narcissism than his greed. When his ties to the "documentary" *Anatomy of a Protest* spurred investigations from independent Russian media, like Garmazhapova's *Novaya Gazeta*, Prigozhin lashed out and planted "spies" in their midst. "He hated the negative coverage," Andrei Zakharov, a Russian investigative journalist who covered Prigozhin said. "And he was obsessed with controlling what people said and wrote about him." Staff at his media companies admitted they "work for one reader alone."

It was no accident that Prigozhin organized his media assets into the "Patriot Media Group." If he was successful in interfering with U.S. elections, or perhaps influencing the Russian public, he could lobby the state to allocate more budget to his companies. He was always after more budget.

But in 2018, Prigozhin was reaching the limits of what was possible in Syria. His mercenary company was butting heads with other Russian institutions, and better-connected oligarchs like Gennady Timchenko were entering the fray, scooping up assets Prigozhin thought he deserved. Prigozhin and Utkin had a product: a battle-hardened and increasingly cohesive mercenary force. Now they needed markets, and Prigozhin had a team in place to pitch new ideas.

III

Diplomats

Figurez-vous, par exemple, que quand nous fûmes capables de lire à peu près correctement le français, une réalité nous apparut qui nous combla de joie et fierté. En effet, au centre même de la localité, à l'intersection de plusieurs axes routiers, une poutre portant plusieurs planchettes directionnelles nous apprit brutalement que nous étions sans conteste le centre du monde, le nombril de la terre.

—Étienne Goyémidé, *Le Dernier Survivant de la Caravane*

Imagine, for example, that when we were almost able to read French correctly, a reality appeared before us that filled us with pride and joy. Indeed, in the very center of town, at the intersection of several roads, a post that carried signs pointing several directions abruptly instructed us that we were, without a doubt, the center of the world, the navel of the earth.

—Étienne Goyémidé, *The Caravan's Last Survivor*, writing from the Central African Republic

In 2016, a Russian national, well-connected to various security services, met Prigozhin at his office in St. Petersburg. The man had worked in several countries, including Syria, and said he found an opportunity to

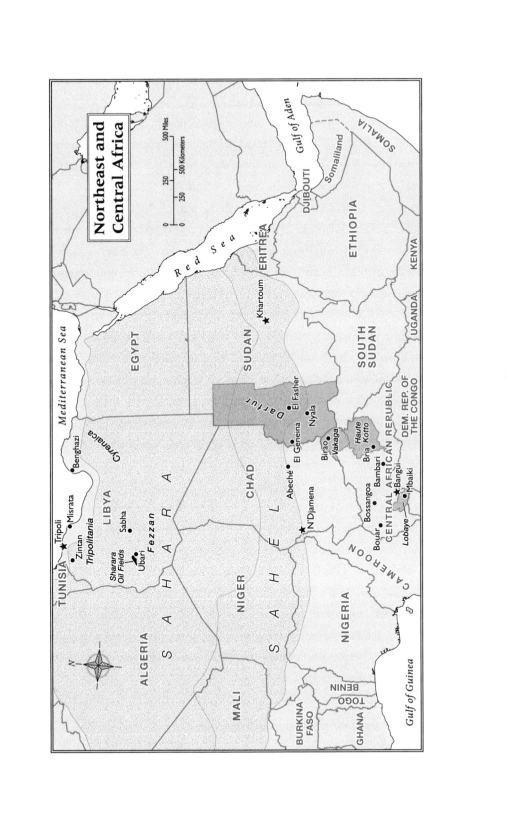

Northeast and Central Africa

Mediterranean Sea

Red Sea

Gulf of Aden

TUNISIA

Tripoli
Misrata
Zintan
Tripolitania
Benghazi
Cyrenaica

LIBYA

Sabha
Fezzan
Sharara
Oil Fields
Ubari

ALGERIA

S A H A R A

MALI

NIGER

EGYPT

SUDAN

Khartoum

ERITREA

DJIBOUTI

Somaliland

SOMALIA

ETHIOPIA

Darfur
El Fasher
Nyala
El Geneina
Abeché
Birao
Vakaga
Haute Kotto
Bria

SOUTH
SUDAN

UGANDA

KENYA

CHAD

S A H E L

N'Djamena

Bambari
Bossangoa
Bouar
Lobaye
Bangui
Mbaiki

CENTRAL AFRICAN REPUBLIC

DEM. REP. OF
THE CONGO

CAMEROON

NIGERIA

BENIN
TOGO
BURKINA
FASO
GHANA

Gulf of Guinea

N

0   250   500 Miles
0   250   500 Kilometers

mine gold. "I have a well-placed contact in Sudan," the man told Prigozhin. "We can go there and dig."

While the identity of that man is not known, it is possible he was affiliated with the GRU, which had been active in Sudan since the 1980s. Presentations show that at least as early as 2017, the MoD had explored several locations for air and sea bases around Port Sudan.

Prigozhin sent another St. Petersburg native, Mikhail Potepkin, to conduct a three-month feasibility study. Potepkin was a staunch supporter of Vladimir Putin since his college days. At twenty-five years old, he became the commissar for Nashi, the pro-Putin youth group. In 2014, he started a tech company, IT Debugger, with an Internet Research Agency employee indicted by Robert Mueller's team. That Potepkin would gravitate to Prigozhin's circle was hardly surprising to those who knew him. "In St. Petersburg, the circle of intellectuals, businessmen, and politicians is quite small," Alexandra Garmazhapova noted.

Potepkin assembled a team of geologists and "a few other guys" and took off. Once on the ground, however, he didn't see the investment opportunity as particularly attractive. When he delivered the report, his boss wasn't happy. "You don't know anything," Prigozhin snapped. "Go back for a while and learn about gold."

"It's true," Potepkin later told me. "I didn't know anything about gold." Prior to Sudan, he had largely worked on domestic political projects.

Like everywhere else, getting things done in Sudan comes down to who you know. The first three-month stint failed because the Russians weren't dealing with the right people. "So, we started knocking on other doors, and the office of Awad al-Jaz recognized the name Prigozhin. Al-Jaz was one of the most important, powerful politicians in the country," Potepkin continued. "He ran much of the regime on behalf of Omar al-Bashir."

Omar al-Bashir came to power in 1989, thanks to the National Islamic Front (NIF) and its ideologue Hassan al-Turabi. The NIF blamed the previous democratically elected government for failing to quash the

Sudan People's Liberation Movement/Army (SPLM/A), led by John Garang, which was, at the time, six years into a major rebellion against the imposition of Sharia laws. Garang called for a secular "New Sudan," a vision in which the country's ethnic and religious minorities would share power with riverine Arabs and Muslims. The conflict continued, however, through the 1990s, while political and economic marginalization brewed tension in the massive western region of Darfur. The SPLM/A was predominantly, but certainly not entirely, Christian and non-Arab Sudanese from the south. Darfur was predominantly non-Arab, but Muslim. Many Darfuris felt excluded from the Arab elite in Khartoum, rendering a power balance untenable.

Amid civil war, Bashir's regime also earned the ire of the United States for reaching out to Iran and harboring Osama bin Laden. The country became a "state sponsor of terror." Sudan was isolated and heavily sanctioned, while Bashir and his former mentor al-Turabi were locked in a power struggle. In 1999, Bashir called a state of emergency and stripped al-Turabi of his powerful post as speaker of the national assembly. To shore up his domestic position, Bashir opened negotiations with the SPLM/A and started to play nice with Western diplomats. Suspecting al-Turabi could develop a rebel base in Darfur, where he was popular, the Sudanese leader began further outsourcing "policing" activities to Arab militias.

The arming and preferential treatment of Arabs in Darfur sparked rebellion among non-Arab communities: first the Sudan Liberation Army (SLA), then the Justice and Equality Movement (JEM). Arab militia leaders like Musa Hilal and Juma Dagalo—who belonged to the same Rzeigat tribe, though different branches—received weapons and funding and coordinated with the Sudanese army to attack non-Arab communities perceived as supportive of SLA and JEM. Their militias— often made up of nomadic Arabs from the Sudan-Chad borderlands— came to be known as *janjaweed*, a portmanteau of the Arabic for "devil on horseback." The *janjaweed* committed mass atrocities against the region's non-Arab populations, especially during the conflict's height in 2003 and 2005.

Meanwhile, the international community was pushing a "north"/ "south" peace deal, excluding Darfur rebel groups from peace talks between the government and the SPLM/A. Bashir's regime, recognizing the importance the international community placed on a peace deal with the SPLM/A, saw he could safely ignore negotiating with Darfur rebels. Instead, he supported the *janjaweed* laying waste to the region. Darfur rebels, seeing no credible offer for a seat at the table, had every incentive to keep fighting. The SPLM/A sent support their way as further leverage over Khartoum. Thus, by simplifying the Sudan's civil war as a "north"/"south" issue, the international community effectively fueled conflict in Darfur, a region the size of Spain. Nonetheless, the clearly uncomprehensive Comprehensive Peace Agreement (CPA) was signed in 2005 and set a timetable for a South Sudanese referendum on independence.

As the war in Darfur progressed, rebel groups split and began fighting among themselves,* while Bashir's concessions to the international community prompted fears among the *janjaweed* that Khartoum was planning to sell them out. One *janjaweed* leader, Muhamad Dagalo, "Hemedti," threatened to join the rebels his militia had been fighting. Hemedti grew up in South Darfur and, by many accounts, was a camel thief before joining the *janjaweed*. He rose through the ranks and, despite his lack of formal education, was a natural political strategist. After his threat, Bashir named Hemedti a brigadier general, then head of his paramilitary force, the Rapid Support Forces (RSF).

Hemedti's rise took place amid major shifts in Sudan's political economy. South Sudan's independence, made official in 2011, prompted

---

★   The SLA, for example, split, at first, along largely ethnic lines between the predominantly Zaghawa under Minni Minnawi (SLA-MM) and the Fur under Abdul Wahid al-Nur (SLA-AW).

a reckoning in Khartoum. The oil revenue that kept Bashir's patronage network running was now greasing pockets of government officials in South Sudan. Bashir needed new sources of income and richer friends. In 2015, he cut ties with Iran and pivoted to Saudi Arabia. The timing was fortuitous, as both Saudi Arabia and the United Arab Emirates (UAE) needed men to fight their war against Iran-backed Houthis in Yemen. Bashir sent up to forty thousand Sudanese mercenaries to their cause, many of which came from Hemedti's RSF, further enriching the paramilitary leader.

In 2017, Hemedti grew even more powerful when he seized a major gold mine in South Darfur, which remained, along with the rest of Darfur, part of Sudan. Bashir granted him permission to sell gold a year later, cementing Hemedti's financial interests with the world's major gold buyer, the UAE. When Potepkin called upon Bashir's money man, Awad al-Jaz, the Sudanese minister would have been well aware of "the growing importance of gold for the regime," notes Kholood Khair, founder of Confluence Advisory. Representatives from his office decided to entertain the Russians' interest. "We know who Yevgeny Prigozhin is," an officer told Potepkin. "Can he fly over here?"

In May 2017, Prigozhin flew to Africa for the first time, where he met Awad al-Jaz and Omar al-Bashir in Khartoum. In the meeting. Bashir told Prigozhin and Potepkin that he needed economic and political advisors and instructors for his security forces. The regime had been looking for instructors for at least two years. Iran had previously provided much of Sudan's security training. Bashir had met with other potential partners but ultimately went with the Russians, reportedly on account of cheaper rates. As part of the deal, Prigozhin's men would gain access to Sudan's lucrative gold trade.

To represent the gold-mining interests, a Wagner subsidiary, M-Invest, was born. Andrei Mandel was named as the director and co-owner. Previously, Mandel ran Evrogrup, a Prigozhin-linked company that managed construction contracts for the Russian military. M-Invest, registered in

St. Petersburg, then opened a Sudanese subsidiary, Meroe Gold. Potepkin became Meroe Gold's director. M-Invest owned 99 percent of the shares, a local Sudanese businessman the remainder.

Through another two subsidiaries, including one state-owned corporation linked to Sudanese minister of defense General Awad Mohamad Ahmed Ibn Auf, Potepkin coordinated the arrival of military vehicles and equipment. Complex financial structures helped obfuscate payments and provision, probably both in Russia and in the West, where Prigozhin's operations were coming under increasing scrutiny following U.S. election interference. Behind the various companies, however, was the same back office. Accountants at both Evro-Polis—the PMC structure for Prigozhin's venture in Syria—and BrokerExpert exchanged emails and reviewed contracts.

According to Potepkin's version of events, Prigozhin's team brought the Sudan project to the Kremlin in early 2017. Other well-connected individuals, however, believe it was Moscow that connected Prigozhin to the Sudanese—perhaps the very individual who suggested an opportunity to mine gold in 2016. The Russian MoD had a long-standing interest in a port in the Horn of Africa. A naval presence in the Mediterranean and Red Sea is paramount to ensuring Russia's shipping and commercial interests in a global economy. A base in Somalia was impossible; the country was too unstable, with an American military presence to boot. The Americans had a base in Djibouti as well, and relations with Eritrea were poor since Russia supported Ethiopia in the 1998 war between the two countries. That left Sudan as Russia's best hope. Sudanese sources suggest Potepkin didn't stumble upon Awad al-Jaz, but rather Omar al-Bashir tasked his energy minister with managing the relationship with Prigozhin.

Potepkin's testimony fits a pattern, whereby sources in Prigozhin's network and state structures each believe they were indispensable to any successful Russian intervention abroad. In the end, both are right. Prigozhin's team probably offered to lobby for a Russian naval base to market their efforts to enter Sudan's gold industry. The prospect of a naval base likely spurred the MoD to support, through funding and equipment, Prigozhin's project in Sudan.

In late November 2017, Omar al-Bashir visited Russia, where he met with Putin in Sochi. The Minister of Defense Sergei Shoigu joined the meetings. Catering, of course, was provided by Concord. Bashir then met Dmitry Medvedev and signed several documents on trade and economic cooperation, including an agreement between M-Invest and the Sudanese minister of mineral resources on gold mining. Now, Prigozhin needed instructors.

Ratibor's First Assault Detachment was tapped to conduct the training mission, along with the Third Assault Detachment, led by Boris "Zombie" Nizhevenok, another veteran of Chechnya and an early Wagnerite who took part in the battle for Luhansk Airport.

"Nazar," born in a small village in Siberia, was another mercenary selected for the Sudanese operation. With a high voice and distinct accent, Nazar told me that prior to joining Wagner, he had only served two years compulsory service in the Russian army. He first learned about Wagner on the internet. He thought, "It might be cool to work for them." A few years later, he met up with a friend who had served and was recruited into the Company.

Nazar was sent first to Syria. But he was there only a few months when his group was brought together and told they were headed for another mission. After some quick pre-deployment training, he and the other mercenaries were bused to the airport. They spent the night in the square outside, cooking and eating dry rations, waiting for the charter flight Wagner had booked from Damascus to Khartoum.

The heat immediately hit Nazar on landing. "It was scorching compared to Syria. We had to wait for several hours, and then we were loaded onto yellow Ural trucks for a long journey through the city and into the desert, with dust swirling in the cargo area."

The soldiers Wagner began to train were conscripts from both the Sudanese army and Hemedti's RSF. "The people were young, very poor, and many were, of course, unprepared," Nazar told me. "Some even wore slippers during training. They always carried water bottles, which looked somewhat odd next to their weapons." The soldiers were armed with Chinese or Korean-made Kalashnikov rifles with folding stocks. Nazar woke his trainees up every morning at 5:00 a.m. to run four kilometers in the desert, followed by exercises. Luckily, the cafeteria had sufficient water and the Russians often showered five times a day. Later, Nazar switched over to tactical training for reconnaissance units.

The heat weighed down all activity. In the distance camels and sheep roamed. "I always wondered what they ate since there was nothing but parched grass everywhere." Flashlights from conscripts catching spiders and scorpions blinked in the dry night. They kept them in jars and sometimes arranged fights.

"The scorpions usually won," Nazar added.

★ ★ ★

Potepkin's 2016 feasibility study in Sudan perhaps sparked the interest, but by the middle of 2018, the Wagner network had traveled throughout Africa, including South Sudan, the Central African Republic (CAR), Libya, Madagascar, South Africa, Chad, and beyond. Prigozhin had recruited Russian experts and academics in African affairs, PR and political consultants, and economists into an informal analytic center, the Association for Free Research and International Cooperation (AFRIC). The center presented Prigozhin with extensive reports on twenty African countries in total.

In Africa, Prigozhin found a unique opportunity. After years of disappointment in Western security providers or United Nations peacekeeping missions, the continent's demand for alternatives was growing. Africa had another advantage, too. Compared to Donbas or Syria, competition from other Russians was light. In the nearly thirty years since the collapse of the Soviet Union, Russian institutions and companies had scaled down their presence in Africa, making it easier for Prigozhin to claim credit for Wagner's success. And since Russo-African relations were not a core national interest, punishment for failures would be less severe.

Wagner still needed Russian military equipment and diplomatic cover for operations, however. The highest chance of launching a project occurred where commercial interests closely aligned with those of the state. "The secret of Prigozhin is that he learned how to sell Putin a dream," an insider told *Proekt Media*, "about the rise of Russian influence in the world." But he wasn't selling a dream to Putin alone. A potential naval port could be leveraged for material support from the MoD, and, in Sudan, the promise of military instructors could be leveraged for access to lucrative mining concessions that would otherwise be out of reach.

Prigozhin was not the type to sit around, waiting for the MoD to come up with further uses for his mercenary force. Nor was he the type to feel comfortable relying on the government to be paid. The goal was to have Wagner projects in Syria and Africa be self-financing, even profitable, in the long-term. His team of analysts and employees back in St. Petersburg were expected to come up with new ideas that would grow the business. They threw many ideas at the wall over the course of 2016 and 2017, and few stuck.

One of the first that did, though, was on the island nation of Madagascar, off Africa's east coast.

Wagner's intervention in Madagascar would be one of the few projects in Africa that likely saw little, if any, cooperation with the Ministry of Defense. In March 2018, Malagasy president Hery Rajaonarimampianina visited an investment forum in Moscow where he met Prigozhin, Putin, and a host of specialists on the sidelines. Rajaonarimampianina requested Russian assistance for his reelection campaign. Prigozhin agreed to send a team.

A month later, fifteen to twenty political consultants took a flight from St. Petersburg to Antananarivo, the capital of Madagascar. One of the consultants was Maksim Shugalei, a St. Petersburg politician who campaigned for the local leadership of the Liberal Democratic Party of

Russia. After a dispute with the district election commission, he ate several documents on live television.

The consultants set up headquarters in a resort hotel and got to work. Shugalei and his team created a newspaper with favorable coverage of the incumbent. They bought ad space, illegally, for their client and distributed pens at rallies misspelling his name. Several team members started lining their pockets by overstating invoices for campaign materials.

It turned out Rajaonarimampianina's prospects for reelection were slim, and so at some point—Shugalei claims he was far from the decision-making process—the Russian consultants began working with other presidential contenders. It is likely Prigozhin told them to hedge their bets. The consultants found and offered "financing" to six other candidates. One of the favorites was Pastor Mailhol, leader of a cult called the Church of the Apocalypse. Twenty years earlier, God had told Pastor Mailhol that he would be the president of Madagascar. The Russians gave him cash and a bodyguard for the campaign trail.

When it became clear that God misspoke or the pastor misheard, the Russians asked Mailhol, as well as the other candidates they backed, to end his campaign and throw his support behind the soon-to-be winner, Andry Rajoelina. There was a good reason why Prigozhin wanted to back the winning ticket. He had set up another company, Ferrum Mining, and signed a contract with a Malagasy state-owned mining company, Kraomita Malagasy, to establish a joint venture: Kraomi Mining. The plan for Kraomi Mining was to exploit chromium, a component of stainless steel. The pivot worked. When Rajoelina came to office, Prigozhin's men were allowed to retain their stake in the operation.

The real business, however, was back on the mainland.

★ ★ ★

In October 2016, François Hollande announced his decision to withdraw two thousand French troops from the Central African Republic. The troops were a part of an intervention, Operation Sangaris, to stabilize the former French colony when the country descended into civil war in 2013. After three years, however, the civil war was hardly over. When Hollande announced the withdrawal, he suggested to CAR president Faustin-Archange Touadéra, semi-jokingly, that Bangui should ask the Russians for assistance. Little did he know, CAR's president took the proposal seriously.

That next summer, when Potepkin was in Sudan, he was approached by an official familiar with the situation in the neighboring Central African Republic. The representative asked him if Prigozhin's team would be interested in similar work in CAR. "What do they need?" Potepkin asked. "Everything," came the reply.

Potepkin brought the idea back to the boss. On August 22, 2017, according to leaks from the Dossier Center, Prigozhin met with CAR's ambassador to Russia. He also sent a Russian academic and a recently hired political operative, Dmitry Syty, to Bangui on a fact-finding mission. "We actually used Hollande's statement—that Bangui should work with Russia—a lot in the beginning of our work in CAR," Syty told me. The mission was a success, and three months later, Yevgeny Khodatov, another St. Petersburg native, registered Lobaye Invest in CAR, naming himself as chief executive.

Lobaye Invest was a subsidiary of Mikhail Potepkin's M-Invest. The new entity almost immediately signed an agreement with President Faustin-Archange Touadéra's administration. Touadéra's chief of staff, Firmin Ngrébada, and his team issued a document summarizing the deal made with Russian representatives, which mirrored, in many respects, those Potepkin brokered with Bashir in Khartoum.

Khodatov's team would build three airports in the provinces outside the capital. The Russians had proposed a landing strip that could handle heavier planes like Boeings or the Ilyushin-76. Bangui promised in return that no later than January 2018, Lobaye Invest would receive a license to explore for diamonds and gold. Both sides agreed that Russia would send information specialists to work with "young people in order to include them in positive social, economic and patriotic activities."

The Russians also pushed for a special unit to protect President Touadéra, though the Central African representatives were more focused on training for the security services. Touadéra officially requested military trainers and weapons in November 2017.

Sending weapons to CAR, however, was not easy, at least legally. The Central African Republic was still under a United Nations arms embargo, a legacy of the 2013 civil war. Prigozhin's men, working together with Sergei Lavrov's Ministry of Foreign Affairs, came up with a clever plan.

In February 2018, at the suggestion of the Russian team working in CAR, Bangui requested the United Nations Security Council lift the arms embargo. The formal request started a debate on the UNSC floor, where Russian diplomats immediately presented a proposition for arms delivery. Paris suggested the Security Council ship AK-47 assault rifles seized in Somalia the previous year. Russia, however, shut that down, on the grounds that weapons seized in violation of one arms embargo could not be given to another country under embargo.

The Americans were more wary. But Syty and his team had "expected the worst possible outcome and planned accordingly." No one at the UN Security Council expected Bangui's request to lift the embargo, so the Russian diplomats worked to resolve it that day, as quickly as possible. The gambit worked, and Russia's proposal was approved. The path was now clear to provide Bangui with weapons and instructors.

As part of CAR's bilateral defense agreement, the Russian government donated small arms, ammunition, and other lethal equipment to the Central African Armed Forces (FACA). The European Union Training Mission (EUTM) in CAR observed the initial deliveries.

"There were teams of EUTM advisors accounting for every cartridge taken down the IL-76 ramp," Syty remembered. "But the guys grew tired after checking the sixth plane, especially when they understood they weren't getting paid extra working through nights."

I asked Syty why the French in particular seemed so unthreatened by the Russians' arrival.

"The French in CAR proved to be unprepared for almost any initiative from any party," he replied. "They had grown too comfortable and soft; they didn't pay attention to anything around them. CAR was French forever. Until it wasn't."

In March, a Russian convoy crossed the border between Sudan's Darfur and the Central African Republic. UN peacekeepers, likely surprised to see Russian instructors coming overland through such a remote area, hesitated to let them pass. Once concerns were alleviated—the Russians had UN Security Council approval for their mission—eighteen creaking trucks and three armored Ural vehicles rumbled into Birao, the capital of CAR's northeast Vakaga province. In the trucks were fifty-five Wagner mercenaries. One of them was Zhandatbek (Zhanat) Tyrgotov, a citizen of Kyrgyzstan. Zhanat had served in his country's national guard before working in Africa as a member of the French Foreign Legion. Around 2017, he went back to Kyrgyzstan to marry. When he didn't receive his expected payout from the legion, he went to Russia, where, as luck would have it, Wagner needed men who could speak French.

Zhanat and the convoy bounced along CAR's dirt roads from Birao to N'Délé, where they met Abdoulaye Hissène, leader of the FPRC, a rebel group. Wagner had a gift for the FPRC: equipment for a hospital. But when Hissène's men searched the trucks, they found a drone. The rebels would not allow Wagner pass if they were carrying weapons for the government in Bangui. Of course, Wagner was arriving to do exactly that. This particular drone and small arms, however, were likely for protecting the convoy. Zhanat worked quickly to translate the misunderstanding between his Wagner commander and Hissène. After some discussion, the convoy moved on, visiting rebel-held Bambari, Bria, and other towns until it reached Bangui.

The decision to send trucks overland was strange. Other shipments, like the IL-76's checked by EU trainers, landed in Bangui. It was also inevitable that the Wagner convoy would encounter the FPRC and other rebels opposed to Touadéra's rule. But the connections

Wagner commanders would make as the convoy passed through armed group territory were worth the risk. It was important to know *all* the powerful stakeholders in CAR's conflict, not just the CAR government.

By mid-2018, Wagner military instructors trickled into CAR, overland or by air. The instructors were part of La Communauté des Officiers pour la Securité International (COSI). COSI formed what was informally called the "Influence Group." Valery Zakharov, a former GRU officer in his mid-fifties, was in charge. Zakharov was not only head of the instructors but also an advisor to President Touadéra. His residence was Lobaye Invest's headquarters.

Lobaye Invest's first mining concessions, a total of seven sites, to start, were in Lobaye province, which was due to receive one of the three airports. The region was more secure from the government's perspective, but the higher quality and more productive diamond and gold mines were in the center and northeast of the country. This, however, was the rebel territory Zhanat's convoy had passed through on its way into CAR. The FPRC held the northeast on the border with Darfur, while 3R controlled the northwest. Gold mines like Ndassima—which, if industrialized, could be worth up to $500 million—were in the hands of Ali Darassa, the leader of the most powerful armed group, the UPC.

Wagner had less than two hundred military instructors in the country. As their title suggested, their job was to offer training to the CAR military. There was no agreement to liberate territory. Yet the fact remained that if armed groups controlled the most profitable sites, little mining revenue would reach the democratically elected government in Bangui. Prigozhin's experts and advisors suggested a way all stakeholders could profit from the country's resources: a peace deal.

In the nineteenth century, the Central African Republic's territory was the target of slave raids, or *ghazawat*, from Muslim sultanates to the north. In the early twentieth century, French officials—often in the name of ending the "Arab slave trade"—ousted the sultans, only to reintroduce *razzia* for forced labor and porterage. The French established a vast administrative territory, French Equatorial Africa, which comprised modern-day CAR, Chad, and the Republic of the Congo.

French officials, inspired by King Leopold's Belgian Congo, introduced the concessionary system to strengthen the colony's economy. Private companies were given swaths of land, and their agents employed brutal tactics to force Central Africans to work for free yet pay taxes and hand over resources. Imprisonment, murder, and rape were common. Facing scandals in Paris, the colonial government ditched the concessionary system but kept the forced labor. It introduced "humanitarian" projects to lift Africans out of poverty, like the Congo-Océan railroad that "marshaled the values, institutions, and know-how of a modern liberal state," to kill up to sixty thousand African forced laborers. Forced labor in the territory of Oubangui-Chari officially ended in 1954.

In 1960, Oubangui-Chari gained independence as the Central African Republic, "six years after [its] first class graduated from its first high school." Considered the least-prepared colony for independence, CAR's first decades saw over ten coups or coup attempts, with Paris participating in many. Structures and styles of governance endured: Elites in Bangui remained comfortable—like colonial officials before them—outsourcing education, healthcare, security—indeed sovereignty in most forms—to whoever offered to foot the bill.

On March 24, 2013, a predominantly Muslim rebel alliance, Séléka, took Bangui. A northerner, Michel Djotodia, became interim president. Having fled, former president François Bozizé worked with networks of ex-army officers and preexisting Christian and animist self-defense groups that formed a diffuse armed movement, the anti-Balaka. The anti-Balaka then began attacking both Séléka fighters and Muslim civilians more generally.

A baffled French government announced Operation Sangaris, and in April 2014, the UN authorized a peacekeeping mission known by its French acronym, MINUSCA. Nonetheless, violence continued. What appeared to many a religious conflict was, in fact, largely a struggle for economic and political power. Alliances formed and re-formed that crossed the anti-Balaka versus Séléka divide in ever more complex ways.

The career of Ali Darassa provides a window into this tangled web. Darassa is a member of the Peul community. The Peul, known in English as Fulani, are primarily Muslim nomadic herders found across West and Central Africa. Before joining Séléka, Ali Darassa was second-in-command of an armed group that, at one point, announced its intentions to overthrow the governments of both Chad and CAR. In 2014, interim president Djotodia disbanded Séléka groups, causing a number of former fighters to rebrand as the Front Populaire pour la Renaissance de Centrafrique (FPRC). Ali Darassa and his colleague, Mahamat al-Khatim, were initially involved, but they split two months later to form the UPC. Then, al-Khatim and his Arab followers split once more from Darassa.

In late 2016, Darassa expanded into territory rich in diamond mines. This prompted his former Séléka allies to partner with their old enemies, the anti-Balaka. Thousands were displaced—in two brutal incidents, anti-Balaka killed fifty Muslim civilians and the UPC, in a reprisal attack, killed forty-five, including ten Red Cross employees.

That same year, after general elections, Faustin-Archange Touadéra succeeded to the presidency. His political and military position was weak. Despite the ongoing violence, the French declared Operation Sangaris a success and withdrew, leaving behind an underfunded and underequipped MINUSCA peacekeeping force. Then in 2017, the U.S.—which had been hunting Joseph Kony and the Lord's Resistance Army in the extremely isolated southeast of the country—also left. Touadéra was "deeply vulnerable to threats of a coup." His government held little territory outside the capital, while powerful armed groups—the UPC, MPC, FPRC, and anti-Balaka—controlled the country's resources.

When the Russian mercenaries first arrived in 2018, many Central Africans welcomed the prospect of territorial integrity and the state's return to the countryside, in other words, an end to the reign of armed groups.

Recognizing that military instruction wouldn't be enough to make a splash in the Kremlin, or grant access the country's most profitable mines, Wagner got to work on a peace process. They started with the UPC—the most powerful, primarily Peul armed group led by Ali Darassa. The meeting was brokered by Darassa's second-in-command, Hassan Bouba. The pair had met years ago working for a Chadian armed group, where Bouba was a photographer and rumored to be a mole for Chadian intelligence. They then fought together in CAR as members of Séléka. In 2017, Bouba was named special advisor to President Touadéra, granting him a lucrative opportunity to act as an intermediary between the weak government in Bangui and Darassa.

In early 2018, Bouba met Valery Zakharov and his right-hand man, Dmitry Syty. The slim Syty cut a striking image in Bangui. Sporting long shaggy hair, the late-twentysomething was a college graduate from St. Petersburg. He had studied abroad in Barcelona and received a master's degree in marketing from Paris. His fluent English, French, and Spanish helped him land a job with Wagner first as an interpreter, then as a consultant, until being named manager of Zakharov's nonsecurity portfolio.

Bouba must have liked what Zakharov and Syty had to say, because after meeting he called his boss, Ali Darassa, to connect everyone. Darassa agreed to meet the Russians on March 13, 2018, in Bokolobo, a UPC stronghold sixty kilometers from Bambari. In the meeting, Darassa requested the Russians build a meat-processing facility. Taxing cattle herders was an important source of revenue for the UPC, and a processing facility would be an additional source of income. Zakharov promised to export Darassa's beef to Russia and, in turn, expressed an interest in access to mining sites under UPC control, like Ndassima. They added that they could build hospitals, schools, and a small airport for the region and assured Darassa that the CAR government was also ready to work with the UPC.

Around this time, Dmitry Utkin arrived in CAR to help set up the military side of Wagner's operations. He connected with Maxime Mokom, one of the most powerful anti-Balaka leaders in the country. Mokom and Utkin discussed setting up a Russian base in the southeastern town of Bangassou. The anti-Balaka militias had a heavy presence there, and there was still significant tension with Ali Darassa's UPC in the area. Following the meeting with Utkin, Mokom met Zakharov, who spoke about the benefits of bringing peace to CAR's people. Mokom said he was interested, so Zakharov flew him in a private jet to Khartoum, where the anti-Balaka commander met Sudanese officials collaborating with Wagner on the project, including the Sudanese minister of defense.

In April 2018, Wagner representatives met with the UPC again in Ngakobo. This time, they emphasized the importance of making peace with all parties, including the government, and they promised they would provide the armed group leaders with whatever they needed to achieve it. Within two months, Wagner had gained permission from armed groups to install four bases in the center and northeast of the country. Soon men began arriving in small planes with big bags of cash.

The impetus for a particular policy or decision rarely has a single cause, and the 2019 Khartoum Agreement encompassed many opposing ideas that were true at once. Prigozhin's team undoubtedly viewed peace in CAR as a good thing, even though the boss also saw an opportunity to make money from the deal. There were plenty of precedents for such an initiative, including broad efforts by the international community and more narrow agreements between armed groups on the ground. More specific to Prigozhin, however, were the benefits, tangible and intangible, of delivering a foreign policy win to the Kremlin.

Recruitment of Russian consultants and experts started in May, one month after Zakharov and Syty first pitched the idea to Ali Darassa and the UPC. Once the decision was made, the pressure was on for the consultants to negotiate terms and get a deal. According to a source close to the negotiations, everything was funded by Prigozhin, though the Ministry of Foreign Affairs and the Ministry of Defense also participated.

Specific Wagner personnel were assigned to manage each rebel leader. Given their prior meetings with the UPC, Valery Zakharov and Dmitry Syty managed the relationship with Darassa and Bouba, while a consultant for the Ministry of Foreign Affairs worked with the leader of the FPRC, Noureddine Adam.

The anti-Balaka leader, Maxime Mokom, was to be managed by Igor Mangushev. In the 2010s, Mangushev was the head of Bright Rus, a nationalist organization that conducted raids on migrants. He then founded his own PMC "ENOT"—allegedly with support from the FSB—before joining Prigozhin's Internet Research Agency in 2013, where he wrote posts on social media denigrating opposition politician Aleksei Navalny. Mangushev reportedly had a tough time dealing with Prigozhin as a boss. When the war in Donbas broke out, he formed his own militia in the DNR, again likely with help from FSB connections. In 2016, Mangushev told a Russian journalist his real dream was to organize a radio station in the LNR and DNR, where he could play the music he loved and broadcast the news he believed in. He began crowdfunding for both the station and his beloved cat, Sasha, who was very ill. Sasha passed, and money was probably still tight, driving him back into the arms of his former boss. In December 2018, Mangushev (call sign "Bereg") touched down in CAR. There his dream was realized in Radio Lengo Songo—a radio station he helped set up to offer pro-Russian coverage—and CAR's famous beauty pageant. In addition to working with Mokom for the upcoming peace agreement, he was also an advisor to the Central African police force.

Another powerful Peul armed group, 3R, did not work with specific Wagner representatives, but became involved following workshops on negotiating techniques sponsored by the African Union (AU) and the Economic Community of Central African States.

In fact, it wasn't easy to convince armed groups to support a peace deal, though the Russians, with the help of Sudan and the UAE, built steady momentum throughout 2018. Prigozhin's men sought an ideological platform that could underpin negotiations. They landed on an inclusive narrative: that to be Central African was to transcend ethnic and religious boundaries. Luckily, inclusive forms of Central African identity had persisted, despite years of civil war. Sango, for example, an indigenous lingua franca that the majority of CAR's over seventy ethnolinguistic groups speak to some degree, remained a point of pride for many.

Still, key points—such as the allocation of ministerial posts—had to wait until formal talks began in Khartoum on January 24, 2019. It took a week of debate before the big breakthrough, when Ali Darassa, representing the UPC; Mahamat al-Khatim, representing the MPC; Noureddine Adam, representing the FPRC; and Maxime Mokom, representing anti-Balaka, met with Omar al-Bashir, who offered his "blessing" for a peace process.

Behind the scenes, armed groups credit both Bashir and Prigozhin with getting the agreement to the finish line. To convince rebel leaders to sign the accords, Prigozhin flew down to Khartoum personally and spoke one-on-one with Ali Darassa, Maxime Mokom, and Mahamat al-Khatim. He also paid the rebel leaders according to their perceived importance. The UPC intermediary Hassan Bouba, according to an armed group source, received $60,000, a carton of Turkish 9mm pistols, and two hundred Android phones. General al-Khatim was paid $100,000. Anti-Balaka leader Maxime Mokom and Abdoulaye Hissène—the FPRC general who first greeted the Wagner convoy driving from Darfur—each got $50,000. Ali Darassa made $250,000 on the deal, still a distant second to Noureddine Adam. Adam was supposed to become prime minister in the new government. But at the last second—perhaps because of his perceived closeness to the UAE—the Russians insisted on giving Chief of Staff Firmin Ngrébada the post. Ngrébada had played a critical role in bringing Wagner to CAR in the first place, and with him as prime minister, there was less of a chance that the UAE could overshadow Wagner in CAR's mining sector. Ngrébada, according to a source, allegedly agreed to pay Noureddine Adam $500,000 to give up the role, and he personally delivered the first installment in cash to Adam's hotel room in Khartoum.

Sidiki Abass, the leader of 3R, refused payment even after Ali Darassa convinced him to sign the agreement, sparking concerns that the group would not adhere to its conditions. Another headache for the Russian team was CAR's leader. Touadéra was seen as uncharismatic and weak, not the anchor such an accord required. His small tribe close to Bangui, the Ngbaka-Mandja, held little political influence. Men like Darassa represented far weightier identity interests.

Touadéra's predecessor was also a problematic force, even after his ouster and exile. Former president François Bozizé hailed from the Gbaya, a community spread across northwest CAR. He was not, however, included in the emerging peace agreement—a decision that all sides had agreed to. "Everyone thought Bozizé represented French interests and would try to hijack the anti-Balaka," a Russian negotiator remembered. "A consolidated anti-Balaka would shift the balance." Bozizé's exclusion, even if it was the right decision at the time, would have serious consequences a year later.

The final signing of what would be called the Khartoum Agreement was on February 6, 2019. All armed group leaders received an additional $16,000, which meant Prigozhin spent well over $1,000,000 to clinch the deal. Some of that money likely came from an MoD slush fund, yet it's likely Prigozhin also used his own funds, betting he would be made whole if he closed the deal. Following the signing, UN Secretary-General António Guterres congratulated the stakeholders and called on "neighboring countries, regional organizations and all international partners to support the courageous steps that Central Africans have made to bring lasting peace and stability in their country."

The agreement included initiatives that covered transitional justice and reconciliation, the formation of an inclusive government, security sector reform, and a program for disarmament, demobilization, and reintegration (DDR). In other words, it was a significant accomplishment.

Some of the most important initiatives, however, were not found in the final published document. These were the distribution of ministerial and prefectural positions, the sharing of territory, and the integration of combatants into the army, outside of formal DDR processes. The division of CAR's gold and diamond mines was also critical.

Armed group leaders agreed that the CAR government would provide the necessary documents for mining companies to work in their territories. Bangui would also allow armed groups to negotiate directly with companies seeking concessions. In practice, this meant that a company looking to exploit a mining site would first negotiate taxes with CAR's Ministry of Mines, then negotiate terms with the armed group in control of the mine itself. The contract with an armed group usually involved a fixed price for access, followed by monthly payments. In return, the armed group provided soldiers to protect the miners and their equipment. Bangui also agreed to let armed groups exploit their own mines if they had the means to do so.

The most serious conditions, however, were laid down by Prigozhin. Wagner wanted free circulation—that is, didn't want to pay for passage—throughout armed group territory and free access to explore mining sites. This vexed armed group leaders: Most of their revenue came setting up roadblocks along key commercial and mining routes and "taxing" those who passed. Wagner smoothed things over again by paying off those who controlled the most important sites, which functioned, in effect, as an advance.

The payments to armed group leaders based on their value to the peace deal—that is, the political and military threat they represented—was an example of what expert Alex de Waal calls the "political marketplace" of the region. Peace negotiations in neighboring Sudan, for example, tend to occur during times of expanding government budgets. After Bashir signed the 2005 peace deal with John Garang, the international community turned its focus to the conflict in Darfur. In 2006, de Waal, a mediator at the time, remembers Abdul Wahid al-Nur—the leader of one SLA faction—talking to his colleague after stalling on a peace deal.

"They offered me $30,000,000! I demanded $100,000,000. But I will negotiate."

De Waal pulled Abdul Wahid into a hotel room, where then-president of Nigeria Olusegun Obasanjo cornered the Darfur rebel. "You let me down, boy!" he yelled. He had already paid Abdul Wahid $1,000,000 a few days earlier.

Prigozhin may well have intuited the political marketplace in which he was conducting negotiations. If he didn't, the many Sudanese advisors working on the Khartoum Agreement could easily show him the ropes.

In the end, Wagner's team was stunned they had succeeded in facilitating an international peace agreement in a country where diplomats had failed to bring peace for years. It was a clear foreign policy win for Moscow and a boon for Russia's international image. Russia was an emerging player—a peacekeeper, even—in Africa. And it was Prigozhin who unambiguously delivered the win. He could now expect more funding from the MoD, in addition to the revenue he anticipated earning from the mines. "Once the agreement was signed, Prigozhin was on the phone with Deputy Defense Minister Ruslan Tsalikov," a Russian participant stated. Tsalikov promised Prigozhin the MoD would deliver whatever equipment was needed for CAR.

A few months after the agreement was signed, I was in Bangui, in one of the city's great informal institutions: the Lebanese-run Grand Café. The Grand Café's infinite shades of dark brown teak offer a chance to cool down with a coffee and croissant. In the café, rumored to be a front for washing diamonds, nefarious-looking businessmen, traders, and plain criminals sit next to bleeding-heart humanitarians and peacekeepers. I was there to meet Georges, a civil society activist. Georges, like many Central Africans, saw the armed groups—and men like Ali Darassa—as the main obstacle to development in the country. "There is no freedom of movement," Georges told me. "And it's the armed groups that are to blame."

Armed groups had committed widespread atrocities, especially during the heights of the civil war. Fear of violence frequently prevented farmers from cultivating fields, or traders from traveling the roads.

Government forces also committed atrocities. Yet on the whole, they still represented an ideal: the return of a state that, in practice, never existed.

Thus the Wagner instructors ordering pastries in front of us were well-received. The training program they'd just opened for Central African Armed Forces (FACA) tapped into a deep desire among Central Africans to see the state assume new authority. A strong FACA, supported by Russia, could end the reign of armed groups in the bush—something the UN peacekeeping mission MINUSCA had failed to achieve. The excitement in Bangui at the prospect that finally something might change was palpable. And yet, among some, a sense of discomfort was building.

"The Russians are collaborating with armed groups for diamonds," Georges whispered in the Grand Café. "Russia is no different from France."

IV

Mercenaries

It happens that every man in a bank hates what the bank does, and yet the bank does it. The bank is something more than men, I tell you. It's the monster. Men made it, but they can't control it.

—JOHN STEINBECK, *THE GRAPES OF WRATH*

When the Khartoum Agreement was signed on February 15, 2019, Prigozhin and his Wagner Group were at the top of their game. In CAR, the team had delivered an internationally recognized peace agreement to the Kremlin. In Sudan, the training program was going well. Potepkin was having difficulty turning a profit in the mining sector, but there was still the prospect of facilitating a naval base. And Wagner had touched down in Libya, where it was working closely with the Ministry of Defense. Prigozhin had concessions to exploit natural resources in both countries as well as Madagascar, even if the political consulting business had occasionally gone a bit sideways. The Battle of Khasham in Syria, only one year before, felt like a distant memory.

The politics and conflict dynamics in each of these countries, however, were highly complex. If the past year had been one of proactive measures, the next two would be spent largely defending what Wagner had achieved.

Facilitating the Khartoum Agreement would be one of Omar al-Bashir's last acts as Sudan's ruler. His regime never managed to recover from the financial loss of the split with South Sudan. Rump Sudan balanced a bloated civil service and military on one end and a population reliant on food and fuel subsidies on the other. The military continued to receive the lion's share of the state's withering budget. Frustration mounted among civilians.

In July 2018, while Prigozhin's team in CAR was working on a peace agreement, Sergei Klyukin, one of Prigozhin's managers for various projects in Khartoum, wrote a thirty-six-page "Conception on the Campaign for Stabilizing the Sociopolitical Situation in the Republic of Sudan." The mission, as outlined in the document leaked to the Dossier Center, included "strengthening the influence of the Russian Federation" and the reelection of Omar al-Bashir in 2020. In the media space, Klyukin recommended creating new TV programs and talk shows that were supportive of the Bashir regime and "fighting opposition press with informational, administrative, and economic methods." Many of Klyukin's recommendations reflected Russia's political system over Sudan's. Some were literally "copy and paste"; there were a few places where the team had forgotten to replace "Sudan" with "Russia."

Klyukin and Mikhail Potepkin were producing reports at a furious pace. The reports, however, were apparently going unread. "We ended up producing a huge amount of research which went nowhere." Potepkin complained to me. "No matter what you think of Russians, we do represent the northern part of European civilization. We are still Europeans. They are Arab-African, and of course, there's a lot of misunderstanding."

Leaving the civilizational rhetoric aside, it is quite possible Bashir was testing his new advisors. The longtime Sudanese leader took pride in knowing what was happening in his country on a granular level; he remembered each military officer and Darfuri politician. It is unlikely the All-seeing autocrat thought the Russians would produce some fact about his country he didn't know.

This did not mean, however, that Wagner ceased to be useful. Bashir's administration announced plans to amend the constitution, allowing him to prolong his rule. This was hardly Wagner's idea, but Bashir could frame Klyukin's recommendations as proof of Russian state support. Training for the all-important security forces marched on. Classes went from morning to evening with a break for lunch. There was one day off on Friday, following the Muslim tradition. Occasionally, Nazar was allowed to go to Khartoum for shopping. "The poverty was shocking," he remembered. "Especially in the slums outside the capital."

In August, rising food prices sparked protests. Sudanese began to organize under the umbrella of the Sudanese Professionals Association (SPA) and neighborhood Resistance Committees. Potepkin's political team furiously built social media sites that lauded Bashir and RSF leader Hemedti. Media operations pushed out content supporting a Russian naval and air base in Port Sudan. The information campaign, though, was coming up short.

In December, protests engulfed the country and Prigozhin flew into Khartoum to deliver the political team's predictions on the crisis. Potepkin had put together a presentation his boss would present to Bashir personally. According to Potepkin, Prigozhin told Bashir he had four months left in office. "In April you'll be overthrown," he said. The predictions were bold, but Prigozhin had confidence in his men, Potepkin thought. Prigozhin pointed a finger toward head of intelligence Salah Gosh, who was also in the room, and said, "This is the man who will overthrow you." Everyone laughed, including Gosh. The only one who kept a stern face was Minister of Energy al-Jaz. He took the Russians seriously and asked for the report after the meeting.

In January 2019, just as delegates were preparing to gather in Khartoum to sign the CAR peace deal, Prigozhin's Africa back office, led by Pyotr Bychkov, presented the Bashir regime with a plan to discredit the protests that had been raging for nearly six months. The document, again leaked to the Dossier Center, recommended the regime "disseminate information about protestors setting fire to a mosque, hospital, and kindergarten." Bychkov's team thought Bashir should label protestors "enemies of Islam and traditional values" and claim they were waving LGBT flags at their rallies. They even recommended public executions for "looters."

Bashir didn't believe the Russians' predictions until Prigozhin's last meeting with him in April. "It was then," Potepkin recalled, "that Bashir told Prigozhin his plans to leave the presidency and allow elections." For the military and many elites, Potepkin knew, this was going to be a problem. A civilian-led government would almost certainly see a decline in the security services' power.

In the end, Wagner was wrong. It wasn't Salah Gosh who launched the coup. On April 10, 2019, the freshly minted minister of defense, First Lieutenant General Ahmad Awad Ibn Auf, called together officials from the security services and broached the idea of Bashir's ouster. Only two men could have vetoed the decision, Salah Gosh and Muhamad Dagalo "Hemedti." Both, however, agreed it was time for Bashir to go. On April 11, General Ahmad Awad Ibn Auf overthrew Bashir, only to step down the next day in favor of General Inspector of the Armed Forces Abdel Fattah al-Burhan. Burhan became chairman of the Transitional Military Council, Hemedti its deputy chairman.

The coup was undoubtedly a blow to Wagner's operations in Sudan. While the training mission was successful, mining operations in the north of the country cost much and yielded little. The political team produced many pages of research but failed to ensure Bashir's "reelection." Hopes of a Russian naval and air base would be delayed, at best. Wagner's reputation with the Sudanese population was in tatters. Mercenaries had been spotted at pro-democracy rallies, sometimes filming protestors. It was clear whose side Prigozhin's men were on.

By the time of Bashir's overthrow, however, Prigozhin had built relationships with the three security services that formed the pillars of

Sudan's ruling class: the army, the intelligence service, and the paramilitary Rapid Support Forces (RSF). This was a testament both to his incessant networking, but also a desire to "never appear one leader's lackey, whether it was Touadéra or the UAE," as one former colleague put it.

When UAE representatives introduced Hemedti to Prigozhin and encouraged him to enter the gold business with the RSF leader, Wagner's boss was initially reticent, lest he be seen as undermining Sudan's ruler. Whatever reluctance there was, however, gave way to a budding relationship and Prigozhin's companies started doing business with Hemedti's family as well. They supplied, for example, Esnaad Engineering, directed by Hemedti's brother, with "riot shields, batons, and helicopter engines."

Prigozhin-affiliated firms still worked with companies linked to the army, of course, and Meroe Gold paid Aswar Multi-Activities, connected to Sudan's intelligence services, $100,000 each month "to facilitate security, immigration, and import activities."

Different institutions have different protocols and preferences for whom they interact with, which can make maintaining contacts across different parties of a civil war, for example, difficult. Prigozhin's ever-expanding Rolodex was useful to the Russian state during periods of change for its allies. Yet Wagner's boss also had a habit of conducting his own diplomacy on behalf of the state: behavior that would often leave diplomats and military officials scrambling to clean up the mess.

★ ★ ★

The siren song of war and reward echoes across Libya's coast, luring great powers, jihadists, armed groups, and mercenaries of all stripes to its shores. It is hard to imagine Libya would not eventually pull in Prigozhin as well. Compared to CAR, even Sudan, the oil wealth at stake in Libya is staggering. Since the fall of Muammar Gaddafi in 2011, and the civil wars that followed, Tripoli—the capital and center of the country's public and private institutions—has been the key prize for a shifting web of warring parties and outside patrons. Libya did not call just Prigozhin, but Putin and many others within Russia's top brass, too, all eager to right NATO's historic wrong.

In April 2019, General Khalifa Haftar, ruler of east Libya, launched a military offensive to take the city. Haftar was part of the group of officers who brought Muammar Gaddafi to power in 1969. Nearly twenty years later, Chadian forces captured Haftar during the Great Toyota War. Gaddafi disavowed him, and Haftar turned on Gaddafi, going into opposition in Chad. When the Libya-backed forces of Idriss Déby swept west from their base in Sudan's Darfur to the Chadian capital, N'Djamena, Haftar fled, eventually receiving asylum in the United States. Living in Washington, D.C.'s Virginia suburbs, he reportedly worked closely with the CIA on the Libya file.

Two decades later, in 2011, the general returned to lead forces against Gaddafi, but his clear ambition earned only distrust from other revolutionary forces. Haftar turned to building up his own military force, the Libyan National Army (LNA), in the east, establishing a base in Benghazi and framing his consolidation of power in anti-Islamist and anti-jihadist terms.

He could point to real threats. In 2014 Syrian returnees and foreign jihadists declared the eastern city of Derna a province of the Islamic State. Haftar rallied the United Arab Emirates and Egypt to his side, which sent funds and advisors. France deployed special forces. The United States, however, was less convinced the Islamic State represented a threat in Libya.

The Egyptians took the Islamic State on their border most seriously. And it was likely Egypt, Libya expert Jalel Harchaoui notes, who first connected Haftar to Moscow. In the twilight of the Arab Spring, Egyptian military forces, led by General Abdel Fattah al-Sisi, overthrew the democratically elected Muslim Brotherhood leader Mohamed Morsi. The U.S. briefly suspended delivery of weapons in response, but it was a wide enough window for Russia to step in. In 2014, the UAE and

Saudi Arabia funded a $3.5 billion weapons deal between Russia and Egypt.

A year later, Egypt, the UAE, and Saudi Arabia were ramping up their lobbying efforts on behalf of Haftar. During Putin's visit to Cairo in February 2015, President Sisi invited a Libyan officer close to Khalifa Haftar to meet the Russians, and the provision of weapons and military equipment was discussed. The UAE then delivered Russian-made attack helicopters. The following year, Haftar's force ordered another eleven.

Haftar needed more and more mercenaries. For his 2016 attack on the oil crescent, he hired thousands of men from the main Darfur rebel groups in Sudan, including factions of the Sudan Liberation Army (SLA), as well as Musa Hilal's forces.

Later that same year, a Russian PMC, RSB Group, landed a demining contract for a cement factory in Benghazi, underbidding a British firm by the equivalent of $25,000,000. RSB Group, founded by Oleg Krinitsyn, a former officer in Russia's border guards, is known to be "the first Russian PMC." Krinitsyn's company offered a wide variety of services: maritime security in the Gulf of Aden and Gulf of Guinea; consulting; demining; and convoy, site, and personal protection. In 2007, RSB worked with American security companies guarding convoys in Iraq. "Everyone has the same task—to make money," Krinitsyn later told Russian state-affiliated media. "Where the U.S. Army appears, private military companies follow. If you imagine a war on foreign territory as a hunt by predators for herbivores, then the American army is a lion, and PMCs are jackals that eat up the carrion of the king of beasts."

Russian contractors cost less than their Western counterparts generally, but RSB's low bid for the cement factory had a little help. Like his counterparts at Moran Group, Krinitsyn and RSB had long-standing connections with the FSB. For the Benghazi cement deal, however, Krinitsyn was essentially a middleman for the Russian Ministry of

Defense; the sappers he recruited came from a special demining center associated with the Ministry of Emergency Situations (EMERCOM), Minister of Defense Sergei Shoigu's brainchild. After signing the contract Krinitsyn received the money and "paid off the right people." Jackals, however, were now circling Krinitsyn's kill.

In 2017, it was clear to many in both Russia's private and public sectors that there was money to be made in Libya, particularly in the region under Haftar's control. After the factory deal was signed, the GRU—which often competed with the FSB—made Krinitsyn an offer he couldn't refuse. "[The GRU] basically said to Oleg [Krinitsyn], 'Look, let us buy your company, and we will work more in Libya,'" a person close to the matter told me.

Krinitsyn sold RSB reportedly for a fair price, paid in cash, then registered a new company, "RSB Security Services." The GRU's Stanislav Petlinsky brokered the deal, which was quickly followed by a change in leadership. Krinitsyn—while not fully beholden to the FSB—was, in the eyes of the GRU, the FSB's man in Libya. They wanted a man of their own. We don't know if Prigozhin was top of mind, yet the change was to his benefit. There was little trust between Prigozhin and the FSB, a far more powerful pillar of Russia's security state.* Though it seems he wasn't directly involved in the GRU's deal, Prigozhin was much better embedded in their network, which had now, effectively, monopolized the Libya portfolio. "It's like when a conglomerate buys a small competitor just to shut it down," the insider mused. Shoigu's EMERCOM sappers, however, were allowed to continue the work. No one, apparently, wanted to piss off the minister of defense.

RSB's new owner would be Jan Marsalek, an Austrian national and GRU asset. Marsalek was the chief operating officer of the German

---

* Wagner recruits were occasionally subject to polygraph tests to prove they weren't FSB plants. As the case of Igor Mangushev showed, however, Prigozhin was not categorically against working with people who had ties, or perceived ties, to the FSB.

payment processing company Wirecard, whose collapse would become the largest fraud case in German history. The Austrian, an investigation by *The Insider* found, wanted his own mercenary company after Petlinsky arranged for him to LARP as a Russian soldier in Syria alongside Wagner's head of intelligence, Anatoly Karazii. Marsalek envisioned his RSB not only demining the cement factory but training an army of fifteen thousand to twenty thousand Libyan mercenaries to guard "the country's southern border and [restrict] migration flows at gunpoint [. . .] mercenaries could be outfitted with state-of-the-art body cams to record 'awesome video material' of them shooting people."

In the end, Prigozhin's capacity to move men and material was far larger than anything Oleg, or the manipulatable Jan Marsalek, could muster in Libya, paving the way for Wagner to service the need for mercenaries. (Thankfully, Marsalek's unrealistic plan for a trigger-happy southern Libyan border force came to naught.) Prigozhin was also enjoying a budding relationship with the UAE, one of Haftar's major backers.

There are two pillars supporting the United Arab Emirates' foreign policy, which its two most important cities, Abu Dhabi and Dubai, represent. The first is security. Abu Dhabi seeks to counter Islamism and jihadism before it reaches its shores. The second, embodied in Dubai, is commerce: the desire to see the UAE as a twenty-first-century Venetian empire. Despite the population boom in places like Dubai, there are few UAE citizens. With only one million nationals, and incredible oil wealth, the country can outsource its foreign policy priorities. In Prigozhin they found a fellow traveler. As one Russian intelligence official put it: "When you have military equipment, military technologies and skills, trained and motivated personnel, and someone has money, then a form of cooperation is always found and easy . . . why not shake the hand with the money in it?" Abu Dhabi would provide the financing in Libya, and Prigozhin would supply the men.

In October 2018, those men were spotted at Al-Watiya Air Base, a slice of land the Haftar's LNA controlled in western Libya. Months later, in early 2019, Haftar's forces launched an offensive on Libya's southern region, officially an effort to oust "Chadian gangs." The LNA took the main cities of Sabha and Ubari and captured the Sharara oil fields, bringing the majority of Libya's oil production under Haftar's control. There is little doubt Prigozhin was interested in this development, though we don't know whether he tried to exploit it. Haftar, though, wanted more than just the south: He wanted Libya's capital.

On April 4, 2019, Haftar launched a surprise attack on Tripoli. The head of the Tripoli government (GNA), Fayez al-Sarraj, promised to resist and launched a counteroffensive, dubbed the "Volcano of Anger." Seizing Tripoli, home to 1.2 million residents and a host of militias armed to the teeth, would prove no easy task. But Haftar had sold outside powers, particularly the UAE—but also the Trump administration—on the notion he could unite Libya. The UAE poured weapons, cash, and drones into the conflict. In mid-April, Haftar left Saudi Arabia with more funding. And while the French denied any connection, the LNA general had met French diplomats just two weeks prior to the attack. Soon French weapons also appeared on the battlefield.

Everyone wanted a slice of the offensive. Security entrepreneurs flocked to Haftar. The Darfuri rebel groups—Minni Minnawi and Abdul Wahid al-Nur's forces, in addition to a host of others—and Chadian rebel groups like FACT were already well represented. Noureddine Adam, the leader of CAR's FPRC, sent some men. RSB's Oleg Krinitsyn even tried to get back into the game after selling his company, but Haftar saw little use in undermining the GRU.

Christiaan Durrant—a former Australian fighter pilot, founder of security firm Lancaster 6, and a good friend of Erik Prince—also had men in Benghazi. According to a confidential UN report, a few days after he started his attack, Haftar met Prince—the founder of American PMC Blackwater—in Cairo. The security entrepreneur proposed

The "Director" Yevgeny Prigozhin (right) shows Prime Minister Vladimir Putin his school lunch factory outside Saint Petersburg in 2010, earning him the nickname "Putin's Chef."

The "Commander," Dmitry Utkin, with his SS tattoos. Utkin's callsign in Donbas, "Wagner," would become the unofficial name for the private military companies associated with himself and Yevgeny Prigozhin.

Armed pro-Russian militants walk in front of the destroyed Luhansk International Airport, eastern Ukraine, on September 11, 2014. The airport's capture would become legendary in the Russian mercenary community.

Marat Gabidullin (front left) together with predominantly Serbian fighters of "the Company's" international unit, taking a break from training at Wagner's base in Molkino, Russia.

Alexander "Granit" Bondarenko (left), Alexander "Ratibor" Kuznetsov (center), and Marat Gabidullin (right) in front of a fortress just outside Palmyra, Syria in 2017.

General Abdel Fattah Abdelrahman al-Burhan (right) and leader of the paramilitary Rapid Support Forces (RSF), Muhamed Hamdan Dagalo "Hemedti" (center) attend a military graduation in Khartoum, Sudan in 2021, when both men were working with Wagner.

Wagner accompanies a motorcade carrying Central African President Faustin-Archange Touadéra through the streets of Bangui. While there has been much deserved focus on Wagner's services as a "praetorian guard," Rwandan soldiers via the local United Nations peacekeeping forces (in blue berets) provide closer presidential protection.

A soldier with the Central African Armed Forces (French acronym FACA). Wagner provided training to FACA and other security forces in CAR.

Members of the Libyan Special Forces, loyal to General Khalifa Haftar (pictured on the billboard), patrol Libya's eastern city of Benghazi in 2017.

United Nations peacekeepers (MINUSCA) patrol downtown Bria, in the Central African Republic's tense northeast.

Beer from Africa Ti L'or, a Russian brewery allegedly owned by Dmitry Syty, in a shop in Bangui.

Left: Wagner's Dmitry Syty with the author (not pictured). Syty rose quickly within Wagner's ranks in the Central African Republic: from translator to advisor to President Faustin-Archange Touadéra. *Right:* Rebels from an alliance of armed groups, the Coalition of Patriots for Change (CPC), January 30, 2021. Two weeks earlier, the CPC failed to take Bangui. Wagner and Central African Armed Forces then launched a counteroffensive, retaking most major towns from armed groups.

Wagner touches down in northern Mali. After arriving in December 2021, mercenaries like Nazar fanned throughout the center of the country and parts of the north, initially to fight jihadist groups.

Left: A recruitment billboard outside St. Petersburg reads, "Join the Winning Team." Volunteers like "Sasha" answer the call, while Wagner recruited men like Sergey and Vlad from Russian prisons. *Right:* A Ukrainian soldier stands in Bakhmut on April 17, 2023, a little over a month before Wagner claims to have captured the city.

A Ukrainian T64 tank moves towards Bakhmut in the town of Chasiv Yar.

Right top and middle: Wagner celebrates wins at Bakhmut while the Ukrainian military reports continued fighting. *Left middle:* "Sasha" and two other Wagner volunteers along the front. *Bottom:* Wagner captured Bakhmut but lost up to 20,000 mercenaries in the process.

Members of Wagner in Rostov-on-Don late on June 24, 2023, just after Yevgeny Prigozhin called off his mutiny, or "March for Justice," upon the intervention of Belarusian President Aleksandr Lukashenko.

Yevgeny Prigozhin is seen for the first time after the March for Justice. "The temperature is over 50 degrees. Everything as we love it," he declared from Mali. Days later, he was dead.

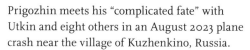

Prigozhin meets his "complicated fate" with Utkin and eight others in an August 2023 plane crash near the village of Kuzhenkino, Russia.

an $80 million contract to the LNA, which would cover the provision of "assault aircraft, cyber capabilities and the ability to intercept ships at sea." Prince outlined a program to kidnap and kill high-value targets in west Libya as well. The plan, according to the UN, swiftly fell apart. The Jordanians cancelled a deal to sell Cobra helicopters, forcing the team to look for backups. They procured some utility helicopters from South Africa, then supplied crop dusters previously outfitted with weapons through Bulgarian and Serbian companies.

Durrant contends the UN investigation mixed up all sorts of time-lines and geographies. "There's nothing 'united' about the United Nations," Durrant later told me. "I've been in countries where the UN is feeding the rebels, criminals really, on the other side." It was Durrant, not Erik Prince, who rolled into Libya quickly, after a separate deal in Jordan fell through. "In our line of work, the first mover picks up most of the business," he continued. "So, we were on the ground early talking not just with Haftar, but with the National Oil Corporation of Libya and U.S. government logistics." As a former associate of Prince's company, Frontier Services Group, Durrant had worked on crop dusters before and was well positioned to purchase planes and other assets for his own company.

After landing in Benghazi to assemble civilian helicopters, Durrant's team were pulled in front of Haftar. "They were told to put a machine gun on the helicopter and fly it over Tripoli." When the team refused—the mission was both "suicide and illegal"—Haftar's men were furious and started waving guns around. The twenty unarmed men decided they needed to get out of dodge. In the dead of night, Durrant's men escaped through Benghazi to reach two small inflatable boats, then crossed nearly two hundred miles of the Mediterranean to arrive safely in Malta.

With Trump in the White House, Durrant believes, there were those in the UN interested in using Erik Prince as a means to link the U.S. president to a "scandal." "Everyone else, Britain, France, is sending in javelins, meanwhile we get reams of reports written up about a potentially armed crop duster." (An Austrian court later found that the crop dusters did not constitute war material.) With regards to the assassination program, Durrant notes there's nothing illegal in proposing business. "I will do any work, as long as it's legal," he added, "and on the side of the right guys. If we are helping the U.S. stamp out terrorism, and we are able to make money doing it, then that's great."

"By August 2019, we knew Russian mercenaries were in the country," Heithem, a militia commander, told me when I met him outside his former base a few years later. Rocket blasts had ripped the building half-open. Concrete, furniture, cooking utensils—the scaffolding of daily life—pooled onto the street below. It was early 2020, and the front line had settled where we now stood, in Ein Zara, a suburb south of Tripoli. In his late twenties, stocky, and shy, Heithem, at the time part of an anti-Haftar militia from Benghazi, stared down the enemy's old position in a whitewashed house a few hundred yards away.

Walking softly across the rubble-strewn courtyard, Heithem waved me over. "Wagner played a logistical role in August, not an offensive one. Then in October, the guys in that white house started to look very different, like special forces. They had special vests, cameras on their helmets, different equipment." The mercenaries started to make a difference. "The LNA usually takes four or five shells to hit a target," Heithem added. "The Russians were hitting us immediately."

Wagner's intervention put Tripoli's forces in a dangerous position. Growing desperate, the head of the GNA government, al-Sarraj, signed a memorandum of understanding with Turkey in November. The MoU established maritime boundaries that effectively cut a direct line between Libya and Turkey and prompted immediate protests from Turkey's rivals in the east Mediterranean—Greece, Egypt, and Cyprus—where Turks and Cypriots were competing for oil blocs. Turkish leader Recep Tayyip Erdogan, in return, ramped up his support to the beleaguered Tripoli government, shipping in air defense systems, the Turkish military's infamous Bayraktar drones, and mercenaries.

Turkish intelligence selected al-Hamzat, one of eight armed groups in Turkish-controlled Syria, to recruit mercenaries for Libya. Al-Hazmat emerged in 2013 as a division within the Free Syrian Army. The group received training and equipment directly from the United States and United Kingdom, first to fight Assad's regime, then to fight ISIS. In 2016, under the leadership of Seif Abu Bakr, al-Hamzat joined Turkey's Operation Euphrates Shield against the predominantly Kurdish SDF.

Turkish military officers put no restrictions on the number of recruits for the Libyan front. An influx of Syrians would provide more time to train Libyan fighters and free up GNA personnel for offensive operations. Syrian commanders quickly took advantage. The more men commanders sent to Libya, the more money they could skim off the top.

One recruit, "Ahmed," had previously fought with al-Hamzat. In Syria, Ahmed recalled, fighters were rarely forced into battle. If conditions in a skirmish became unfavorable, many would simply fall back and fight later. In Libya, however, Ahmed discovered this was not the case. Seeing the front line in south Tripoli, the barrage of artillery and the drones hovering overhead, he asked to go home. His commanding officer told him: "Coming to Libya was your choice, going back is not." Together with fellow recruits, Ahmed reluctantly moved into an empty villa close to the front line. The first disbursement of his salary would be in three months, upon his return to Syria. Food became an issue, and it didn't take long for Ahmed to understand how things worked. "A shopkeeper introduced us to the black market," he said, "where we could sell our bullets and weapons to pay for groceries."

Turkey's Syrian mercenaries found themselves under-equipped for the fight ahead. "We were given old machine guns from home," one fighter recalled, "not due to lack of higher quality weapons, but because those weapons had been sold off on the black market." On the enemy's side, Haftar's LNA employed sophisticated surveillance drones—likely provided by the UAE, but also Wagner—to map targets. Back in Syria, "neither the regime nor rebels had the ability to target precisely."

Turkish officers told the Syrian recruits they were fighting not just Haftar, but Assad—there were Syrians on the other side loyal to the regime. They weren't wrong.

In September 2019, "Basil," a twentysomething Syrian from Syria's Latakia region, was in Deir ez-Zor with Wagner's ISIS Hunters unit when an order came to head to their base in Homs. "The Russians told us about [another] mission, but no one knew where exactly. We thought we were maybe going to Raqqa." The ISIS Hunters took a bus to Hmeimim Airport, then boarded a military plane packed with men and coffins. Three hours later, they landed. The Syrians were loaded in pickups and brought to Al-Karama base where they were finally told where they were: Libya. The starting salary was $500 per month. Twenty of the ISIS Hunters immediately refused to fight. "They said it was because of the low salary, but really they were afraid of the whole situation." More ISIS Hunters joined them in a strike, forcing a Russian commander to raise salaries to $1,000 a month: low by international standards but good money in the overwhelming poverty of Assad's Syria.

The same twenty fighters still refused to participate. They eventually flew back to Syria. The commander of the brigade collected the mobile phones of the others. Basil's family had no idea where he was, but that was pretty normal given "all the secret work" he did. Still, he was terrified. "I thought it might be another Conoco incident," he said, referring to the Battle of Khasham. The men were given weapons and piled into another plane, this one heading for al-Jufra. Everyone was given a fake name. From there, they hopped onto small buses and drove twelve hours to the front line in Tripoli. The trip shouldn't have been that long, but various "clans" put up roadblocks on the way.

Like their fellow Syrians across the front line, Basil and the ISIS Hunters were put up in civilians' houses. The next day, they visited one of the field hospitals that had an operations center. The first floor was for injured Russians and Syrians and food supplies, provided by the UAE. The floors above were for communications. There were Sudanese mercenaries, who, annoyingly for Basil, were earning $1,500 dollars, as well as Chadians. After a few days, it was time to fight. "The Russians were advancing during the day and withdrawing at night. I don't know why," Basil remembered.

"The real war was in the air, and the Turks controlled it."

Basil and his unit stayed in a ransacked house, everything picked through by either the Libyans, Russians, or Syrians. In December, he got a vacation, and he traveled the same winding path back.

At the beginning of 2020, the program ramped up. "The Russians began shipping in Syrians in large numbers, one company after another." When Basil returned to Tripoli for his second tour, Nazar had also arrived, having finished his contract training soldiers in Sudan. Flights were landing on small farming runways since the skies were becoming more and more dangerous for the LNA and its backers. Nazar remembers charred trucks and equipment along besieged roads, the work of Turkey's Bayraktar drones.

In May 2020, the Turkish intervention had made a serious difference. Pro-Tripoli forces pushed Haftar's LNA out of the capital's southern suburbs. Heithem thanked the Turkish drones more than the mercenaries. "They cut off the logistical supplies for the Russians and the LNA. They ran out of ammunition, even food." At the end of the month, Wagner's 1,500 mercenaries, a number that did not include Syrians under their employment, made a sudden and hasty retreat from Tripoli. From what Basil had heard, there had been a truce. "The Russians learned the GNA and Turks wanted to attack Sirte. Sirte had oil and was more important to Wagner than Tripoli, so they made a truce, and we were given seventy-two hours to withdraw." For now, it seems unlikely that Wagner had a direct stake in those oil fields. The bulk of Wagner's funding in Libya likely came from the Russian military, not Haftar. It is still unclear, too, whether Wagner brokered a deal with the Turks or simply made a hasty retreat. Soon, though, fires were lit at Russian headquarters.

Smoke from laptops and documents filled the air. Haftar's campaign against the capital collapsed a few days later.

Ahmed—who had fought for the Turks and the GNA—went back to Syria with a shattered pelvis. He was paid $2,500, a quarter of the $10,000 he was owed. "When I complained, they said this is what we have for you. If you don't like it, file a complaint." When the fighting in Libya was at its peak, a recruiter for one of the Turkish-backed militias reported he was told to "send as many fighters as we could recruit . . . so, we started sending kids with zero military experience." But once the battle was won, "commanders confiscated salaries," he confirmed.

After visiting the white house, Heitham and I drove a few minutes to meet Abdul Rahman. Abdul lost two brothers to the mines Wagner left behind. He showed us the car, speckled with small holes where shrapnel sliced through. He pointed to the trip wires in his garden, and the booby traps behind his doors.

"Was it possible this was the LNA?" I asked.

"We don't know for sure," he responded. But the sophistication hinted at the Russians. "Libyans themselves wouldn't leave these mines behind; society is not structured that way."

In the backyard we saw an unexploded shell. Abdul covered it with a rusty bucket and put a rock on top to keep it in place. His neighbor lost two children the year before when they picked up a mine. Frequent petitions to demine Ein Zara had gone unanswered by the government in Tripoli.

We then drove past several buildings destroyed by Emirati drones and fighter jets. On the street, groups of African migrants congregated, some on break from rebuilding Ein Zara, earning money to pay for boats to Europe. They bore the brunt of injuries from unexploded ordinances.

In October 2020, representatives from Libya's two rival camps signed a United Nations–sponsored action plan committing to the withdrawal of foreign mercenaries. A Wagner force stuck around, however, keeping some of its Syrian fighters. Basil's unit was transferred to Sirte, to wait for an attack from the Turks and GNA that never came. They were bored almost immediately, even more so after commanders cut everyone off from hashish. Most Syrians opted to go back, but a few signed new contracts to fight in Africa. Together with Nazar, they went south to the Central African Republic.

The offensive on Tripoli was a failure for Haftar, but not for Wagner. Prigozhin's men were paid for their services—likely through the UAE and the Russian state. While the Kremlin and Prigozhin would be happy for Haftar to take Tripoli, there was no interest in throwing all the necessary resources behind him. Russian military planners knew Haftar's chances of taking the city were limited. In the spring of 2019, Prigozhin received a report stating the LNA lacked the capacity and motivation to seize the capital. It was more important to maintain Haftar's dependence on the Kremlin and, therefore, Russian influence in an important country on NATO's southern flank.* In proxy warfare, outside powers are typically willing to invest enough resources to ensure their preferred proxies won't lose, but not enough for them to win. In this sense, Russia and Turkey have made the conflict in Libya more intractable. Ironically, it is also Russia and Turkey's intervention that produced a military stalemate and prevented the eruption of another war after 2020.

Neither at war nor at peace, the real winners in Libya are those comfortably straddling the two, feeding belligerents' demand for men and material.

★ ★ ★

In Libya, the wealth at stake is so high, it's worth going to war. In CAR, the stakes are high because wealth is so hard to come by. In

---

* This is not to discount the ways in which General Haftar, too, used the Russians to his advantage. The Russians were frequently frustrated with Haftar's outreach to other countries like France and his willingness to cut them out of lucrative deals with the UAE.

December 2020, I was back in Bangui, where the atmosphere was tense. The Khartoum Agreement was feeling increasingly vulnerable to collapse. Rumors of rebellion filtered in from the countryside.

The agreement, of course, was far from perfect to begin with. Just two months after signing, 3R killed at least forty-six civilians in three attacks. And while the agreement had called for establishing pastoral routes, it could do little to solve structural issues like the conflict between cattle herders and farmers over land and resources.

In the months that followed, President Touadéra came to conflate the success of the agreement with his own rising star. The Russians had thought Touadéra a weak, technical figure at first. But soon, the president was leveraging Wagner's muscle to centralize his own power. Prigozhin's men became, in many respects, victims of their own success. "We began resting on our laurels," one participant remembers. And armed group leaders, hardly democrats themselves, grew frustrated with their integration into the government.

Of course, a look through CAR's history yields little precedent for democracy and peaceful transitions of power. Successive governments rarely had the capacity or interest to govern outside the capital. The farther one travels from Bangui, the more power diffuses across multiple sources of authority. CAR's citizens both suffer from and take advantage of the state's absence, temporarily aligning with authorities that benefit them the most.

The political elite in Bangui, in turn, leverage their access to more powerful outside authorities—historically France, but that was now changing—to enhance their domestic political and economic position. The prosperity of Bangui's elite, however, always came first and foremost from the countryside, not geopolitical maneuvering.

It would be unfair to expect Prigozhin's few years in CAR to significantly affect these structures of governance. The country's head of state, political elite, and powerful armed actors all saw themselves using Wagner as a means to their own ends, few of which included making life better for CAR's citizens. Outside interventions like Wagner's simply create new equilibria. And even among all the constraints that exist within a small village in the world's poorest and least developed nation, people often, but not always, have power in choosing how to interact with Wagner or other intervenors. Many used the mercenaries to their advantage, or swindled them.

Language barriers, for example, were a constant problem and finding translators was no easy task. Former French legionnaires constantly had to assist their monolingual Russian colleagues. One time, commanders in the northwest town of Paoua hired local interpreters for $600 a month—an excellent salary by CAR standards. Once hired, the translators rarely showed up for work. Whenever they were called for, there was always some excuse, an internal investigation found. "Oh, he's gone to the market. He fell ill; took a drink; had a day off, etc.," a Wagner mercenary reported in frustration. There was not much the Russians could do.

After significant delays from the CAR government, the construction of Ali Darassa's meat-processing facility began in March 2019. But it too was plagued by challenges, though they were more specific to Wagner. Three men working on the project—Malyshev, Ponomarev, and Barabkin—arrived in June and immediately began consuming large amounts of alcohol. They drank, an internal Wagner investigation concluded, practically every day, except for the two or three days a month when they were part of supply columns.

A local translator told Wagner investigators that the three men, when they had money, drank until late at night. Sometimes they urinated and vomited in the tent where they slept. The senior project member, Sasha Ponomarev, was forced to sleep outside. The men often forgot where they put their belongings and told UPC guards that the workers had robbed them. The guards would beat up the workers. Later, when the Russians found their belongings, they wouldn't mention it to the guards.

Ponomarev and his men often sent the translator to find alcohol at night, an uncomfortable task, Wagner's internal investigators pointed out, for a Muslim in the town. Whenever he tried to refuse, Ponomarev threatened to fire him. The job fed his family, so he did what he was told.

In August 2019, the three Russians began purchasing 186-proof pharmaceutical alcohol, typically used to disinfect wounds. Later that month, they found a batch of pharmaceutical alcohol with a different appearance, that "emitted a strong smell of burnt rubber." This was hardly a problem; it just needed some lemon to remove the smell. The next day a blind, blabbering Ponomarev was transported from the meat-processing facility to Bambari. He tested negative for malaria. After a medevac, he died at the Chinese hospital in Bangui. A day later, Barabkin also showed up in Bambari, his friends claiming he had malaria. The medevac was delayed until the following morning, too late for Barabkin, who passed away that evening.

These deaths were extreme, but they still reflected a general problem the organization faced. The fighters Wagner recruited ranged from relatively courteous professionals to violent sadists, teetotalers to low-functioning alcoholics, and leaked internal documents show Wagner's commanders and managers constantly policing their men, likely to the detriment of other tasks. Drinking, drug use, corruption, and gratuitous violence all carried fines and punishments. Whether those punishments were carried out on the ground, or simply "corrected" on paper is hard to tell. If previous colonial administrations are any precedent, the latter is more likely.

Despite the discomfort men like Ponomarev and Barabkin fostered in some communities, and a lingering distrust surrounding the Khartoum Agreement, Wagner remained broadly popular. Western officials divined disinformation the reason for such popularity. This was not without merit. Local journalists, like my friend Maka Gbossokotto, were growing anxious about the rise of "fake news" in Bangui. Facebook shut down both Russian and French networks peddling fake accounts. Igor Mangu-shev's Radio Lengo Songo and new print media pushed editorial lines favorable to Touadéra and his Russian partners and articles blaming

France and the UN for CAR's crises. In response to the increasingly polarized environment, Maka founded a newsletter, *Anti Infox*.

It would be a mistake, though, to attribute anti-French sentiment, or disappointment in MINUSCA to mere "disinformation." Central Africans did not need Russians to understand France's deleterious role in their history, or MINUSCA's inability to bring peace. While the effectiveness of Wagner information operations is difficult to measure—not least because CAR features one of the lowest percentages of internet penetration, and one of the highest rates of illiteracy in the world—Wagner's little media empire in Bangui was a window into Prigozhin's thinking.

Wagner's boss saw tangible value in soft-power initiatives. Favorable coverage of the intervention ensured buy-in from the local population and continued access to government officials the Company could do business with. It was ultimately in CAR where Prigozhin worked to perfect this model of complementary businesses and operations. No one would call him an academic, but Prigozhin was a reader. He was particularly taken with Antonio Gramsci's theory of "cultural hegemony," or, that the dominant class in a society rules through norms and values.

Yet even if there was a method to Prigozhin's madness, events on the ground rarely follow tidy theories. "Everyone has a plan," said Mike Tyson, "until they get punched in the mouth." Prigozhin's carefully crafted peace deal would soon take a hit.

On December 31, 2020, New Year's Eve, I stepped outside of the Grand Café to meet my friend Jean-Paul. We hopped in his Ford F-150. *"I gui na ndo wa?"* I asked in Sango. Where are we going?

"Na Bimbo."

Though he doesn't look a day over forty-five—a fact he attributes to "judo, soccer, and samba"—Jean-Paul will soon be sixty-six years old. He is from Manza territory, one of the areas most devasted from slave raids 150 years ago. In the 1920s, French officers kidnapped Jean-Paul's grandfather and shipped him to Congo, where he built a railroad through the jungle, bare hands clawing earth under vast vaults of green. His grandfather survived but never went home.

Jean-Paul wanted to show me the Catholic mission in Bimbo, just outside Bangui. On the way, he told me how in 1979, he was shot in the leg when Jean-Bédel Bokassa—a general who took power in a French-backed coup, then crowned himself emperor of Central Africa—and his army put down a student uprising. Around one hundred children were massacred. The French military toppled the emperor later that year, but Bokassa got his revenge when he divulged he had gifted French officials scandalous amounts of diamonds during his reign.

On our way back to Bangui, someone leaned on the horn behind us. Jean-Paul checked the mirror and skidded off the road.

A Toyota pickup screeched past. Men in green balaclavas and dark sunglasses stood behind a machine gun nailed to the cargo bed, a large Ural truck trailed them. The mercenaries in the back were covered in dust, exhausted, returning from a countryside in chaos. They stared back; cheap blue surgical masks a reminder there was also a pandemic.

The truck was waved through the checkpoint into Bangui, never slowing down for the city's clogged streets, horns blaring. We were stopped, and men peered into our vehicle looking for rebels. Some of the soldiers were Syrians coming through Libya. A few months before, they were fighting for Wagner to capture Libya's capital. Now, they were defending CAR's.

Touadéra's former boss-turned-rival, Bozizé, emerged from exile in late 2019. In July 2020, he had announced his intention to run for president again, despite an international warrant for his arrest. On December 3, CAR's Constitutional Court ruled against his candidacy. In response, Bozizé contacted the leaders of armed groups and tried to convince them to overthrow Touadéra.

Following the discussions, Sidiki Abass (3R), Mahamat al-Khatim (MPC), and Maxime Mokom (anti-Balaka) were on board. For Mokom, the decision was easy. Over the past year, as part of Touadéra's centralization of authority, pro-government militias such as *les Requins* (Sharks) had popped up in Bangui. Mokom was frustrated by the slow pace of disarmament and reintegration into the army, as well as the allocation of ministerial posts, all of which was agreed in Khartoum. His friend Igor Mangushev concurred. After voicing his opposition to Russia's support for Touadéra, Mangushev broke from Prigozhin yet again and moved to Lebanon, where he opened a small business dealing with drones. In July, one of Mokom's houses was ransacked by CAR authorities, likely a show of force given his perceived closeness to Bozizé.

Abass, al-Khatim, and Mokom became the cornerstone of the new rebel alliance. Mokom, who had worked closely with the Russians on the Khartoum Agreement, now helped persuade the Peul armed groups, especially Ali Darassa's UPC, to join the plot. To sweeten the deal, Bozizé promised money to the armed group leaders and claimed the French supported his plan. Both were convincing, and untrue.

On December 15, Sidiki Abass, Maxime Mokom, al-Khatim, UPC and FPRC representatives, members of anti-Balaka, Bozizé's family, and old allies met with more than three thousand fighters in Kamba Kotta and agreed to take Bangui. Ali Darassa's UPC was to handle military operations in the south, southeast, and center of the country. The MPC would route the CAR government and Wagner from the Chadian border, while 3R would seize the northwest. Noureddine Adam was responsible for the northeast, while the anti-Balaka would be distributed in all sectors, coordinated through Maxime Mokom. Four days later, the six armed groups announced a new alliance, La Coalition des Patriotes pour le Changement: the CPC.

Despite incredible levels of insecurity, the U.S., France, European Union, UN, and African Union (AU) pushed ahead with presidential elections, elections being one of the few concrete ways international interventions can mark progress. Meanwhile, town after town began falling to the CPC, while hundreds of FACA deserted and joined the rebels through a battalion led by Bozizé's sons.

Back in Bangui, Wagner met with President Touadéra. "We promised the president we would protect him," Vitaly Perfilev, head of
security, told me. Touadéra, according Perfilev, requested support from
the French, the Americans, and Moscow. France allegedly said it would
continue to observe the situation. The Americans allegedly did not
respond. "Within one day Russia had a plane landing in Bangui.
Russia kept its promised. We were disappointed with the Americans
and the French."

Rwanda—which has a security cooperation agreement with CAR—
deployed hundreds of bilateral forces, while UN peacekeepers under
MINUSCA called in reinforcements from South Sudan. Each night
Jean-Paul and I sat waiting for the attack on the capital. Little did I know
at the time, but one of the planes landing in CAR that week carried
Dmitry Utkin. The head Wagner commander would personally oversee
the defense of Bangui, though one source says he was mostly there to
scare the shit out of his own men. "Boys, if you can't win here. Then
don't come home," he reportedly told his commanders.

Meanwhile, armed groups were closing in on the capital. A UPC
fighter remembered: "We used all possible means to advance on Bangui.
Cars, motorcycles, horses, donkeys, and on foot. We passed through the
transhumance corridors [cattle trails], the roads that are inaccessible to
FACA and MINUSCA, attacking towns along the way."

From Bozizé's hometown of Bossangoa, some rebels walked nearly
two hundred miles. In their wake marched the children and the poor;
when Bozizé took Bangui, they would have permission to loot the
capital for a few days. They were also promised a gun when the person
in front fell in battle. The French embassy's defense attaché told the
rebels if they reached the city's gates "something would be done." Just
like Bozizé's promises of French support, it was false.

On the morning of January 13, the CPC attacked Bangui from the
north and Bimbo in the south. From the start, the operation suffered
from poor execution. First, not all the armed groups followed through

on their commitment. Both al-Khatim's MPC and the FPRC bailed, claiming Bozizé still owed them money. The rebellion had little heavy equipment since the Chadians didn't want to invest much, either.

Ordinarily such a coup would cost a few million dollars: small by international standards but still serious money in CAR. It is possible the ex-president simply didn't have the funds. Regardless, the UPC, 3R, and anti-Balaka would have to fill the void.

Wagner, together with MINUSCA peacekeepers and Rwandan troops, pushed back the ill-equipped assault. "We didn't care about counting their dead," said Perfilev.

It was an awkward moment for the UN peacekeeping force, which a few days earlier denied any level of cooperation with Wagner when I asked them. Western officials and humanitarians admitted only in private that without the Russian mercenaries, Bangui would have fallen. The dark days of CAR's 2013 civil war could have returned. Instead, Touadéra won a second term by a slim majority, in an election where 40 percent of the regions were unable to vote due to insecurity.

★ ★ ★

"Jacque," a native of Bozizé and Mokom's hometown of Bossongoa, had long made his living selling groceries. A father of four, he sold soap, biscuits, and cigarettes on Bangui's dusty streets until 2018, when he recognized a business opportunity back home. For a year, Jacque sold his goods to workers at a gold mine just outside of town. Business thrived, allowing him to build up a small savings of gold dust. Then a new mine opened farther afield. The miners followed, so Jacque went for a few months to set up his business on-site. When he returned, Bossangoa was under the control of Bozizé's CPC. "We could no longer walk in the street; we had to hide our phones and motorcycles to avoid being robbed or killed."

In early February 2021, the Russian counteroffensive arrived in Bossangoa to the crackle of gunfire. "After the defense of Bangui, we met with Touadéra," Perfilev told me. "And we came to a joint decision. The CPC, these were Chadian and Sudanese mercenaries. They needed to be ousted from the country."

Wagner came in pickups and trucks, dressed in uniform, faces masked. The CPC fled into the bush when they heard the warning shots. "We could no longer bear living under the CPC," Jacque told me. "There was so much insecurity. Everyone thought that the Russians would improve our lives."

For two weeks, the Russians killed everything they could eat: goats, pigs, sheep. They occupied private properties, schools, the town hall, and the prefecture. They raped women and arrested young people suspected of being part of the CPC. Some men were found lifeless in the nearby river. They stole motorcycles, rode them into neighboring villages to hunt down the CPC, then offered to sell them back to their owners for $100, an unaffordable sum. The actual rebels were long gone in the bush.

In July 2021, Jacque went with his wife to the Léré market, one of the largest in the region. "We wanted to buy pumpkins to store and sell them at an opportune time," he said. They left in the early morning given the long road ahead. It was a decision that likely saved their lives.

Later that day, three Russian mercenaries hid their motorcycles behind trees and concealed themselves on the other side of the road, fifteen kilometers outside Léré. Twenty young Central African men on motorcycles fell into their trap. The mercenaries held them at gun point and forced them to sit in a line. Then one man at a time was told to stand up and run away. Each one was then shot in the back. Only the last man managed to escape and reach Bossangoa in time to warn others from taking the road.

Jacque and his wife were in Léré when the massacre happened, and they waited until the prefect arrived on the scene before they returned home. They left the pumpkins behind for fear of being robbed or killed. When Jacque arrived back home in Bossangoa, he learned two of his friends were among the victims.

After the attack, Jacque, like many in Bossangoa, was wary of the mercenaries "whose language we couldn't understand." But he still needed to feed his family and pay for his daughters' Catholic school education. He returned to the mine.

In December 2021, just before the Christmas holidays, Jacque woke up around 7:00 a.m. It was his last day of work before heading back to his family. He set up his stall, as usual, next to a construction site and checked that his gold powder, around $350 worth, was well-hidden in his pockets. "We were a group of four men and a woman. I was not the only merchant that day." Three successive gunshots snapped through the air before Russians arrived on motorcycles, metal detectors in tow. People started to flee.

The Russians approached Jacque and pointed their guns at him. He raised his hands while another stripped him of all his belongings. His money, his phone, and his merchandise. They found the gold powder: his life savings. A helicopter buzzed overhead. The mercenaries looked up and Jacque sprinted for the bush. Running frantically, he injured his foot. He has yet to recover. "I am alive. That is all I know," Jacque said.

Jacque no longer felt safe in the countryside. He packed up his family and moved them to Bangui. "I lost everything that day. You know what breaks my heart the most?" he added. "It's feeling like a bad parent. My daughters' school keeps reminding me to pay the last two quarters tuition for them. But I have no way to pay. I know my children will resent me, and I'm ashamed. I live in fear. Living with the rebels is dangerous, but at least they are Central Africans and can sometimes have pity on a situation or understand us."

The same week Jacque lost his savings, Land Cruisers carrying Russians, Central African Armed Forces, and former anti-Balaka and UPC militants (who had not joined the CPC) pulled into Boyo, a village in the center of CAR. The militants were trained and recruited by Wagner, then organized by local leaders into new pro-government militias.

The militias came to be nicknamed "Black Russians." Over the course of 2021, Black Russians played an increasingly prominent role in Wagner's operations. Partnering with local armed groups to fight an insurgency is, of course, standard practice among the world's militaries. They know the terrain and enemy behavior better than foreigners. But civilians preferred not to see former anti-Balaka and UPC fighters rewarded for past violence. They continued to commit human rights abuses; the only difference was that now they did it for the government.

Before entering the town, the mercenaries reportedly brought the pro-government forces together. "They told us that drones flew over the villages, and all the men in the villages are CPC rebels," a participant told *The Sentry*. "They have just hidden their weapons in the bush . . . so the Russians told us to kill all the men." Over the course of the operation, men and women were raped and killed. Homes were destroyed and looted. A UN investigation found at least twenty individuals were murdered, though participants told *The Sentry* the death toll was far higher.

Violence was a tool. "The success of Wagner Group in Africa comes down to the total cleansing, or mopping up, of all opposing armed groups using extremely harsh but effective military force," a former Russian officer told me. Toward the end of the Soviet war in Afghanistan, special units of the Soviet Army of the KGB developed a counterinsurgency strategy that would prove influential in both Afghanistan and Chechnya. The basic principle of the strategy was "the destruction of the enemy at any cost and by any methods and means, with no sentimentality."

The logic was that only extreme measures can force insurgents to lay down their arms. Thirty years later, Russian instructors told Central African soldiers it was necessary to kill women and children "in order to terrorize the other rebels, who will be afraid to settle in the villages." These brutal methods can bring stability. But that stability, the former Russian officer noted, "is always only temporary. Without a full-fledged peacekeeping operation, it cannot give permanent or long-term results."

It is difficult to get an exact picture of who led the counteroffensive against the CPC. We know Boris Nizhevenok, "Zombie," who had been with Wagner since its beginnings in Luhansk, led the Third Assault Detachment in northwest CAR along the border with Cameroon. Alexander Emalyanov, or "Emalya," who had survived the Battle of Khasham, was based around Bangui along with Nikolai Budko, or "Bes." Anton Elizarov, or "Lotus," led Wagner's Sixth Assault Detachment and was present around Bambari. The men who served under them often had little idea, or curiosity, where they were or what the mission was.

In 2021, Nazar arrived in CAR. He told me CAR rebels only had a few beat-up RPGs maybe some *kalash*, or AK-47s. "To be honest," Nazar added, "I can't remember the names of the places we were. At some point we were in the east, marching through jungles and liberating towns from Séléka."* Every unit worked on its own, and Nazar had little idea who the commanders were in other units, let alone what Wagner leaders like Vitaly Perfilev or Dmitry Syty were up to in Bangui. "You would never know what you were going to do or where you were going to go until the last second," he said. "Suddenly, you'd just get the order: 'Pack up boys let's go.' And you wouldn't get back until dark."

Just a few weeks after the massacres in Bossangoa and Boyo, I returned to CAR. I decided to drive from Bangui to the northwestern town of Bouar, close to the border with Cameroon. I was told it was now possible thanks to Wagner's counteroffensive.

As I drove north, we passed FACA checkpoints and Wagner bases— dirt berms topped with barbed wire enclosing a few sparse buildings. I slept in a village thirty miles outside Bouar, where Wagner mercenaries lived in small huts that dot the roadside. They lounged about, sunburnt, grilling meat, drinking beer. The masks were gone, the atmosphere relaxed.

---

* Central Africans often use the defunct "Séléka" as shorthand for any Muslim armed group, a term Wagner picked up as well.

In the center of town, I met Omar, a Peul recently returned from Cameroon, where he was for years a refugee. Next to us, children sat on colorful rugs laid over packed earth, learning the Quran by rote. "Here in the center of town, there's security," Omar told me. The major problem, in his mind, was 3R and anti-Balaka in the countryside. Armed groups continued to steal cattle along the herding trails.

While many of CAR's citizens suffered at the hands of Wagner, particularly in places viewed as supportive of the CPC like Bozizé and Jaque's Bossangoa, other Central Africans saw opportunity. Some fighters in pro-government militias ransacked towns, others positioned themselves as intermediaries between Wagner and communities such as Omar's. One commander told me he had the task of "sensitizing" the Russians to Peul issues. "I explained to them that armed herders coming from Cameroon are protecting their cattle, they are not part of armed groups."

After a few days in the northwest, I met a few Central African friends to make the drive back to Bangui. It's a distance of 240 miles that, in a disintegrating pickup, takes the whole day. In every hamlet, my friend haggled with women over the price of *gozo* (manioc in Sango) and *nyama ti ngonda* (bushmeat), including *deku ti ngonda* (rat) and *ngbo* (snake).

After a full day, we stopped on the outskirts of Bangui for fried fish. "Our trip, traveling like this by road: None of this would have been possible without the Russians," one friend told me, hand stretched toward the laughing and shouting Friday night crowds. "The Russians brought security."

My friends were not ignorant of the dark rumors from the countryside. But for them, after decades of civil war and failed international interventions, the Wagner mercenaries were still the best chance of ridding the country of armed groups.

Later, I sat down with Vitaly Perfilev, head of operations in CAR. Our meeting would be hosted at a Wagner hangout: the Ledger Hotel. The Ledger lays nestled against rolling hills that circle Bangui's sprawl before sliding into the Oubangui River below, where wooden pirogues, pressed within an inch of the water's surface, haul goods from Congo. Bangui itself is a symphony of horns, shouts, and Cameroonian pop crackling out of cheap Chinese speakers. Smoke from trash fires and sizzling meat hang suspended in thick heat.

For those who can afford it, the Ledger offers a brief respite from the city's brimming life. After a half-hearted search for explosives from security, drivers deposit clients under a shady portico. To the right of the white marbled lobby sit some of the Central African Republic's most reliable ATMs, often out of cash. Around the corner, a café looks over one of the country's few pools, with a small bakery, a jewelry store, and a gym down the hall.

The Ledger remains one of the few hotels foreign governments and NGOs consider safe for their personnel. It is, therefore, an excellent venue to discuss or listen in on important matters. When Prigozhin's men arrived, the Libyan hotel manager and astute businessman, Ziad al Zarzour Khalifa, provided them with several suites. Staff send Vitaly Perfilev a list of guests each night, and his personal bottle of Jack Daniels sits in a safe behind the café bar. Only the Americans forbid their personnel from staying there, believing that the rooms given to Western officials are bugged.

Vitaly, in many respects, does not conform to most people's image of a Wagner mercenary. The man shaking my hand that day sported a clean shave. He wore, as he often does, a beige nylon button-down shirt and pants. Day-hike boots remind one of a German tourist flying to Nairobi in full safari gear.

Vitaly, of course, was no tourist. As a young man, he signed up for the French Foreign Legion, serving as a paratrooper in Africa until perhaps 2017. In 2018 he joined Wagner and, thanks to his fluent French, found himself in CAR. By the time I sat across from him five years later, he had risen through the ranks, and was now one of President Touadéra's closest advisors. He is sharp and taciturn, someone who creates a void for others to speak into. After a few minutes, he warmed up slightly and conceded: "When we first came here, we had to learn everything. We knew nothing. Everything we learned, we learned through experience."

The 2021 counteroffensive against the CPC returned almost all major towns to CAR government control. "In a few months, we ousted them." Vitaly told me. "For the first time, FACA reached the borders of Chad, Cameroon, and Sudan. That had never happened before." Infrastructure and banditry, Vitaly claimed, were the main obstacles to CAR's development. Indeed, the lines between armed group members and bandits were often blurred in the countryside. Many fighters left the CPC to return to racketeering.

Ironically, in the attempt to overthrow the government and their mercenary backers, the CPC rebels turbocharged Wagner's penetration of the political system and economy. Touadéra drew even closer to his mercenary backers. Perfilev deepened ties to the minister of defense and the head of intelligence. The mercenaries, for a time, held CAR's customs agency and received subsidies on fuel and food totaling $35,000,000 per year.

Strangely, prior to the counteroffensive, Prigozhin's team did little to invest in the mining sites for which they owned concessions. If there was a strategy, it was largely ad hoc. Either Lobaye Invest leased the concessions it owned to other companies, or the mercenaries simply followed the armed groups' method of taxing artisanal miners for access to the mines. Often, Wagner seemed more interested in shaking down mines, the "smash and grab" operation, of which Jacque was a victim.

At some point during the counteroffensive, Wagner's trucks rolled into Ndassima, the only gold mine in CAR that could operate on an industrial scale. Darassa's UPC—who had allowed artisanal miners to the site—had retreated and were no longer an obstacle. The mercenaries chased away Chinese miners linked to the mysterious Madame Zhao in Bangui and claimed Ndassima as their own. (Madame Zhao, however, got her men back in.) A Prigozhin-affiliated company, Midas Resources SARLU, received a preferential mining allowance, and as early as 2021, Prigozhin's team began building a "state of the art" processing plant, following recommendations from a feasibility study conducted by the Canadian firm that held Ndassima prior to Darassa's takeover. At full capacity, the mine could generate up to $100 million in profit per year, though Wagner was still far from reaching those levels.

While investment in gold seemed largely concentrated on Ndassima, Prigozhin and his team still ventured into other natural resources, such as timber. Through a company called Bois Rouge, huge trucks filled with logs began making the trip from CAR to Cameroon. Each carried up to $200,000 of lumber.

Wagner also expanded into distilling and brewing. In 2021, a new vodka producer appeared in Bangui, "Wa Na Wa," made "in the heart of Africa with Russian technology." Then "Africa Ti L'Or" hit the beer scene. Africa Ti L'Or was owned by Dmitry Syty, who launched the business just after a letter bomb, sent to the Russian embassy, exploded, leaving him in critical condition. Russian media immediately produced photos from the crime scene, where a perfectly intact letter read in Russian: "This is from the French. Russians will get out of Africa." Western officials suggested the Russians staged the operation. The injury, however, was real, a fact Syty was keen to assure me of. He lost a few fingers and began wearing a black glove.

I asked Vitaly what led to all this success in CAR. "The most important thing is respect," he responded, brushing aside the brutality of the counteroffensive against the CPC. "Take, for example, Russia in the 1990s. We were poor and a lot of foreigners came thinking we're idiots who need to be taught. You need to be open and talk about serious things openly. I'll give you an example," he continued. "The Russian soldier is very different from the European soldier, or trainers here. The Russian soldier can sleep in the dirt, he can go without water. We live with the FACA in the bush. We help them in the field; we fight with them. The European soldier wants to stay on base."

He paused, then added: "By the way the Ukrainian soldier can also live in filth, that's why the fighting between us is so fierce."

V

Liberators

"Thus we do disagreeable things, but we are defensive. That, I think, is still fair. We do disagreeable things so that ordinary people here and elsewhere can sleep safely in their beds at night. Is that too romantic? Of course, we occasionally do very wicked things"; he grinned like a schoolboy. "And in weighing up the moralities, we rather go in for dishonest comparisons; after all, you can't compare the ideals of one side with the methods of the other, can you, now?"

—JOHN LE CARRÉ, *THE SPY WHO CAME IN FROM THE COLD*

By early 2021, all actors—from small-time political entrepreneurs to great powers—recognized the utility of the "Wagner threat" to Africa. African governments leveraged the discourse to position themselves as either "cooperating with" or "countering" Wagner, to extract further support or concessions from Russia, the West, or both. Yet much of the fearmongering was advanced by Western journalism. The opaque nature of Prigozhin's dealings with African governments, and of Wagner's relationship to the Russian Ministry of Defense and President Vladimir Putin, ignited intense speculation. Western media and pundits described Wagner as Putin's shadow army, a tool for Moscow's pursuit of "influence" in Africa.

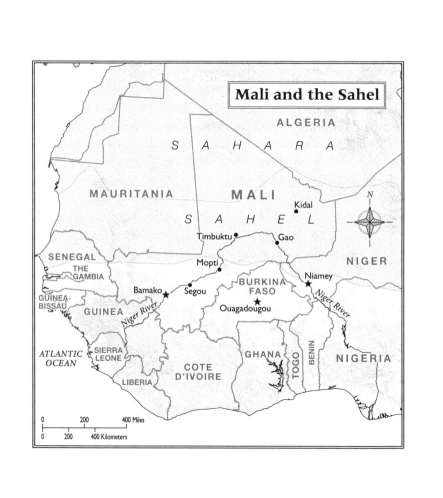

Mali and the Sahel

ALGERIA

S A H A R A

MAURITANIA

MALI

Kidal

S A H E L

Timbuktu
Gao

SENEGAL

THE
GAMBIA

Mopti

NIGER

GUINEA-
BISSAU

Bamako
Segou

BURKINA
FASO

Niamey

GUINEA

Niger River

Ouagadougou

Niger River

ATLANTIC
OCEAN

SIERRA
LEONE

GHANA

BENIN

NIGERIA

LIBERIA

COTE
D'IVOIRE

TOGO

N

0   200   400 Miles
0   200   400 Kilometers

The Central African Republic became a hot spot for what one Western diplomat termed "Wagner tourism." American and French media churned out articles that painted CAR as a "laboratory" for Russia's hybrid warfare, or worse, a "zombie host for Wagner." Implicit was the belief that Central Africans had no agency. Only Russians had the capacity to control events.

Such reporting on Russia's return to Africa united two great *others*. First, the Africa of Joseph Conrad's *Heart of Darkness*, where, as Chinua Achebe wrote, the continent is "a metaphysical battlefield devoid of all recognizable humanity, into which the wandering European enters at his peril." Second, Russia as home to the irrational, where, Virginia Woolf concluded, the soul is "confused, diffuse, tumultuous, incapable, it seems, of submitting to the control of logic." To these journalists, Russian and African societies were a window into a distant past, one that revealed certain truths about mankind's predisposition to violence. It followed that Wagner's goal in Africa was to sow chaos, even though chaos is hardly good for something as capital-intensive as gold mining.

CAR officials were frustrated. Journalists came to cover Wagner and their human rights abuses, events vital to call attention to. Less interesting, however, were the abuses of the armed groups. Africans killing Africans made far fewer headlines, and Central African lives were only meaningful to the extent they suffered from or supported Wagner.

Their country, too, was relevant only in relation to larger neighbors: the Democratic Republic of the Congo, Cameroon, Chad, and, farther afield, the Sahel. Wagner's operations in CAR weren't important; CAR's potential to facilitate Wagner's spread elsewhere was. Policymakers, pundits, and think tanks recommended ways the West could contain the Russian PMC. The threat of Wagner became more powerful than Wagner itself.

In 2021, waxing fear of Wagner coincided with the waning threat of jihadist terrorism. The year prior, the United States began further drawing down troops from Iraq. ISIS, or at least its territorial caliphate, had been defeated. The Biden administration then committed to a chaotic withdrawal from Afghanistan. The pivot to Asia was underway. "Great Power Competition"—the strategic rivalry between the United States, China, and Russia—had taken center stage.

The "Great Power Competition" narrative was a boon for political and security entrepreneurs working in Africa. Journalists and pundits could get clicks discussing shadowy Russian influence. African governments could position themselves as bulwarks against Russian or Chinese malign influence to attract further resources. Paris and Washington could avoid defining what their policies in Africa were, stating instead what they were against.

Wagner benefited perhaps most of all. The threat Prigozhin represented to the West was proof to the Kremlin that his initiatives were a worthy investment. Their effectiveness was less important than the West's reaction to them. The Internet Research Agency's social media campaigns had little influence on American voters, but the coverage Russian election meddling received in U.S. media undoubtedly contributed to further polarization between Democrats and Republicans. Heightened awareness of Russian influence at home carried over to fear of Russian influence abroad. The U.S. Treasury sanctioned Wagner for its role in undermining the territorial integrity of Ukraine. Prigozhin was placed under personal sanctions for his role in interference in the 2016 U.S. presidential election. In 2021, the U.S. sanctioned a number of Prigozhin's entities in response to their malign operations in Africa.

While sanctions certainly made logistics more difficult, they were useful for Prigozhin's virtue signaling back home. The "Great Power Competition" narrative was only reemerging in the West, but in Russia it had never quite left. Many, if not most, Russians believed the sacrifices the Soviet Union made in defeating Nazi Germany endowed their country with a unique claim to shaping world order. And throughout his first three terms, Putin's administration cultivated and derived significant political legitimacy from restoring this unique claim to *derzhavnost'*, or great power status. According to pro-Kremlin historians and talking heads, the poverty and instability that followed Soviet collapse was the product of Western interference and meddling—something Vitaly alluded to at the Ledger—not its own internal contradictions. Gorbachev had been a naïve fool to cooperate with the West, while Yeltsin was simply a Western proxy.

Putin embodied the restoration of a strong state, capable of defending Russia's singular history and mission. U.S. and EU sanctions confirmed the West's jealous, futile plans to impede Russia's return. Men like Prigozhin positioned themselves to aid Putin in this just crusade, and the personal sanctions against them signaled they were doing something right.

Thus, Wagner was both ideologically and materially incentivized to push the motherland into new worlds. But entrepreneurial spirit and hard work are useless if there's no demand for one's product. Timing is critical, and Prigozhin's team landed in Africa at a particularly propitious time.

During the age of European empire, African rulers and elites lever-aged their privileged access to colonial officers to enhance their own wealth and power—a phenomenon the scholar Jean-François Bayart labeled *extraversion*. This is not to say that relations were equitable, far from it. Rather, it explains, in part, why an unfair system like colonialism could last. Independence had little initial impact on these structures of governance. African rulers and elites continued to utilize their access to the metropole to secure their regimes. European powers kept troops in their former colonies and provided budgetary support to the newly independent governments. In return, they often maintained their privileged access to natural resources and, especially in the case of France, a symbolic standing as a great power. In Francophone Africa, the cozy relationship between French government and intelligence officials, French companies, and autocratic African elite took the collective term *Françafrique*.

The twenty-first century, however, saw a shift. France became an increasingly reluctant partner in military interventions, especially against opponents who did not represent a terrorist threat to the homeland.

A new generation of Africans were critical of France's support for the geriatric kleptocracies that ruled them.

United Nations peacekeeping missions, too, were undergoing an existential crisis. While there were countless people with good intentions working for the UN in places like CAR, it was well-known that UN peacekeeping missions often failed to keep the peace and protect civilians. Rape and sexual assault committed by UN staff was an open secret. Peacekeepers received danger pay in the field without putting themselves in danger, while Central African soldiers could be killed with salaries months in arrears. Some UN officers in Bangui could earn compensation packages equivalent to $20,000 per month without having to pay local taxes, raising legitimate questions as to who was really a war profiteer.

Skepticism of peacekeeping missions often took the form of conspiracy theories. A common conspiracy in CAR, which Wagner fighters believed as well, was that MINUSCA aided armed groups. Such claims were easily dismissed by the peacekeeping community. Yet the conspiracy did reveal an underlying structural issue that academics were just beginning to tackle. In countries such as CAR, the state is the main employer. Most of the population, of course, was shut out of state positions. Peace talks were a chance to redistribute government posts and the patronage networks associated with them. The international community did not consider bandits legitimate political actors. So, many armed groups, which were closer to racketeering networks, went political. They wrote manifestos, named themselves liberation movements, and declared themselves in opposition to the government, thus ensuring a seat at the negotiation table. Peacekeeping missions and peace dialogues, therefore, could increase rather than reduce the number of armed groups in a conflict.

Security partners in Africa were changing, too. For almost three decades following Soviet collapse, security providers came from the West. China invests but is reluctant to intervene in any conflict. Turkey tends to stick to exporting arms and hardware, like the Bayraktar drones so effective in Libya, while Gulf States like the UAE insert themselves liberally through financial networks and mercenaries. In 2017, Russia became the only alternative security partner with a United Nations veto and the ability to put boots—albeit through men like Prigozhin—on the ground. Prigozhin's network slipped seamlessly into Africa's ecosystem. Wagner was not an aberration within African politics but what the scholar Graham Harrison called a "part of the repertoire of techniques of governance" African leaders use to manage instability and international balancing.

In 2021, Prigozhin matched supply and demand, and his organization was truly global. He had representatives or mercenaries working in eastern Ukraine, Syria, Sudan, Libya, Madagascar, and the Central African Republic. Thousands of men had passed through Wagner's ranks. They, together with fans, came together in unofficial forums and Telegram channels, like Reverse Side of the Medal, that had thousands more followers. A unique mercenary culture developed, with its own lingo, imagery, and ultranationalist views. Wagner boosters shared the latest interviews and gossip and sold unofficial merchandise like T-shirts and patches. One patch, the infamous black and red, smiling skull in crosshairs, was lifted from the ISIS Hunters in Syria and popped up on FACA uniforms in CAR. Another popular patch depicted the grim reaper, his skeletal fingers wrapped around a placard that read: "Our business is death, and business is good."

Prigozhin had laid the groundwork for Wagner's rising fame, largely through efforts to control both his and his businesses' image. Some measures, however, were decidedly brutal.

On July 28, 2018, three Russian investigative journalists, Kirill Radchenko, Alexander Rostorguyev, and Orkhan Dzhemal—sponsored by ex-oligarch Mikhail Khodorkovsky's London-based Center for Investigation—arrived in CAR to investigate Prigozhin's investment in diamond fields. For reasons unknown, the group decided to travel outside the town of Sibut after dark. (It is axiomatic in CAR to use roads only in daylight.) They were shot dead. The official response from

Moscow and Bangui was that the attack must have come from rebels or bandits. This was certainly possible given the dangers of traveling in rural CAR. But Khodorkovsky's team found extensive evidence of an assassination plot. The driver for the three journalists trained at a Wagner camp in Sudan and the CAR officer who followed in a car behind the group had close ties to Russian trainers. The murders sparked outrage in Russian media and internal documents show Prigozhin's men followed the investigation obsessively. The scandal didn't stop Wagner from intimidating independent journalists, but it appears Prigozhin refrained from murdering them thereafter.

Prigozhin created his own media initiatives, too, such as Igor Mangu-shev's Radio Lengo Songo He was also a fan of one genre heavily steeped in ideology: action movies.

A few months after he worked on the Madagascar presidential campaign, Maksim Shugalei landed in Tripoli. "The Russia-Africa Summit was coming up in 2019," Shugalei told me, referring to the October event in Sochi attended by forty-three African heads of state along with Putin and top Russian officials. "From an investment stand-point, Libya was very interesting to us. But the western part of Libya was an unknown entity." The decision was made, therefore, to conduct surveys and hold interviews with key stakeholders in the west, while Wagner mercenaries arrived on the ground in the east to support Haftar's offensive.

One person of particular interest to Shugalei was Muammar Gaddafi's son Seif al-Islam Gaddafi. Seif was considered second-in-command and the chosen successor. After the death of his father and brother, Seif was captured by Zintani militias in southern Libya. Released from prison in 2017, though still in hiding, he began to move a bit more freely about Zintan and slowly tiptoed back into politics, at one point even trying to recruit a Tuareg militia. "We thought he might be a pro-Russian leader who could deliver the west of Libya," Shugalei said. Meeting Seif, however, was risky. Gaddafi's son was a symbol of the old regime, which made him no friend to the militias that fought against his father and now controlled Tripoli. It made him a political threat to Haftar as well. After years of civil war, Haftar portrayed himself as a provider of stability, an attempt to cultivate nostalgia for Libya under Gaddafi.

Prigozhin and Shugalei, therefore, were going behind Haftar's back in meeting Seif. Unfortunately for Shugalei, he was in territory controlled by the Tripoli militias when Haftar launched his attack on the capital. On his way back from meeting Seif, he and his translator were arrested and thrown into Tripoli's notorious Mitiga Prison.

While Shugalei listened to Haftar's bombs on the outskirts of Tripoli, Prigozhin's think tank kicked into gear to lobby for his release. *Shugalei*, an action film shot in Tunisia and Russia, premiered on NTV one year after his capture. Filming took only forty-eight days, a record for the Russian film industry.

In the movie, a gutsy, jaded Shugalei travels to western Libya, under the control of the Government of National Accord (GNA). There, he learns that, following the overthrow of Gaddafi, the population has suffered under the brutal regime of militias and jihadists. Shugalei succeeds in meeting Gaddafi's urbane son Seif, who benevolently lectures the sociologist on how his father kept terrorists at bay. In Tripoli, Shugalei discovers dangerous information: the GNA is working with al-Qaeda. Worse, Libya's president, al-Sarraj, is the richest man in Libya. The Americans then organize Shugalei's kidnapping through a Tripoli militia. After months of torture, Shugalei escapes Mitiga Prison thanks to General Khalifa Haftar's daring mission to save his "Russian friends."

The film is, in essence, a bad 1990s action movie, with plenty of the orientalizing tropes about Arabs and the Middle East that one finds in Western counterparts. But behind the clunky dialogue was a real narrative Prigozhin was trying to sell.

"The Russians never completely trusted Haftar," Kirill Semenov, a Moscow-based expert on the Middle East and North Africa notes. "He turned, after all, on Gaddafi in Chad, then became a CIA asset in Virginia. He was among the first to arrive to fight Gaddafi." Major Russian state-owned companies like Gazprom and Tatneft, even if they worked in the east, needed to maintain relations with the internationally recognized government in Tripoli to keep pumping oil and gas. *Shugalei,* therefore, sought two objectives. The first, certainly, was to free Prigozhin's sociologist. The second was an effort to convince the Russian government and public to throw its weight behind Haftar, and not Tripoli.

Of course, the movie failed to convey the real reason Shugalei was in Zintan meeting Seif: that Prigozhin was looking for other ways to access the west if Haftar failed to unite Libya. The real Haftar was reportedly livid when he found out about Shugalei's shenanigans in Zintan—the field marshal had no benevolent plan to liberate him from prison. Nor was the Russian MoD aware of Shugalei's adventure. "The idea came from Yevgeny," Shugalei told me.

After *Shugalei,* more films followed, including Prigozhin's most famous movie, *Tourist,* which was filmed in CAR. In *Tourist,* Wagner mercenaries valiantly defend Central Africans from nefarious armed groups led by François Bozizé. Unlike *Shugalei,* which was directed more toward a Russian audience, *Tourist* was screened to crowds in Bangui.

The decision to make a movie about Wagner's foray into Mozambique, *Granit,* however, was more curious. There were few episodes from that brief intervention that Prigozhin could cast a success.

Granit opens with a conspiracy theory widely accepted in the former Portuguese colony. In 1986, a Soviet aircraft carrying the Mozambican president Samora Machel crashed in South Africa, killing the president and many members of his cabinet. Many still hold South Africa's apartheid government responsible. Prigozhin's film added a new twist—the Americans gave South Africans special technology that lured the Soviet plane off course.

The film cuts to its eponymous hero, "Granit," a Wagner mercenary stationed in Sudan. Wagner's chief of staff, Andrei Nikolaevich Troshev, "Sedoi," tells Granit that Mozambique needs the Russians' help against a shadowy insurgency in the north of the country. Troshev tells his men that the Mozambican military (FADM) needs only instruction. "No heroics," he tells steely Granit.

On the ground in Mozambique, Granit finds the FADM under-equipped, in a fight against an insurgency they barely understand. Eager to hide their ignorance, the generals refuse to say which villages have been attacked: "That information is classified," they tell the exasperated Russians. The mercenaries decide they need to make sense of the situation themselves, but FADM is too scared to join them. Driving on dirt roads through the thick jungle, Granit and his companions realize their drones and advanced equipment provide no advantage.

While obviously a work of fiction, the film reflected many of the genuine frustrations Wagner felt in Mozambique.

In 2017, President Filipe Nyusi was negotiating a major deal between his ruling FRELIMO party and RENAMO, with which it had been at war nearly since the country gained independence from Portugal in 1975. The agreement was to be Nyusi's great legacy. But while focus was on peace with RENAMO, an insurgency was growing in Mozambique's northern province of Cabo Delgado, where the local population continued to suffer economic and political marginalization.

Nyusi was Mozambique's former minister of defense, but he was not a military man. As in other former Portuguese colonies in Africa, the military played an outsized role in politics and the economy following independence. "Nyusi saw what was happening in CAR, and he saw in Wagner an opportunity to create a praetorian guard that would decrease his dependence on the military," a Russian close to events recalled. Personal security was particularly important to Nyusi, since he was seeking reelection in October 2019.

Prigozhin's team, however, believed they could extend their services far beyond coup-proofing, and it appears they focused on solutions to the crisis in the north. Prigozhin's associates weren't the first to pitch a private military intervention in Cabo Delgado. In 2010, vast natural gas fields were discovered off the coast. Nine years later, the French energy giant TotalEnergies announced it would invest $20 billion in the

Mozambique Liquified Natural Gas (LNG) project, just as insurgents declared their allegiance to ISIS. It was the perfect setup for a private military intervention.

Erik Prince reportedly came up with a proposal, and he wasn't alone. "Everyone and their uncle were pitching to the Mozambicans," a South African mercenary remembered, and Wagner was clearly one of them. These proposals may have planted in Nyusi's mind the idea of a small, outside force to deal with the sideshow conflict in Cabo Delgado. Prigozhin's men beat out all the others. "We couldn't compete," a rival PMC source admitted. "They could source equipment from the Russian military that we had no access to. They could do it cheaper, and they had a major state backing them."

It appears, however, that the Russian state was less enthused on Prigozhin's venture than competitors thought. At least within the Russian MoD, those who knew Mozambique told Prigozhin to back down. Relations between Russia and Mozambique had been strained for years, and MoD officials were aware of divisions within the country's security forces.

Despite the warnings, Prigozhin forged ahead, perhaps thinking these obstacles would make victory that much sweeter. In August 2019, Nyusi traveled to Moscow, where he and Putin signed energy and security deals. One of Prigozhin's think tanks got to work on an opinion poll for Nyusi's reelection campaign and 160 military instructors touched down in Maputo.

Once on the ground, no one seemed to know what Wagner's mandate was. The mercenaries moved north and found themselves almost immediately over their heads. One month into the mission, the real Granit, Alexander Bondarenko, was killed in an ambush on Cabo Delgado's dense, forested roads. More deaths—including reported beheadings of Wagner soldiers—and frustration followed. A few weeks later, Wagner withdrew from the country.

When Prigozhin pulled his men out of Mozambique, the loss was not significant, at least in Wagner's terms. There were a few deaths, and probably some money that wasn't coming back. Prigozhin's real failure was never managing to get the MoD on board with the project. The Kremlin invested little in equipment and resources, and Prigozhin's team couldn't find the paths necessary to working independently.

In short, Mozambique lacked a narrative that could justify Wagner's adventurism. Maputo's former colonial ruler was now a relatively poor European backwater. Framing Prigozhin's intervention in anti-Portuguese terms carried little discursive weight with the Kremlin or the world more generally. Neither Prigozhin nor the Russian state were in a position to push TotalEnergies off its $20 billion LNG project, and far smaller assets came with significant local obstacles and headaches. Even with a movie to memorialize Granit's heroism, Mozambique was soon forgotten.

France's former colonial territories, however, offered a far catchier story. Unlike Portugal, France had a seat on the UN Security Council. It was a world power, fighting its own forever war against jihadist insurgencies in the Sahel. The Sahel itself was home to Europe's two great existential fears: immigration and terrorism. Planting a flag in such an important geopolitical arena would show Russia was back.

★ ★ ★

The Republic of Mali emerged from French colonialism in 1960. A rebellion in the northern region of Kidal came only three years later. The uprising had multiple causes, researcher Alex Thurston notes, "ranging from ambiguous French gestures toward the possibility of creating a Saharan polity in the 1950s, to the racism and contempt that Tuareg 'whites' felt for the 'blacks' in southern Mali, to the centralizing and authoritarian policies of the administration of Mali's first President Modibo Keita."

Since then, politics in the north cycles from rebellion to negotiation. Despite their small size—making up around 7 percent of Mali's population—Tuareg traders and pastoralists play a critical role in the Saharan economy: from Mauritania to Niger, Algeria, and Libya. Tuareg society is traditionally divided into socio-professional castes—including nobles, non-nobles, and slaves—though French authorities banned the formal practice of slavery under colonial rule.

In 1990, a new Tuareg leader, Iyad ag Ghali, led a short-lived insurgency. Ag Ghali belongs to the noble caste, but he was entering politics at a time when many traditional social hierarchies were being challenged. Not only in Tuareg society, where non-nobles were seeking more political power, but across Mali. The arrival of charities and Salafism from the greater Islamic world, for example, presented religious clerics a chance to upset the status quo of hereditary government offices. New alliances formed. The Algerian jihadist group, al-Qaeda in the Islamic Maghreb (AQIM), descended south into northern Mali, and their arrival was met with "strategic engagement" from local elites like ag Ghali, who could profit from a burgeoning kidnap economy. Meanwhile, herders, farmers, hunters, and fishermen competed for decreasing resources in Mali's center, already strained by climate change and a population boom.

In January 2012, a younger cohort of Tuareg, many from non-noble backgrounds, and older Tuareg fighters returning from Libya launched a rebellion. Iyad ag Ghali, unable to get a leadership role with this new National Movement for the Liberation of the Azawad (MNLA), leveraged his connections to AQIM to form an armed group with fellow nobles who feared the MNLA's popularity. The MNLA, together with ag Ghali and AQIM, pushed the Malian military out of the north. But the partnership was short-lived. Soon the jihadists ousted the secular separatists from major northern cities and moved toward the country's center.

In 2013, the French intervened. Operation Serval put the jihadists on the backfoot and precipitated a shift in northern alliances. The MNLA and "moderate" Tuareg nobles previously affiliated with Iyad ag Ghali formed a coalition of secular armed groups acceptable to the West. Ag Ghali stuck with the jihadists, perhaps, Thurston posits, because it was the only way he could stay politically relevant.

Meanwhile, Operation Serval; its successor, Operation Barkhane; a United Nations peacekeeping mission (MINUSMA); and an alliance of Sahelian states (G5 Sahel) all failed to stem growing violence in the center of the country. In 2015, Iyad ag Ghali teamed up with the Salafist cleric Amadou Kouffa, whose call to jihad attracted poorer Peul from the Mopti and Ségou regions. Together they formed Jama'at al-Nusrat al-Islam wal-Muslimin (JNIM).

Jihad masked what was fast becoming a complex ethnic and socioeconomic conflict. In response to JNIM's attacks, Dogon and Bambara hunting societies, known as *dozo*, formed self-defense groups. The Malian military provided sporadic support and encouragement. The Dogon and Bambara were largely farmers, hunters, and fishermen, which placed them in competition over resources with the (largely) pastoral Peul and their herds of cattle. The *dozo* enacted collective punishment. In one particularly brutal incident in 2019, "self-defense" forces killed at least 157 Peul villagers. These and other atrocities only pushed more Peul into the arms of the jihadists.

In 2020, the military ousted President Ibrahim Boubacar Keita in response to mass protests against corruption and insecurity. Generals promised a transition to civilian rule, which the French accepted, but nine months later, Colonel Assimi Goïta arrested the interim civilian leaders, in a "coup within a coup." Both MINUSMA and France condemned Goïta's actions, and a war of words ensued. Behind the scenes, Goïta wanted France to recognize his government. But in public, anti-French rhetoric helped build political legitimacy for his regime.

Anti-French sentiment was especially pronounced in the capital, Bamako. France's Operation Barkhane had failed in its mission to defeat jihadist groups. The Malian military (FAMa) was continuously reeling from attacks that left scores dead. EU missions to train FAMa often used wooden guns, humiliating given the crisis they faced. In September 2019, an attack on forces near the border with Burkina Faso killed perhaps eighty-five soldiers. A month later, the Islamic State of the Greater Sahara (ISIS-GS) killed fifty-four more near the border with Niger.

Worse however, from the perspective of the Malian military, was that France had quietly worked with Tuareg separatists (MNLA) to oust jihadists from northern Mali. Government leaders saw that cooperation as a violation of Mali's sovereignty and territorial integrity. Intervenors and those intervened upon could not agree on who the terrorists were.

Colonel Goïta's regime rode to power on a wave of anti-French sentiment that was surging through France's former colonies in Africa. Over the years, protestors in CAR, Chad, and across the Sahel started waving Russian flags and holding up signs with Putin's picture to protest France's military presence in their countries. In CAR, Prigozhin and his associates had stumbled upon a useful political talking point: French neocolonialism and the ineffectiveness of the UN peacekeeping missions. They funded protests against MINUSCA in Bangui and pushed out articles and posts on social media denigrating France. In 2021, they ramped up messaging on Mali. Wagner was not responsible for the rise of anti-French sentiment in the Sahel, but like the regime in Bamako, they worked hard to cultivate and exploit it to their own ends.

Anti-French sentiment presented both opportunities and obstacles. As relations with the French soured, Colonel Goïta and his entourage, despite their popularity in Bamako, faced a massive challenge. The Malian military could not fight JNIM and ISIS-GS—an offshoot of the Movement for Oneness and Jihad in West Africa, itself a 2011 offshoot of AQIM—on its own, even with JNIM and ISIS-GS fighting each other throughout 2020. A renegotiated partnership with France was off the table. Goïta, however, had a card up his sleeve.

In 2021, there were only two African countries where the Russian Ministry of Defense kept a small group of military advisors: Guinea and Mali. For at least twenty years, one military insider noted, both these countries were a halfway home to retirement: a destination for decorated dinosaurs. These officers, not subordinate to military attachés at the embassy, forged relations with the local officer corps. They also worked closely with the Russian state-owned arms manufacturing company, Rosoboronexport, which supplied Mali and Guinea's militaries with weapons. Malian and Guinean officers trained in Russia, and many spoke Russian, including Goïta's Minister of Defense Colonel Sadio Camara.

Potepkin claims that it was he who brought Mali to the Russians, just as he had Sudan and CAR. "Everything in Africa," he told me, "was our initiative." Members of the Russian MoD who were directly involved in the negotiations disagree. Long before Prigozhin's men began arriving in Mali, Russian military advisors were preparing a potential intervention.

In the eyes of the Russians, Western military-humanitarian initiatives, including Operation Barkhane, lacked specific goals. "Despite all the dependence on Western initiatives, there was no actual interaction between the Malian army and Western interventions," an insider said. "One could even notice a conflict of interest between the two." An overreliance on pro-government militias such as the *dozo* had also "led to a loss of state control in the provinces."

The situation in Bamako, according to the source, was reaching the point of no return. The military advisors decided conditions were ripe for a Russian intervention, though there was no consensus on what such an intervention would look like, even among the pro-Russian officers within FAMa. "It was decided," a person close to the negotiations told me, "that for the external audience, the intervention would be a private company initiative. For internal consumption, it would be a government initiative."

Once the terms were agreed with the MoD, the initiative was transferred to Prigozhin's structures "in such a way that the preliminary work remained unexplained." In other words, Prigozhin and his team were unaware of the initial work that went into facilitating their arrival. If such a statement is true, it helps explain why Potepkin's team believe they alone brought Wagner to Mali. But even the MoD source admits: "It is certainly possible that, without Prigozhin's influence in the Kremlin, the intervention in Mali could not have taken place." As always, Prigozhin's team and the MoD needed each other to succeed.

Potepkin, Alexander Ivanov (based in CAR), and Shugalei all traveled to Mali. In September 2021, rumor spread of an imminent deal. The MoD decided on a structure similar to the one that fought the CPC in CAR. (Malian military officers had been visiting CAR in secret to assess the structure.) The intervention would be built around instructors who could simultaneously take part in combat operations as commanders. Such instructors would be integrated within units of the national army, and these units would be the tip of the spear against "illegal armed formations." They were provided with heavy equipment and weapons, as well as communications and reconnaissance equipment. Unlike in CAR, however, the Russian military would have a more meaningful presence in Mali. The intervening force would utilize aviation, including Russian pilots and technical personnel, and employ military advisors for planning operations.

The Ministry of Defense would be responsible for ensuring the activities of forces on the ground. They handled analytical work, strategy, and coordination with the Malian military. Prigozhin and his well-seasoned network of Africa hands would be responsible for logistics: the replenishment of personnel and more quotidian problems like coordination with military police and FAMa.

In December, the U.S. government announced that Goïta's regime had reached an agreement with the Russian PMC worth $10 million per month. Sources close to the deal, however, are not sure of the financing structure. "There weren't exact figures. It was obvious that the Malian government was making some payments, including for the supplied weapons and equipment, but the volume and form of this material remuneration is unknown. It was understood, however, that Wagner did not receive money directly from the Malians; this money went to Russia's account." Equipment and weapons were shipped in from China and Turkey. The same Bayraktar drones that halted Wagner's advance in Tripoli would now aid them in the fight against JNIM and IS-GS in Mali.

As in CAR, geologists arrived, including Sergei Laktionov, who had worked for Prigozhin in Bangui. He quickly connected with a young executive who served as minister of mines and energy during Goïta's transition. The executive resigned after accusations that he used his office, and proximity to his brother-in-law, Defense Minister Camara, to collect rents. The resignation didn't stop him from working with Laktionov to renew a mining license that had been seized from a Canadian firm. Andrei Mandel, who worked with Potepkin under M-Invest in Sudan and CAR, structured the Malian mining portfolio.

Starting in December 2021, Wagner mercenaries touched down in Bamako and began building a base close to the international airport. Nazar was among them. He had just finished his contract in CAR and took a brief leave back home in Russia. Once in Mali, he and the other mercenaries stayed on the new base while more arrivals and equipment came. Then, they fanned out to central Mali, in the Mopti region, Ségou, and Timbuktu.

"For the most part, our enemies were al-Qaeda and ISIS," Nazar told me. "And it was interesting, because they were even fighting among each other, quite seriously." The enemy in Mali was very different from CAR. JNIM and ISIS-GS were more mobile, had better weapons, and knew how to mine roads effectively. In January 2022, Wagner suffered its first casualties following an IED explosion in the Mopti region. "They were mining roads whenever and however they could," Nazar remembered. He went flying one time when a mine exploded under his truck. It resulted only in a concussion.

Unlike in CAR, the Russians were always embedded within FAMa units. The mixed force was constantly on the move, chasing the jihadists and conducting mopping up operations. Their losses, says Nazar, were not too serious, but the battles were fierce. They were under constant threat of ambush. "It was their territory, not ours."

The jihadists, according to Nazar, had informants in every village, and they knew right away when a Wagner column left camp. They could organize quickly, and with their motorcycles, materialize out of nowhere.

By February 2022, the gig was up for the French, and the military began its long-threatened withdrawal. A month later, FAMa, backed by Wagner forces, launched an operation on Moura, a town in central Mali with a population of ten thousand. Moura had been partly under the control of JNIM. After entering the town, over the course of several days FAMa and Wagner forces executed men, predominantly Peul, in small groups. One trader who was in Moura at the time told Human Rights Watch: "A Malian soldier kept saying, 'You kill us at night, then by day pretend to be civilians.' Each night people were taken out and shot."

Another trader was sipping tea with his brothers when the helicopter's arrived. After lecturing the men on how all Peul were jihadis, the Russians began picking people out. "I thought they were going for interrogation," the trader continued. "They took them several meters away and executed them, point blank."

Roughly three hundred men were executed, the largest massacre in a war that saw civilians constantly caught in a spiraling cycle of violence between terrorists and a counterterrorism operation. There was no reprieve.

Despite applying shocking levels of violence, Prigozhin's network had trouble achieving their commercial goals in the country. Just one visit to Bamako reveals how much more development even Mali has experienced than the Central African Republic. The paved streets and, comparatively, tall buildings bely stronger institutions, even accounting for corruption. Of course, as in CAR, levels of development drop drastically once one travels outside the capital, but Mali had a history of democracy, a strong civil society, and developed industries that were difficult to muscle into.

Prigozhin's efforts to profit from Mali's natural resources bore little fruit. Many of the top mining assets in Mali were in the hands of foreign firms like the Canadian mining company Barrick Gold. Laktionov and Mandel, frustrated by legal obstacles in gaining control over concessions, at one point proposed nationalizing Mali's mining assets in a bid to oust foreign competitors. But Goïta's government showed little interest in scaring off international investors whose taxes provided a stable source of government revenue. For the time being, Prigozhin and Wagner had to settle for counterinsurgency in a geopolitical hot spot.

Malian perceptions of Wagner depended on one's socioeconomic status, ethnicity, and location. The northern regions of Gao and Ménaka were among the few in which the French Operation Barkhane had been successful. The terrorists were pushed outside of major cities, bringing a degree of safety and stability. Barkhane's withdrawal saw jihadists take outlying villages, prompting frustration with the new regime in Bamako and its Russian partners. The French departure also left an impact on the local economy. Foreign bases created demand for goods and services: food, translators, and much more. That was now gone.

For farmers in the center of the country, especially outside major towns like Ségou, the departure of the French made little difference. "It was bad before, and it's bad now," one resident told me when I visited in early 2023. For Peul and other pastoralists, Wagner's intervention was terrifying, news of Moura and other massacres spread like wildfire.

The drive between Bamako and Ségou is only 150 miles. On each side of Route nationale 6 is the Sahel, the semi-arid belt between the Sahara and the tropics that runs nearly across the continent. In the dry season, warm, glowing oranges give way to hot yellows at noon. Short, brackish acacia shrubs dot the sienna expanse, only mango trees offer small patches of shade.

Given the kidnap risk from JNIM, my friend Henri decided I best cover as much of my German Irish skin as possible. If the ransom didn't end me financially, the dermatologist's bill certainly would.

I received a loose, comfortable kaftan. A navy *tagelmust*, the traditional turban of the Tuareg, covered my head and face. Dark sunglasses filled in the remaining gaps. Once fitted, we set out at sunrise to meet local self-defense forces, or *dozo*, fighting JNIM just outside Ségou.

I sat down with one of the leaders, who wore a beige bucket hat and a brown, greasy leather kaftan. A mirror and leather pouches carrying amulets hung from his neck. "There are no longer any animals in the bush to hunt," he began. Then, the jihadists arrived. "We were there to protect the community. We were never paid."

The *dozo* initially fought the jihadists with homemade weapons. They had to sell their cattle to purchase better arms. Then they began to work with FAMa, but the relationship was unequal. "If things get too hot, the soldiers just disappear and leave us to fight," he complained. The arrival of the Russians saw continued collaboration, though not in a systematic way. "They will come to an area and partner with the *dozo* for a day or two then leave."

A mayor from a nearby village surrounded by JNIM complained, "The Peul can't come into the village, and the Bambara [farmers and hunters] can't leave." When war descended, people first thought the Peul wanted to make war, but they soon realized the Peul, too, wanted peace. "Yet the actions of some *dozo*," he said, calling back to the self-defense forces and their widespread atrocities, "forced the Peul to become jihadists. They joined JNIM after the *dozo* killed their parents and children."

"We never had security, under any regime: Barkhane, the first president, the second president, under the *dozo*," the mayor added. Nonetheless, the situation now was more dire than at any time before. The jihadists prevented villagers from going to their fields. They had no food, water, or medicine. And the government, as part of its pro-sovereignty movement, was kicking out the last NGOs that could provide it. The *dozo*'s protection costs money or goods in exchange. "We need the FAMa to come, to secure our fields."

While experiences of the war differed greatly in the north and center of the country, residents of both felt disconnected, both literally and figuratively, from Bamako. Speaking with government ministers and politicians, one had the sense that the fight against the jihadists had turned a corner; that Mali had shed its unequitable partnership with France for a truly independent future. Much of this rhetoric was thanks to the fact that

Bamako, like Bangui and other capitals around the world, is a bubble. But there were structural reasons as well. Views from Bamako dominated social media. Many Malians in the periphery, without consistent electricity and internet, struggled to counter dominant narratives.

Wagner's arrival in Mali further exacerbated the conflict's separate realities. Western analysts had difficulty understanding what attracted Malian officers to Wagner, because all media reporting from CAR had painted the Russian intervention there a failure. Metrics for judging success were very different. Outside analysts focused on the government's control of territory, while Goïta's circle was more concerned about retaking the north from Tuareg separatists and protecting the regime in Bamako from another coup.

The day after I met *dozo* leaders, I was waiting in the hotel lobby for Henri when a man in green camouflage and an olive balaclava approached. "I'm with the gendarmerie," he said flashing a badge. "Can I ask a few questions?" We stepped outside the hotel, where several other plainclothes officers closed in and pushed me into a Land Cruiser. Blindfolded, with a bundle of AK-47s stacked between my legs, I was whisked through Bamako at breakneck speed before turning into an interrogation facility.

I fumbled into a small room and was placed in a chair. Still blindfolded, I heard two men sit across from me. "*Qu'est-ce que vous savez de Moura?*" they asked. "What do you know about Moura?"

Over the next two days I was accused of being a spy, a journalist, or both at once. "You know, I'm also a writer," a beady-eyed intelligence officer informed me, when they finally allowed me to take off the blindfold. "I publish articles, and I work for intelligence. The difference between journalism and espionage is simply a matter of who you write for."

It was a difficult point to argue, and the prospect of two steady paychecks compared to the zero I enjoyed then was certainly enticing in theory. But the logic of an American spy risking jihadists and Russian mercenaries to visit Moura was beyond me. Investigations into the incident were reported and published—a few interviews would have hardly tipped the scales in favor of credibility. And yet, my interrogation, and the accusations that I intended to visit Moura, showed a lingering sensitivity around the incident. Despite the jingoistic rhetoric from the regime, the tough language on fighting a dirty war, there was a sense that what happened in Moura was wrong, an awareness that seeped through the rooms' cracks and endowed this downtown black site with a hollow vulnerability.

In between questioning, I peeked through a slit in the door and looked out into the courtyard. Periodically, an SUV would pull in and soldiers would spill out, a blindfolded man in tow. Another blindfolded man would be led into the vehicle before it sped off. There was no shortage of potential traitors to the regime, and slowly the questions directed at me shifted from what I was researching to what other Malians were saying in front of me.

The West, my interrogators believed, was hell-bent on discrediting Mali's sovereignty movement and Bamako's partners. Roughly a month after Moura, the French military claimed to have footage of Russian mercenaries digging a fake mass grave near a former French military base. If the claim is true, Wagner's logic would have been not to deny FAMa and Russian crimes, but show that everyone, including France, commits war crimes.

"We have information you were planning to make contact with Iyad ag Ghali," my interrogator then declared, referring to the jihadist leader of JNIM.

"No, I'd rather the jihadis not hold me hostage for five years."

"Hm," came the reply. Paranoia was rife.

After two days, I was blindfolded and bundled into another car. We rushed through the thick night. The driver stopped and started, pulled into back alleyways, and waited, for what I didn't know. It became clear only later they were engaged in evasive maneuvering.

After an hour, we stopped. I was pulled out and pushed into another vehicle, a slightly unnerving development. Then, after another hour, the blindfold was pulled off. I had been deposited, much to my surprise, back at my hotel.

I never got the sense that Prigozhin's men were behind my detainment. Vitaly made no clever allusion to it when I saw him again in Bangui; an opportunity I doubt he'd miss. The military junta was very much in charge, and the sensitivity around Moura was their own. Wagner was a tool—a particularly violent one—employed by the Malian regime to prosecute a dirty war as they felt needed to be done. It was their political legitimacy, not Wagner's, at stake. Neither Prigozhin nor anyone else needed worry much about coverage of Moura back in Russia.

To be fair, the Malian government likewise need not have shown so much concern. The world had little time for Africa now. All eyes were on Russia's full-scale invasion of Ukraine. It would be a war unlike any other, and one that would launch Prigozhin and his mercenaries to dizzying heights.

VI

Heroes

У штрафников один закон, один конец
Коли-руби фашистского бродягу!
И если не поймаешь в грудь свинец
Медаль на грудь поймаешь «За отвагу.»

—Владимир Высотский *«Штрафные батальоны»*

Penal soldiers have one law, one test:
Kill the fascist savage!
And if you don't catch lead in your breast,
They'll put a medal on it "for courage."

—VLADIMIR VYSOTSKY, *"PENAL BATTALIONS"*

On July 12, 2021, a little over one year into the COVID-19 pandemic, Vladimir Putin "penned" a verbose article, "On the Historical Unity of Russians and Ukrainians." Russians and Ukrainians are "one people," the president wrote. Together with Belarusians, they are the descendants of Ancient Rus and share the Orthodox faith. "Modern Ukraine was entirely the product of the Soviet era," part of an effort by the Bolsheviks to detach Russia from its historic territories. The government in Kyiv considered World War II Nazi collaborators national heroes: an insult, according to Putin, to the Ukrainians who served in the Red Army against Hitler's Germany.

In the seven years that followed the annexation of Crimea and the start of the war in Donbas, politics in the Kremlin took an increasingly illiberal turn. The nationalist narratives and methods of control unleashed on the periphery came back to the core, an imperial boomerang.

"Of course, Putin had to borrow phrases and slogans from the far-right," Vorobyev, founder of the Russian Imperial Movement (RIM) noted. "Putin has no principles and is only interested in money. Still, he must justify his rule to a domestic audience and refer to history to do so. But he knows if he declares Ukraine the illegitimate product of Soviet rule, then so too is the Russian Federation which he leads." It is unlikely that Putin, a man who has held an extraordinary amount of power for over two decades, is still capable of such introspection. His article on the history of Ukraine reflects both his own contradictory views and the broader mish-mash of historicized anecdotes Russian officials use to construct state identity. Mythmaking, of course, is hardly unique to Russia. "Forgetting," the nineteenth-century French orientalist Ernest Renan wrote, "is a crucial factor in the creation of a nation." Yet following the annexation of Crimea in 2014, the Kremlin began to treat historical memory as a security issue.

Under Vladimir Medinsky, the former minister of culture, the shared legacy of Soviet victory in World War II, or the Great Patriotic War, was further politicized. The West, in Medinsky's view, wanted to erase Russia's sacrifice in the struggle against fascism, and cast instead its liberation of Eastern Europe as an occupation. To defend against such slander, Medinsky and others worked tirelessly to drag the Great Patriotic War into the present, through documentaries on television, military camps for children, patriotic marches, and war reenactments. It was as if the Second World War never ended, the fight against Nazism was real, and it was happening today.

Then came COVID-19, and the famously germophobic Putin disappeared from public. The president and an old friend, the billionaire Yuri Kovalchuk, scurried away to Valdai palace, where they sipped wine and steeped themselves in Russian history. Putin stopped taking visitors and lost interest in the more mundane issues of running a country, like the economy. Instead, he dwelt on restoring Russia's glorious past. By then, according to Russian journalist Mikhail Zygar, plans for a full-scale invasion of Ukraine were already in place, though they were "known only to a very narrow circle."

Prigozhin was far from these mystical, late-night musings. His men were on the offensive against the CPC in CAR, an enemy who would be lucky to have a few 4x4 trucks. Of course, Prigozhin had logged several foreign-policy wins and was working hard with the Ministry of Defense to facilitate Russian intervention in the Sahel. But it's difficult to imagine a quarantining Putin and Kovalchuk sitting in a gaudy palace, poring over a map of Mali. It is unlikely, too, though not impossible, that Prigozhin was able to meet with Putin personally over the pandemic. One of the president's oldest friends, Igor Sechin, had to quarantine weeks each month for just a few meetings.

Putin had no cell phone, no email. Access to "the body," as Putin was nicknamed, was controlled by Sergei Kiriyenko, chief of staff of the Presidential Administration. That was bad news for Prigozhin. Putin's Chef had been butting heads with Kiryenko, Russian journalist Lilia Yapparova reported, following the latter's support for St. Petersburg governor Alexander Beglov. Beglov had recently passed over Prigozhin's companies for some choice government tenders.

Whether tensions lingered between Shoigu and Prigozhin after Khasham is debated, but a certain amount of running antagonism would be in keeping with Putin's style of rule. The pair kept each other in check. Shoigu wanted to keep preparation for an invasion of Ukraine by the book, within Putin's closest set of advisors.

In 2021, Russian military intelligence, or GRU, subordinate to the minister of defense, began creating new "PMCs," separate from Wagner

Group. Prigozhin had shown the utility of the PMC structure; now the MoD would copy the idea and avoid dealing with its pesky patron. The initiative was spearheaded, according to Russian outlet *The Insider*, by deputy head of the GRU General Vladimir Alekseyev. General Alekseyev had worked closely with Prigozhin in Donbas and in Syria. In the first half of 2021, Alekseyev tapped Wagner's former head of intelligence, Anatoli Karazii, reportedly his relative, to manage the recruitment drive.

Karazii was successful in recruiting many Wagner fighters over to his "PMC Redut," which made Prigozhin furious. One of those men was "Adam," who first joined Wagner from the military in 2017. Adam was deployed to Syria, where, luckily for him, he was only guarding Wagner's headquarters during the Battle of Khasham. In 2019 he had some issues with debt back in Russia, but his commander wouldn't let him take a leave of absence to address it. He quit the PMC and went home, where he became a security guard and construction worker. Then, in 2021, he heard from a few friends that another "PMC" was recruiting for a big operation, and he leaped at the chance.

Karazii also approached members of Gennady Timchenko's PMC of the same name. These included Marat Gabidullin, who had joined Timchenko's Redut after resigning from Wagner. He disagreed with the first war in Ukraine and refused to join the new Redut on principal. Other commanders working in Syria accepted the offer.

"Each Redut unit is like its own family," said one commander, in that they really function as groups of mutual connections. They carried names like the Hooligans, Axes, and Wolves. The Wolves—the unit Adam joined—were led by Marat and Branko's old nemesis from Luhansk, the Bosnian Serb Davor "Volk" Savičić.

Sensing something was amiss, Prigozhin visited the GRU's Moscow offices to complain. There he told General Alekseyev he would "finish off Karazii," but the general called his bluff and led him to another office, where Karazii was waiting. Alekseyev offered to work it out between the two men on the spot, and Prigozhin backtracked on his threats. A month later, Karazii had built out "Redut" to include thousands of mercenaries.

The mass of troops on Russia's border with Ukraine was clear for all to see, but only a few men within Putin's narrow circle knew whether the buildup was preparation for a real invasion or a bluff designed to extract concessions from Ukrainian President Volodymyr Zelenskyy. Russian diplomats making last-ditch attempts to negotiate with Kyiv, for example, seem to have been left in the dark. Western diplomats and intelligence officials were convinced, however, that Russia would invade. In early February, Putin told Chinese president Xi Jinping of his decision. Xi asked him to wait until the end of the Beijing Olympics.

We don't know when Prigozhin understood the invasion was real, but it seems clear that he knew where the winds were blowing at least a week or two before. His men, however, had yet to be tapped for the operation. On February 20, Prigozhin was desperate to get General Alekseyev on the phone. The general didn't pick up his calls.

Four days later, on February 24, 2022, Russian troops and Redut units crossed into Ukrainian territory. In the early morning of February 25, with Russians pressing toward Kyiv, President Zelenskyy posted a video to social media, declaring his determination to remain in the capital. "The president is here. We are all here. Our troops are here," he told Ukraine's citizens. Zelenskyy also said Moscow had plans to assassinate him. Amid the mayhem and rocket attacks, rumors swirled four hundred specially trained Wagner mercenaries were roaming the capital, looking for the president.

In hindsight, it's highly unlikely Wagner was given such a task, though the Ukrainian claims speak to the emotive powers the "Wagner" label carried. At the time, the GRU, and the Russian Ministry of Defense more generally, thought they didn't need Wagner in Ukraine. All the stories over the years of brotherly relations between Ukrainians and Russians pushed out by pro-government media affected the Kremlin's analysis.

In other words, the Kremlin consumed the same "disinformation" it produced. Putin and his circle believed the government in Kyiv would collapse in three days, and that Russian soldiers would be greeted with open arms.

In his speech to inaugurate the "Special Military Operation," known by its Russian acronym SVO, Putin addressed Ukrainian soldiers: "Your fathers, grandfathers and great-grandfathers did not fight the Nazi occupiers and did not defend our common Motherland to allow today's neo-Nazis to seize power in Ukraine [. . .] I urge you to immediately lay down arms and go home." To those outside enemies thinking of interfering in the SVO, "they must know that Russia will respond immediately, and the consequences will be such as you have never seen in your entire history."

For Vorobyev and his RIM, there was no question that they would join the SVO, even though the Kremlin had spent years prosecuting the anti-Putin far-right in the country. That prosecution came despite a 2020 U.S. State Department decision to designate Vorobyev and his men a terrorist organization, citing RIM's training of white supremacists and neo-Nazis in Europe, including two Swedes who bombed a refugee center. "Let's get something straight," Vorobyev told me. "We are using Putin; he's not using us. The most important thing is to reunite the Russian people and return Russia to its 1917 borders." RIM's militant wing prepared for the front. Arkady, who had spent the intervening years in Syria with Wagner, returned to his old unit.

If there was a well-thought-out plan to support Putin's braggadocio—most evidence suggests otherwise—it would fall apart with surprising speed. While the first advance saw Russian troops and Redut units reach the outskirts of Kyiv, unexpected Ukrainian resistance took its toll. The vast majority of Ukrainians were showing what they felt about "brotherly relations" with Russia. In the first weeks of the invasion, Redut suffered significant losses. "We were not prepared," Adam remembers. As a result of the disaster, General Alekseyev lost command and the

Redut project was taken over by deputy defense minister Yunus-bek Yevkurov.

Prigozhin's luck began to turn. This time, it was General Alekseyev who called him. On March 19, Wagner was in the fight.

Prigozhin knew he had to shine. He would show his boss why Wagner Group was better than all the Russian security services put together. And the rewards would be great. "He kept repeating to associates," one source notes, "that the future of Wagner is in Ukraine."

Once Prigozhin got the green light in March, he brought in some of his top commanders from Africa. For CAR, the timing was fortuitous. In early 2022, the northwest, southwest, and center of the country were experiencing a degree of security and calm. This allowed several experienced commanders like Boris Nizhevenok, "Zombie," and Nikolai Budko, "Bes," to head for the front in Ukraine, ceding more power to Vitaly Perfilev and Dmitry Syty. A few hundred fighters from the Fifth Assault Detachment in Libya were also transferred.

In Mali, however, Wagner was still engaged in a deadly conflict with JNIM and ISIS-GS. "The Ministry of Defense did not initially set plans to use Prigozhin in the Northern Military District," a source remembered. "But nonetheless, once Wagner's operation started, the most qualified, combat-ready and young employees of the PMC were sent to Ukraine, since this became a higher priority for Prigozhin." Nazar was in Mali when the war broke out. Several fighters in his unit opted in; many of the mercenaries were from Donbas themselves. Others simply believed in the cause. Nazar, however, decided to stay in Mali, and the commanders soon closed the door on further transfers to the Special Military Operation. Despite Ukraine's priority, "the question of stopping the operation in Africa was never raised."

In early April, Redut was told to retreat from Kyiv. The mission to seize the capital had failed and Russian generals refocused on controlling Donbas. Wagner first entered Mariupol, a city that became famous the world over as hell on earth. Viktoriya, a friend from Mariupol's small

Greek community, hid in a basement for forty-five days with no electricity and barely any food or water, under constant bombardment. On April 9, she escaped, but only through a humanitarian corridor to Russia. She and her family were forced to hide as "tourists." Many refugees, especially Ukrainian children, were receiving Russian documents against their will. Finally, they collected enough money for a flight to Greece, where they received asylum. Viktoriya was lucky—up to twenty-two thousand civilians were killed in Mariupol. Ukrainian forces, particularly those burrowed in the massive Azovstal steel plant, would hold out, surrounded and under siege, for a remarkable eighty days before surrendering. Wagner lost up to sixty men.

It took some time for Prigozhin to gather men from various parts of Africa, but these represented only a few hundred from each theater. Wagner had to open recruitment to former fighters and new volunteers. Boyar, who had fought in Mariupol with a local militia from 2014 to 2015, jumped at the chance. After the Minsk ceasefire in 2015, he joined the French Foreign Legion but was injured in training. "I decided to join the Wagner PMC because they had the best system for training fighters, logistics, and evacuation," he told me, from a hospital bed. "The glory of the company was, say, even higher than the French Legion with its 170-year history."

Once Prigozhin had gathered a critical mass, the MoD decided to concentrate his forces on Popasna, a key link between Russia's advance to the north and south. Wagner commanders would have significant freedom to command their men, but the Russian generals oversaw the invasion. In early April, parts of the Fifth Assault Detachment, and perhaps men with Wagner's Fourth Assault Detachment, were deployed toward Popasna. Ratibor and his First Assault Detachment were sent to the southern flank. In a video uploaded to social media, Ratibor, a man who, at the very least, flirted with fascist ideologies, claimed he and his fellow Wagnerites were worried for the safety of the people of Donbas, exposed as they were to the Nazi threat from Kyiv. They wanted to help, "and in one incredible moment, I received a call from our brigade commander [Utkin]. 'Well, Ratibor, are you ready to defend the motherland?' Of course, for us it was great news."

The fighting was vicious, and close. "It was in Popasna that I killed my first man from a distance of ten feet," said Boyar. "That was probably the most intense moment. I had never had to kill so close before." Groups were formed in fives and threes and were mobile. Boyar had support from anti-aircraft guns and artillery mortars. After mop-up operations, his unit moved in the direction of Klinovoe, southwest of Popasna. There, the fighting was even more difficult, moving through forests and fields. Boyar was wounded twice, the first, a light wound, the second, severe. After recovering, he took a contract to work directly for the MoD as an instructor.

In early May, Popasna was taken, but at great cost. Wagner had lost some of its most experienced and talented fighters. Still, it was a rare victory for Russia three months into the SVO. Wagner Group went public. Billboards sprung up all over Russia with catchy lines: "The 'W' Orchestra Awaits You," or, "PMC Wagner, Join the Team of Victors." Wagner's unofficial social media channels, tolerated, at the very least, by Prigozhin over the years, gained thousands of followers. The Ministry of Defense, low on manpower, had no choice but to lean on the Wagner "brand" for recruitment. Wagner was now cool among young nationalists at home. Prigozhin was awarded Russia's highest honor: "Hero of Russia."

Putin's Chef stepped out of the shadows. Almost immediately, he and Wagner Group were everywhere. State television pushed out glowing coverage of the Russian mercenaries on the front line, paying the ultimate sacrifice in the struggle against Nazism. Prigozhin's enemies could no longer keep him from "the body." Prigozhin loved the limelight. To stay there, he needed more victories. To deliver those victories, he needed more men.

★ ★ ★

Correctional Colony No. 6 in Samara Oblast is colored in mute pastels, a palette typical of Russia's regional offices. Off-white brick soaks up stains from the year's mud and snow. Smudged, robin's-egg walls bear rusting barbed wire.

Inside, a ruling criminal caste and the prison administration are locked in a perpetual struggle over the right to enforce order among prisoners. Prison is boredom punctuated by bouts of impulsiveness and intense violence, a culture built upon myths of the days when *vory v zakone*, or thieves in law, adhered to their own systems of governance.

On September 27, 2022, the cameras in prison colonies across the Samara region were switched off. Administrators called on a few prisoners and threatened "harsh" punishments if a single photo emerged of whatever was to come. Then, the prisoners, or *zeky*, of No. 6 were called into the yard. A helicopter landed.

A man walked into the colony, surrounded by armed security. The *zeky*, like a weather barometer attuned to the smallest shift in atmosphere, immediately picked up on prison officials' behavior. The guards were nervous, tense. This man must be a serious *uncle*. Even some of the more powerful *vory* were acting differently. Whoever the man was, he carried weight.

The man walked up to the assembled convicts. A baseball cap in hand. Then he began to shout, in a blunt style *zeky* know well. "I am a representative of a private military company," he yelled over the crowd. "You've probably heard of it . . . it's called PMC Wagner. And I have the permission from higher authorities for a prisoner-to-soldier program."

The war the man was recruiting for was harsh. The Chechen campaigns Russians were familiar with didn't come close. My losses, the man said, are two-and-a-half times greater than Stalingrad.

The rewards for those who survive would be profound. "I can take anyone out of this prison. And in exchange for six months of fighting, you get a clean record and pay up to 240,000 rubles [$2,700] per month.

Your children and family will be eligible for government benefits, and you'll have access to credit again."

He told the prisoners that the first group of convicts had fought on June 1. Forty men—repeat offenders from a maximum-security colony in St. Petersburg—participated in an assault on Vuhledar southwest of Donetsk. They jumped into Ukrainians' trenches and cut the enemy up with knives. Of the forty, three died, including a fifty-two-year-old serving a thirty-year sentence.

"He died a hero."

To date, there are no known official documents or decrees granting Prigozhin the right to recruit prisoners for the war. In fact, Prigozhin's actions were illegal at the time, which led many to believe he got a "secret decree" from the Russian president. At the very least, Russia's Ministry of Justice received a verbal communication from Putin, or someone representing Putin's office, not to prosecute Prigozhin for convict recruitment.

It is also unclear whose idea it was to ship *zeky* to the front. But in the history of Russia, the use of prisoners in war is nothing new. In September 1941, following Hitler's invasion, the Soviet High Command was looking for new recruits. The head military prosecutor office of the Red Army suggested convicts from the Gulag, Joseph Stalin's network of prison systems formed seven years earlier. Stalin issued Order No. 227 calling for the formation of penal battalions. The forces were sent to the most dangerous areas of the front, so the convicts could "atone for their crimes with their blood."

Punishments for penal soldiers tended to be harsher than for soldiers in regular units. "Any officer," researcher Alex Statiev wrote, "had the right to summarily execute any soldier." After the victory over Japan, penal units were disbanded, but they lived on in Soviet culture, immortalized by singer and poet Vladimir Vysotsky.

The Kremlin's years of effort to bring the Great Patriotic War into the present made the recruitment of convicts almost inevitable. The Special Military Operation was, in many respects, one giant World

War II reenactment, and everyone got to don a costume and play a character.

Life in Russian prisons is brutal. Most infrastructure dates to the 1970s or earlier. Overcrowding is widespread. The Federal Penitentiary Service's (FSIN) use of torture is systemic. Research by human rights advocate Marina Litvinovich indicates that prison officials take advantage of the *vory* code, which stipulates that a prisoner raped by another man automatically descends to the lowest caste: roosters. The rapes they allow, or perpetrate, are then recorded for blackmail.

"Prison makes you a worse person," a twenty-six-year-old named Vlad told me. He was serving three and a half years in Samara Maximum Security Penal Colony No. 6—for fighting with a man harassing his wife and her friend while they were out shopping—when Prigozhin arrived with a contract. He took a quick look and signed right away. To him, it was a chance "to atone for one's guilt before the motherland with blood." The language surrounding the convict recruit program had changed little eighty years later.

Prigozhin, or one of his representatives, visited every minimum- and maximum-security colony except for those in Chechnya and the far-eastern region of Kamchatka. At each, he outlined the rules behind the offer, or, as he sometimes put it, the three sins forbidden during six months' service. The first sin: never turn back. "Those who show up and claim they made a mistake will be considered deserters and shot." The second: no drugs or alcohol in a war zone. The third: no marauding, including sexual relations with local women, "flora, fauna, men, and whoever else."

Olga Romanova, head of Russia Behind Bars, estimates Wagner recruited forty-eight thousand to forty-nine thousand convicts to fight in Ukraine. By the time Wagner came to thirty-three-year-old Sergei's prison, they were arriving on the front en masse. Like Vlad, Sergei found joining Wagner to be an easy decision. "You're sitting in a penal colony, and some guy shows up, offering to free you for six months' work," he remembered. "You'll go home to your wife and kids, have your life back . . . Of course, you have to go."

Sergei was eighteen when he first served time for fighting at school. Once freed, he boxed, and "did the family and kids thing." Work was behind the counter at Sweet World, a chain of Russian candy stores. But sweets couldn't keep him out of prison.

"Twenty years for fighting?" I asked him when we met.

"Well, it was a murder too. They made a big deal about it, hiding the body and stuff."

"Oh."

Prisoners at Sergei's facility had to decide that day whether to put their name down. Some of the guards told them they were doing a great thing, going to war. Others advised against it. Most prisoners declined. For those who didn't, a week later it was time to go.

Vlad and Sergei were taken in buses to the local airports, then flown to Rostov-on-Don. They were given new clothes and brought into Ukraine for training. Recruits got five or ten minutes each day for breakfast, lunch, and dinner. There was little time for sleep. As convicts, however, they were used to a regimented schedule. They were first shown how to handle automatic rifles. After that came drills, which grew more and more complex each round. They were taught tactics for storming trenches, mining and demining, and how to move in groups of two or three through the woods. Instructors were either experienced Wagner commanders who had fought in Syria, Africa, and elsewhere, or former Russian special operatives.

Given Russia's mandatory service for men, most of the convicts had at least some familiarity with automatic rifles and tactics. Many had served longer stints in the army or fought in previous wars. "I loved it. I kept thinking what an idiot I was for ever leaving the military," one convict told Reuters.

Dmitry, who was convicted of kidnapping, had served with the border forces earlier in life. During training, the other convicts voted him commander. He worked to bring the rest of the men up to speed. "We had around fifty in our training unit," Dmitry said. "About twenty had served previously and knew everything already. There were others who had no idea what was going on, but many of them figured things out." There were still some, according to Dmitry, who you could tell right away were "200," meaning they weren't going to survive. "It was clear they came to the war thinking they could just wait out their six months in a trench."

Wagner's "code" was stressed again. No rape or abuses against civilians. No drugs or alcohol. No desertion.

After two weeks, it was straight to the front.

★ ★ ★

Following the battle for Popasna, Wagner joined other regular Russian units storming Lysychansk and Severodonetsk. The two towns—the last Ukrainian holdouts in the Luhansk—were taken two months later. And on July 3, Minister of Defense Shoigu informed Putin that Russia had captured the entirety of the Luhansk region.

Bakhmut, fifty-five kilometers southwest of Lysychansk by road, was next. It was Ukraine's only defensible position before Slovyansk and Kramatorsk, whose capture would give Moscow the whole of Donbas.

In speeches at the penal colonies, Prigozhin told convicts he only needed assault troops. "Sasha"—a volunteer who had worked in finance before quitting to join Wagner in Ukraine—noticed that all the convicts he met were part of the assault detachments. Prigozhin had also told prisoners they would be treated the same as all other fighters. Sasha remembers "comradely" relations. "For me personally," Sasha said, "I grew to have a good impression of the convicts; they were always there to help, and there weren't many cowards among them." Other Wagner fighters, however, told me a different story. Wagner "considered [the convicts] meat. They say *zeky* are trash and no one pities them, so they started throwing them into hell right away."

Tactics were designed to never give Ukrainian forces a break. First, Wagner units softened Ukrainian positions with artillery, often using drones to help target them. Then they sent small assault groups of convicts. Once the first group engaged the Ukrainians, another group would arrive.

When Vlad showed up in October, convicts were divided into groups of ten. He was first stationed along the Lysychansk line, likely to the west of town. (Those fighting outside of cities had difficulty differentiating one field from another.) Everyone in the group was "fresh" and inexperienced, other than the two-week training course. The order to attack came on the first day.

"In the beginning, it was terrifying. You start hearing explosions all around you, and you don't know which way to go. Then, you start to conquer your fear, and you realize that the more you run, the tougher you are to hit. You get used to it quick if you want to live."

When the shooting started during Sergei's first assault, he froze. "I couldn't budge," he said. Someone picked him up and shouted, "You can't just stand here, you gotta move!" It got better with each assault.

Losses depended on how difficult the Ukrainian position was to attack. Sometimes, a group had no losses. If the position was tough, on higher ground, there were many. There's no time to think about the fallen. "I didn't feel anything; you just keep trying to move forward. Sure, maybe there's a moment when a thought flies through your head. But then there's a drone, or a plane and it disappears."

Dmitry spent only four days on the front before he was seriously wounded. But those few days for the commander were absolute hell. Along the Bakhmut line, he saw green guys look at shredded corpses and break into tears. Others vomited or were too scared to climb out of the trench. Dmitry knew that if you want to survive, you spend most of your time lying flat, crawling from one position to the next. "The bullets fly by so fast; you don't have a chance to lift your head."

Dmitry and his group of eleven were tasked with taking a gas station located at an intersection outside Pokrovskoye, a village on the outskirts of Bakhmut. They took it, and he was soon reinforced with another twenty fighters. He sent his men to cover each side of the crossing, but they were under constant fire from Ukrainian tanks and mortars. Drones buzzed overhead. One of his men was hit, and Dmitry went out to pull him back. He was then hit himself and evacuated. He lost several fingers on his right hand and doctors had to "amputate his balls."

On the other side of the front line, in Kostiantynivka, a small city fifteen miles from the center of Bakhmut, I met Sam. Smoke rose from the rubble on the horizon and soldiers streamed out of the convenience store with stacked cases of Red Bull. Inside there are burgers. A few feet outside, a crater.

In early 2014, Sam retired from the Ukrainian military. That "dick Putin," however, had other plans, and a couple months later he was fighting in Donbas. He and his force retook Slovyansk from Igor Girkin, or "Strelkov," after four months. Like many career soldiers, Sam speaks to the uninitiated in a laconic, casual style. "*Nu, a scho ya mozhu skazat'*, what can I say, there was a mop up, *tut tut tuh*." Eventually, the front settled, and he was back in retirement. When the *polnomashtabka** broke out he volunteered again. His brigade had been relieved from Bakhmut three days prior to our meeting. Their losses were significant from artillery and drones.

"And Wagner never stops crawling out of the trenches."

Sam had never seen such an intensity of warfare: the scale of artillery, aircraft, the technology. The madness. The enemy, he told me, was motivated. "They climb out in waves. They know that a certain number

---

*   The colloquial term in Ukrainian is *povnomaschtabka*, like the Russian it is short for *povno-mashtabna viyna* (full-scale war). A clever shorthand for differentiating the covert war in Ukraine (2014–2022) from the overt invasion.

of them will live and go home free. They know that if they turn back, their own will shoot them."

We heard the rumble of a rocket. Sam didn't look up, instead he took a draw from his vape. "Ours," he whispered.

When he arrived from Soledar, the Ukrainians held 80 percent of Bakhmut. When we were speaking in April, that number had dwindled down to 10 percent.

"What is the plan, can you retreat and reposition?"

"There's no going back," Sam responded. "Home is only one hundred kilometers away."

His eyes were those of many soldiers on the front. Imminent tears that never arrive, tiny whirlpools that collapse into nothing. The trauma and PTSD hardening in real time.

We drove a short distance to meet Salam. Mud-stained camouflage hung loosely over his wiry frame. Dirt buried deep into nails curled over a yellow cigarette.

"Five days they stormed our positions. We'd shoot into the wave of meat, and *vsyo*, bodies lying there. Not a hand moving. Thirty minutes later, another wave." One *zek* they captured said he wasn't worried about the Ukrainians killing him in captivity, something he couldn't say for his side.

Salam's company was convinced all *zeky* were addicts, that Wagner was feeding them drugs to fight. "There's no quality, just quantity," he added. "They're meat for the meat-grinder."

His eyes flashed and his voice rose in an arc: "Fuuuck, there's nothing better at night than watching HIMARs land on the Russians. It's so beautiful, shiiit!" A minute later, the light was gone. "They made it into our trench; we didn't stand a chance. Lost seven."

The next day, I made my way to Druzhkivka to meet an Azov Battalion commander. To move through the checkpoints more quickly, we bought ten pizzas: a special delivery for the boys. Erik, in beige camouflage, hopped out of a pickup and quickly removed his *wolfsangel* patch. Tattoos climb up his neck—a skull licked by flames over his Adam's apple—and spill down his right hand.

Erik was born in Sevastopol, Crimea, and prior to the war worked as an electrician in the city's trolley depot. After the Russians seized the peninsula, he fled to the Ukrainian city of Mykolaiv.

In June 2014, Erik was in Mariupol when the then-nascent Azov Battalion, together with two National Guard companies and Ukrainian special forces, pushed around eighty pro-Russian militants out of the city. One of those men was Boyar. Seven years later, the two were facing off again in Bakhmut.

"The first assault, we call that meat." Erik said. "The first assault finds out our position, where we are. And it's just numbers. They climb out day and night."

"And what motivates them?"

"They kill them if they turn back."

Wagner's tactics, according to Erik, were simple in Bakhmut. Take four guys, tell them to run to a position. An explosion. After a few minutes, another group runs.

"So, is it effective?"

"Of course, it's effective," Erik replied. "As long as you don't care about your own men."

★ ★ ★

Yevgeny Nuzhin was born in Kazakhstan but moved to the Russian SSR in early childhood. After mandatory military service, he stayed in the army until 1995. In 1999, he found himself in a "kill or be killed" scenario. He murdered one man, wounded another, and was sentenced to twenty-four years. Following a failed escape, another four years was slapped onto his stint. Prigozhin visited his penal colony, the Federal Strict Regime Penal Colony No. 3 in Skopin, Ryazan region, in July 2022. A month later, Nuzhin joined the Seventh Assault Detachment, fighting alongside Sasha.

Nuzhin's relatives in Russia were confused at his decision to sign up with Wagner. His daughter-in-law asked the BBC, "A man sits 23 years in prison, and then he agrees to go do this? He only had four years left to serve, such a small amount of the time." His wife cried when she learned of his decision.

On September 4, Nuzhin was sent from his position to fetch corpses. Taking advantage of the chaos, he escaped and handed himself over to the Ukrainians. This, he claims, was his plan all along. "I decided," Nuzhin told Ukrainian journalist Yuri Butusov, "I'll surrender and try to make it to the Russian Legion." Nuzhin then concluded, "It wasn't Ukraine that attacked Russia. It was Putin who invaded Ukraine. I can't go to war against you—I have relatives here."

Little of Nuzhin's past reflected this attitude on the war in Ukraine. Online, Nuzhin often waxed nostalgic for life in the Soviet Union, he even posted photos of the Russian imperial flag. Looking back, there's a certain theatricality to Nuzhin's interview with Butusov. Long pauses and deep sighs, a tendency to speak in absolutes that would please a Ukrainian audience. "Here, on the front line, if you spill your soul, you'll be executed."

A few months later, the Wagner-affiliated Telegram channel Grey Zone posted a video of a pale Nuzhin positioned vertically, head taped to what looked like concrete. "I went to the front," he told the camera, "to switch to the Ukrainian side and fight against the Russians." He said he was walking the streets of Kyiv when he received a blow to the head. "I came to, here in this basement, where they informed me that I will be sentenced."

For a while, Wagner assault detachments contained more "regular," or professional, Wagner fighters than convict recruits. But as the war progressed, Sasha believes convicts became the majority. Boyar agreed, his detachment had become 80 percent "Project K," Wagner's codename for prison recruitment, while he was in the hospital. These convicts almost certainly brought the brutality of Russia's prison system to

Ukraine, and, in the case of Nuzhin, their own courts for meting out punishment.

When Nuzhin finished his words, a man in camouflage wound up, then slammed his head and neck with a sledgehammer. Nuzhin collapsed onto the floor. The executioner then lifted the sledgehammer one more time high above his shoulders before driving it into Nuzhin's skull.

If Nuzhin's execution was meant to dissuade Wagner fighters from switching sides, it failed to reach its audience. Wagner fighters located in the war zone weren't allowed cell phones. When Sasha and others returned and found out about the video, they didn't really care. "He's not the first, and he won't be the last," Sasha told me.

The video was more likely intended for an outside audience. Back home in Russia, Wagner's popularity was surging. Sites like Telegram and VKontakte—a Russian version of Facebook—were an important source of information on the war. Russian military generals didn't "get" social media. In contrast, Prigozhin and Wagner were in their element, entertaining audiences with patriotism, thrills, and gore.

That attracted attention from abroad, too. Telegram channels translated Western media reports into Russian, and Wagner personnel kept track of articles written about the organization.

For Western journalists, Wagner was an easy story. Prigozhin looked like an evil villain, and better yet, he was constantly on social media saying the quiet parts out loud. "Putin's Chef" could rest assured that Reuters, BBC, and every other major media outlet would reprint and relay his social media messages to a worldwide audience. The West's great boogeyman would stay relevant with Putin and the Kremlin.

Rather than prevaricate, therefore, Prigozhin embraced Nuzhin's gruesome demise. He even issued a statement on the day the execution aired: "A dog receives a dog's death." Nuzhin, according to Prigozhin, "betrayed his people, betrayed his comrades, betrayed consciously." He didn't stop there. Less than two weeks after the video, Prigozhin "sent" a bloody sledgehammer to the EU Parliament, a rebuttal of sorts to a debate on labeling Wagner a terrorist organization. A few months later, Sergei Mironov, leader of a political party close to the Kremlin, "A Just Russia," published a statement thanking Prigozhin for gifting a sledge-hammer. Etched into the metal was a pile of skulls. Mironov, a former paratrooper, proposed legalizing Wagner in Russia.

As he became the face of Russia's war at home and abroad, Prigozhin's arrogance grew. His rivals needed to check him. As early as September 2022, the Ministry of Defense began recruiting convicts on its own. They targeted special prison colonies that housed members of Russia's security forces and offered the same terms as Wagner, but with a kicker: "a higher chance of survival."

In April 2023, I was in Kyiv with my friend Marian—the activist who took part in the Maidan Revolution—and two Ukrainian officers working in intelligence. We jumped into a 4x4, drove across the Dnieper River, and parked behind a nondescript building. A woman came out, shook our hands, and led us into a basement. Around the corner, a man stood with a sub-machine gun pointed to the cement floor, his black balaclava in stark relief against whitewashed walls. Across the room, a faux-wood desk reflected bright LED lights, where two skinny guys in camo sipped coffee from thin paper cups. Once they saw us, they rushed to put on their masks. Just between a balaclava and collar I could make out the beginnings of a dark blue Swastika.

It was in that basement that I sat across from Sergei and Vlad, pris-oners, now, of war. Detained by the Ukrainian Ministry of Defense, they showed no regrets for having signed with Wagner. They found their two-week training "top-notch." Prigozhin, in their minds, had laid out all the dangers and chances of survival prior to the front. It was a fair exchange, and they continued to revere the man. When I asked whether *they* took advantage of Prigozhin, their eyes lit up: "Yes! Yes! We took advantage of him!"

Around this time, a video had emerged of decapitated Ukrainian soldiers around Bakhmut. The video was attributed to Wagner, though it could not be independently verified. Prigozhin denied the allegations.

Russian journalist Vladimir Osechkin also reported that a Wagner commander, possibly drunk, had admitted to murdering Ukrainian children on orders. He later recanted the testimony, but Ukrainian POWs, like Bogdan with his Wagner tattoo, have testified reliably to Wagner's use of torture.

Vlad and Sergei denied seeing any human rights abuses or war crimes. When presented with Osechkin's piece, they said it was impossible for the commander's confession to be valid. "If his testimony was true, he'd be dead," they agreed. "Both by Wagner's code and by criminal code."

Over the course of our interview, Sergei and Vlad frequently referred to, and clearly believed in, the "Wagner Code." Always carry out orders. No rape or abuses against civilians. No drugs or alcohol. No desertion. And yet, I sensed that if our roles were reversed, and I were their prisoner, they would not hesitate to execute me on order. The most important lesson in life, Sergei told me as we concluded our meeting, was to not be a coward.

Other convicts were luckier than Vlad and Sergei. They'd served their six months and were now returning home, where Russian citizens were growing anxious over their sudden freedom. In a particularly public incident, Ivan Rossomakhin, convicted of murder in 2020, came home from his service in March. He was seen shortly after carrying a pitchfork, axe, and knife around town. A few days later police arrested him, believing him the murderer of an eighty-five-year-old woman.

In another case, Giorgiy Siukaev returned to Tskhinval, a small city of roughly thirty thousand and capital of the de facto independent Republic of South Ossetia within the Republic of Georgia. In 2014, he had gone to the Donetsk People's Republic (DNR) to fight as a volunteer. That December, he was wanted for murdering his commander. In 2022, Wagner recruited him from prison. In April 2023, he was free again, until being named lead suspect two hours after the murder of a beloved local.

Wagner released its own investigation into the stabbing, finding Siukaev, unsurprisingly, not guilty. The man, Tsugri, according to

Wagner, was often drunk and "rude" to passersby. These conclusions, Ossetian journalist Alik Puhati noted for the *Guardian*, were absurd. Tsugri had a developmental disability. "He was loved by everyone in our tight community," Puhati wrote. "A welcomed guest at weddings and dinners, people really took care of and protected him." His death was devastating.

Fear spread while Prigozhin maintained that of the twenty-six thousand convicts released by Wagner, only fifty-four committed crimes (a number that included "stealing bicycles"). This recidivist rate, according to Prigozhin, was twenty to forty times less than the typical rate of repeat offenders prior to the military operation in Ukraine. It's a statistic that human rights activist Olga Romanova disputes: "Simply look at the murders that have taken place."

To many convicts, Prigozhin had given them a new lease on life. Zhenya, an inmate serving twenty-nine years for multiple counts of theft, was wounded and spent the rest of his six months in the hospital. In his mind, the decision to go to war paid back many times over. He told Reuters: "The last time I landed in prison, I thought: well, here I am again, and what next? One, two, three years I'll sit and what then? I get out of here, and who needs me? . . . And now I'm clean. I have a bit of money. I can think about the future, think about buying an apartment. Could I achieve this by myself before? Of course not, I got all this thanks to our esteemed Yevgeny Viktorovich. He delivered on all his promises."

Dmitry, who had spent those four days in hell capturing a gas station outside Bakhmut, also "turned a new leaf." While recovering, Dmitry told me he was focused on raising his two daughters and finding work. "I don't regret anything," he said. "I knew everything would work out for me."

Zhenya and Dmitry were lucky, of course. All told, Prigozhin sent twenty thousand men to their deaths in the Bakhmut meat grinder. And their bright futures came at the expense of Sam, Erik, and thousands more Ukrainians forced to defend and die for their homeland. Sam, when thinking about Zhenya's luck, was more cerebral than I expected: "Some philosopher said pity humiliates a person," he told me. "I feel sorry for them."

VII

Traitors

— Милостивый государь . . .—сказал Ковалев с чувством собственного достоинства,—я не знаю, как понимать слова ваши . . . Здесь все дело, кажется, совершенно очевидно . . . Или вы хотите . . . Ведь вы мой собственный нос!

Нос посмотрел на майора, и брови его несколько нахмурились.

—Вы ошибаетесь, милостивый государь. Я сам по себе.

"Dear sir . . . ," said Kovalyev, feeling self-confident. "I don't know how to understand what you're saying . . . The issue at hand, it seems, is entirely obvious . . . Or you want . . . I mean, after all, you are my own nose!"

The nose looked at the major, and slightly bent his brow.

"You are mistaken, dear sir. I'm on my own."

—Nikolay Gogol, "The Nose"

When Wagner recruited Pyotr from a maximum-security prison colony, he had already served eight years of a twelve-year stint for assault and robbery. Like the others, Pyotr received a few weeks' training before he was thrown into the *bakhmutskaya myasorubka*: the Bakhmut meat grinder. Prigozhin's commanders were sacrificing hundreds of men to move meters through the rubble. Kyiv had withdrawn its troops from Soledar, north of Bakhmut, in late January. But on February 3, Zelenskyy declared Ukraine would fight "as long as we can" for Bakhmut itself. There would be no easy victory.

That same month, Prigozhin announced he was halting the convict recruitment program, allegedly in response to a request from the Russian military to make his fighters sign contracts with the MoD. The MoD, however, was stepping up its own enlistment of prisoners. Prigozhin had no legal ground to enforce "Project K." The Ministry of Defense did. In March, Putin's party, United Russia, introduced legislation guaranteeing a clean record if a "volunteer from prison" fulfills his service in the special military operation. The law allowed the MoD to keep its hands clean, something Prigozhin lacked the influence to achieve. Minister of Defense Shoigu, it appeared, was starting to turn the screws.

Conditions for Wagner's operations in Bakhmut only deteriorated from there. Videos began appearing on social media in which masked mercenaries identifying as Wagner spoke to the camera about supplies. When journalists inevitably questioned Prigozhin's press office his response was measured. "Please note that these wonderful fighters are heroes who die for our Motherland, they did not call anyone indecent names, and in no way discredited the Ministry of Defense. They simply asked their colleagues for ammunition and gave a detailed list of what was needed," Prigozhin wrote to Live24, a media outlet.

Just beneath the surface, though, tensions were evident. President Putin had relieved General Sergei Surovikin—a man seen as particularly close to Wagner—of his command as head of the SVO. Surovikin, nicknamed "General Armageddon" after his brutal air campaigns in Syria, was one of the more competent officers within Russia's top brass. During his brief tenure he had made prudent, politically unpopular decisions, like withdrawing Russian forces from Ukraine's southern city of

Kherson. Surovikin's competency was a threat and he was relieved, perhaps in part, because "he was becoming very powerful and was likely bypassing Shoigu when talking to Putin."

Replacing Surovikin was an old Ministry of Defense stalwart, Chief of the General Staff Valery Gerasimov, the same Gerasimov who penned the article on the West's "hybrid warfare" tactics a decade before. And while General Gerasimov's reputation was that of a sharp military strategist back then, many within Russia's military circles felt he had lost his edge over the years. Certainly, his academic theories failed to predict the political and organizational risks of outsourcing military operations to private individuals like Prigozhin. That lack of vision and inability to turn think pieces into real world victories was secondary, however, to his loyalty to Shoigu.

Officially, the Ministry of Defense's decision to replace Surovikin was grounded in an effort to organize "closer contact between different branches of the armed forces and improv[e] the quality and effectiveness of the management of Russian forces." The statement suggested that some of the top brass had become uncomfortable with the personalities dominating the airwaves with regards to the Special Military Operation. Chechen strongman Ramzan Kadyrov, who contributed forces through "Akhmat Battalion," had also grown critical of backseat generals in Moscow. On the front itself, thousands of men had joined a host of "PMCs" or volunteer battalions that were first under the management of GRU deputy head General Vladimir Alekseyev, then Deputy Defense Minister Yunus-bek Yevkurov. Thousands more convicts flooded the front. Unified command and control were needed. Yet Prigozhin simply couldn't shut up and fall into line.

Bakhmut, the city on which Prigozhin was staking his reputation, was not itself strategically significant; there were other places along the front that were more important. But the world's eyes had turned to the once beautiful, small city that had become a twenty-first-century Stalingrad. Ukraine's leadership decided to defend Bakhmut, justifying the move as a worthwhile battle of attrition. Each day the bodies piled higher, Bakhmut acquired more weight. In Western media and the Russian blogosphere, Bakhmut began to embody the war itself, a story about a clash of wills between Prigozhin and Zelenskyy. But the battle over what Bakhmut meant was always somewhere in the ether: high above the smoke rising from its ruins. On the ground, there was no neat metaphor or allegory to capture the experience. "I just try not to remember it," Pyotr said.

Wagner continued its ruthless tactics: softening a Ukrainian position with artillery while storm troopers like Pyotr crawled close. Grenades were lobbed when Pyotr was within meters of the Ukrainians, then he and fellow convicts leaped into the trenches. Ukraine was losing some of its best and most talented soldiers in the struggle for Bakhmut. The Russian state, in the eyes of its generals and commanders, was losing some of its worst. For the convicts to get close enough to Ukrainian positions, lots of shells were needed. In March, Prigozhin started directly criticizing the MoD. "I am worried about ammunition and shell starvation not only for the Wagner PMC, but for all units of the Russian army. It's not just my guys who are dying, of course. My men demand ammunition and die more because they are the very tip of the spear biting into Ukrainian forces."

In interviews with fighters present in Ukraine, and with those who worked closely with Prigozhin and his associates, I've heard a wide range of accounts regarding the supply of ammunition and shells. Pyotr, who participated in the last months of the Bakhmut campaign, remembers artillery being a serious problem, but he, like most of Wagner mercenaries, even commanders, were not privy to conversations about supply and strategy. The nature of Wagner contracts meant few served over the entire course of the campaign. Those who did, commanders like Ratibor, are unlikely to comment. Sasha, the financier turned volunteer, did not remember equipment or shells being an issue, and he felt that the relationship between Wagner and the MoD was cooperative during his time on the front. But Sasha also finished his contract in early 2023, when the problem likely began.

"Shell hunger" was hotly debated in Russia, even within pro-war circles. Members of the "ultra-patriotic" community, like the commander of Vostok Battalion, Alexander Khodakovsky, believed Wagner only felt "shell hunger" because the PMC received more ammunition than any other unit in the previous months. Khodakovsky conceded that Prigozhin's men were playing an outsized role in Bakhmut, but "to be honest," the commander wrote, "we genuinely envied the Wagnerites when they had their own front-line aviation . . . when they were bringing in prisoners from across the country . . . We envied them but understood that not everyone given such support would produce the same results."

It is possible that Wagner was receiving the same allocation of shells as everyone else, but no other unit was taking on so great a task as Bakhmut, which made equality hardly "fair." But there are also some within Prigozhin's network who believe their boss was politicizing supply issues as leverage in his personal vendettas.

On March 20, Prigozhin wrote an open letter to Minister of Defense Shoigu. "Currently detachments of PMC Wagner control 70% of Bakhmut," the letter read. But Ukrainian forces, Prigozhin warned, were preparing a massive counterattack at the end of March or early April. "We ask you to take all necessary measures to prevent Wagner's cut-off from the main Russian forces, which would have negative consequences for the Special Military Operation."

The open letter was yet another shock to the Russian public and undermined the chain of command. Prigozhin was positioning the minister of defense at fault in case of Wagner defeat or failure. The likelihood of Wagner's being cut off in Bakhmut, too, was low; the Russian Air Force provided cover along its flanks to prevent any encirclement. Shoigu shot back, telling Russian media the production of supplies had increased several times over to fulfill Russia's needs. Prigozhin was incredulous: "Neither I nor the fighters of the Wagner PMC have ever doubted the amazing qualities of the Minister of Defense as an outstanding builder and production worker," he stated, alluding to Shoigu's civilian background. "It would be important for us to understand the future fate of this ammunition."

If the supply of men and munitions weren't enough, Prigozhin was feeling the heat from other "PMCs" that were popping up on the front. Redut, meant to take Wagner's place in the SVO, was no longer the only competition. Large state-owned companies and rich Russian businessmen began funding private military companies as well. Most of these "PMCs" were simply volunteer battalions, vehicles for unofficial mobilization of recruits to the front.

On April 21, Prigozhin, livid with the trend, published another dispatch. "The main problem that exists with PMCs [is the effort] to dilute PMC Wagner in some way, so that there isn't one large force capable of playing a role in domestic politics. [People are saying] there might be a struggle for power, and everyone needs a private army." For the first time, Prigozhin tacitly linked Wagner to domestic political power. He added, "The people who have money think that this is a cool topic now—to assemble PMCs. Therefore, they are starting to multiply. Gazprom PMC Potok, PMC Redut. They need to report to the Kremlin how fucking cool they are, that they created their own PMC. But there is no aviation, no artillery, no electronic warfare, no ammunition, there are no drones, [and] no doctors."

In a few lines, Prigozhin pithily described Putin's system of governance, in which Russian elite fund private, patriotic initiatives to maintain their stake in the state's largesse. Of course, the pot was calling the kettle black, and Prigozhin wasn't, or at least he shouldn't have been, complaining about the system that made him rich. He was mad that he now had competition. Luckily, he knew the best way to handle it: control the narrative. In the same dispatch, he visited an unnamed "PMC"—presumably one of his new competitors—next to Wagner on the front lines. There in a basement, he met exhausted mercenaries in dire need of artillery, medicine, air support, and other supplies. "These guys need to report back to the Kremlin," Prigozhin told the pathetic-looking men before him, "what a fucking amazing mess of a PMC they've created." The men nodded in agreement.

Two days later, masked men, claiming to be members of one of those competitors, made a video appeal directly to Putin. They said they were sent to Bakhmut to support Wagner's flanks. Due to the lack of supplies and the irresponsibility of their commanders, they had to withdraw from their positions. When Wagner found out about their decision to withdraw, they blocked their route and forced them to continue fighting. The empathy Prigozhin displayed earlier only extended so far.

The Ministry of Defense responded to Wagner's complaints with an inventory of the thousands of various munitions Prigozhin's men had received. Prigozhin disputed the letter's authenticity. Even if the list were authentic, he added, the numbers weren't large enough for the tasks PMC Wagner had been assigned. In each confrontation with the MoD, Prigozhin chose escalation and theatrics. Every day, clad in military fatigues, a flak jacket, and a helmet, he provided updates on territory taken in Bakhmut and the casualties Wagner had suffered.

Here, Prigozhin was in his element. His assessments of the war from close to the front line, certainly closer than Shoigu or Gerasimov dared go, were in stark contrast to the sanitized version of the Special Military Operation Russians watched on state television. Despite his reputation for lies and disinformation, it felt like Prigozhin was telling the truth about the war. Western media ate it up too and "Putin's Chef" made the front pages of newspapers the world over. Not a day went by that the *New York Times*, the *Wall Street Journal*, or CNN weren't sending Prigozhin's office requests for comment.

Ever since the first articles about "Putin's Chef" in St. Petersburg, Prigozhin avidly read what people wrote about him and his projects, including articles and reports from his employees. "You had to be ready to answer for every sentence," Shugalei remembered. Journalists working for Prigozhin's media outlets had a feeling they were writing for an audience of one.

Prigozhin, according to associates, rewarded employees who agreed with him and berated those who didn't. He was mercurial. The most successful in his orbit tended, over time, to be sycophants. He was a narcissist long before the full-scale invasion of Ukraine. But the international fame that accompanied Wagner's intervention whipped his ego into ever more dangerous proportions and he started losing his ability to calculate risk effectively. "His popularity," a former associate remembered, "was ultimately his downfall."

On May 4, in the middle of a pitch-black night somewhere around Bakhmut, Prigozhin glared into the camera. Its harsh light cast sharp shadows onto the contours of a face twisted in rage. "Shoigu! Gerasimov! Where is the fucking ammunition?" he roared. The camera panned to lines of fresh corpses lying on the grass. "They came here as volunteers and die for you to fatten yourselves in your mahogany offices." In a country where it would be unthinkable to publish true casualty figures, Prigozhin was filming the dead.

Casualties were growing in "geometrical progress" every day, Prigozhin told the camera. He also claimed tens of thousands of his men had been killed or wounded in Bakhmut. The U.S. government itself estimated ten thousand men had died fighting for Prigozhin in only four months. The expletive-filled transmission divided opinion within Wagner. "The majority of people clearly believed what he was saying," Sasha told me. "But for me and a few friends, we already suspected we had more supplies than other units. The MoD just reduced Wagner's allocation to what others were getting. We didn't approve of his reckless behavior."

The following day, standing before a group of masked Wagnerites, Prigozhin listed Wagner's victories in the Special Military Operation and declared his men were leaving Bakhmut on May 10. The date was symbolic, one day after Victory Day, which celebrates the Red Army's defeat of Nazi Germany. Taking his men out of the SVO was a serious decision; Prigozhin's political relevance at that point rested on his contribution to the war effort. Withdrawing his forces from the battle-field would leave him vulnerable to other oligarchs and securocrats who had invested in the war through their own PMCs and volunteer brigades. Even the anti–Putin Vorobyev conceded his need to keep at least a small force of Imperial Legion in the SVO; "you need to have your finger on the pulse, politically speaking."

If Prigozhin was simply manufacturing a crisis and politicizing the struggle over resources to undermine Shoigu and Gerasimov, then publicly removing his forces from the SVO defied logic. It would take a staggering amount of self-confidence to assume Putin and his inner circle would beg Wagner to reenter the war. We can't exclude, therefore, that a part of him cared, or believed he cared, about the corpses strewn before him. Prigozhin was convinced that he and his men were patriots, fighting not only Russia's enemies on the frontier, but Moscow's decadent elite as well.

That elite had shut Prigozhin out. Yet the public was hanging on his every word. It was only natural that he play the populist. Prigozhin had been hell-bent on joining the elite, now he was a man of the people, increasingly critical not just of Shoigu and Gerasimov, but the entire Russian system.

Less than twenty-four hours later, he issued another video. He claimed he had received a letter from the MoD, threatening to charge his men with treason if they left their posts. Russian army units had already fled their own posts thanks to the criminal and idiot decisions of their commanders, he raged. "Why can't the Russian government protect the country? We have a Ministry of Intrigue, not a Ministry of Defense." He also took a swipe at Putin himself. May 9 is the Victory Day of "our grandfathers," he said. There is another "happy grandfather" on whom the future of Russia depends, who "thinks that he is good" but may just be "a complete asshole." Russian media outlet *Meduza* noted to readers that "grandfather" or *ded*, was a well-known nickname for Putin.

Wagner failed to take Bakhmut by the tenth, and so the mercenaries kept pushing to seize the small sliver that remained. On May 21, Wagner's top commander, Ratibor, climbed to the top of a bombed-out building on the "last street in Bakhmut" and—Russian flag in one hand, Wagner flag in the other—roared into the necropolis below. Prigozhin announced a new departure date, May 25.

Pyotr and his comrades returned to their rear base in Luhansk, where they had initially undergone training. They hung out and waited for orders to go home. They didn't have their cell phones, of course, but Pyotr knew something was afoot between his boss and the MoD. What he didn't know was that Wagner claimed the MoD had mined its path back to the rear base. On June 4, Wagner mercenaries captured and beat up a Russian officer who they claimed attacked their forces.

Prigozhin was still playing hardball.

Wagner was out of the SVO. But Middle East and African operations were still at stake, and the MoD had plans for those, too. According to a source familiar with the matter, around the time of Wagner's departure from Bakhmut, the decision was made to turn it into an official MoD project.

Prigozhin wasn't going to let that happen without a fight. The public bashing of Shoigu continued, it was his attempt to convince the Kremlin and the Russian public that the defense minister couldn't be trusted. On June 12, Prigozhin published "his side" of what happened during the Battle of Khasham. Shoigu, according to Prigozhin, avoided telling Wagner the Americans had picked up on their advance on Conoco. Worse, the minister of defense did not pass along Americans warnings. Of course, Prigozhin failed to mention Wagner's cut of oil and gas revenues in the campaign against the Islamic State. Instead, Wagner's presence in Syria was an altruistic effort to return the country's riches to its people.

Africa was even more important. And now it was important to the MoD, too. Prigozhin had drawn the Russian state to the continent, and the state wanted to stay. Talks began on what structure operations in Africa would take. The Ministry of Defense decided to create an official entity, Africa Corps, which would subsume Wagner's operations on the continent. The question was chain of command. Prigozhin wanted Africa Corps to operate separately from Shoigu. Shoigu wanted Africa Corps under him. Finally, on June 11 a decision was announced. All PMCs and volunteer fighters would be required to sign a contract with the Ministry of Defense. The writing was on the wall. Africa Corps, Wagner, or any other entity Prigozhin could lead would answer to Shoigu.

"Prigozhin and Shoigu were not necessarily always enemies," a former associate noted. "But at some point, he decided he wanted to get out from under Shoigu's thumb." In other words, Prigozhin was done being an implementer. He wanted his own position within the government, with his own budget, and no more intermediaries between himself and Putin.

The official subordination of Wagner to the MoD was the last straw. Prigozhin's men were now Shoigu's. He had spent all this time talking about how a PMC gave him political power. Now he had no PMC and was destined for irrelevance— tantamount to death, or worse, poverty.

Within the week, unbeknownst to Pyotr sitting across the base in Luhansk, Wagner's Council of Commanders voted to take a stand. In the days that followed, Western intelligence watched and listened in disbelief as Wagner amassed ammunition, tanks, and armored vehicles. Prigozhin, Utkin, and the Council of Commanders initially planned to capture Defense Minister Shoigu and Chief of the General Staff Valery Gerasimov when they visited Russia's Southern Command in Rostov, just across the border of Luhansk. The plans, however, were leaked and, according to reporting from the *Wall Street Journal*, the FSB discovered the plot two days before it was to take place. The discovery forced Prigozhin to act more quickly than he and his fellow leaders anticipated or planned.

On June 23, Prigozhin's social media channel published another explosive interview in which Wagner's boss divulged to the Russian public the "truth" behind Russia's war in Ukraine. "There was nothing extraordinary happening on February 24," Prigozhin told Russians, referring to the date of the full-scale invasion. "The Ministry of Defense is trying to deceive the public and the president and spin the story that there were insane levels of aggression from the Ukrainian side and that they were going to attack us together with the whole NATO block," he added.

The Ukrainians, Prigozhin charged, were ready to negotiate before the war. "When Zelenskyy became president, he was ready for agreements. All that needed to be done was to get off Mount Olympus and negotiate with him," he said. The special operation, therefore, began for a very different reason: "The oligarchic clan that rules Russia needed the war." The war in Ukraine was an asset grab, designed to enrich and keep in power Putin's close inner circle. "The task was to divide material assets in Ukraine. There was widespread theft in the [industrial eastern Ukrainian territory of the] Donbas, but they wanted more."

Prigozhin left out only his own desire, at least until quite recently, to partake in the division of Ukraine's assets. He also neglected the role Putin's delusions of grandeur played in the full-scale invasion; the blame lay solely with the tsar's wicked advisors. But the rant was close to the truth, or certainly closer than Russians were used to. Prigozhin was exposing the inner workings of the Kremlin and was laying his cards on the table.

That same day, Pyotr and his fellow Wagnerites were given the order to board a plane. He thought he was going to another training base, perhaps the last stop before finally returning home. He would have no such luck.

While Pyotr was on the move, Prigozhin's Telegram channel published a video showing what appeared to be a rocket attack on Wagner's camps. Prigozhin said there were many losses, though the footage showed a blast not typical of such attacks. It was the justification Prigozhin needed, however. Around 9:00 p.m., he made an announcement:

The Council of Commanders has decided to put an end to the evil
carried out by the military leadership of this country [. . .] they have
forgotten the word justice, and therefore we will bring it back. All
those who destroyed our guys today [. . .] will be punished. I ask no
one to put up resistance. Anyone who tries to resist we will consider
a threat and eliminate immediately, including any barriers in our
path, any planes above our heads. I ask everyone to remain calm
[. . .] and stay in your homes. The government, the Ministry of
Interior, the National Guard, and other structures will continue to
work as usual. We will deal with those who destroy Russian soldiers,
then return to the front.

A slew of audio messages followed on Telegram as thousands of
Wagner fighters began to make their way across the border of Luhansk
and into Russia. First, Prigozhin claimed that Shoigu had fled Rostov
like a coward, and that Wagner's convoy, numbering twenty-five thousand men—surely an inflated number—had been attacked by helicopters
sent by the Ministry of Defense. He called for Russian soldiers who
agreed with him to join, something he desperately needed.

Prigozhin was walking a dangerous line: Was he leading a mutiny?
Or a military coup? He was adamant to deny the latter, broadcasting,
"This is a March for Justice." The Ministry of Defense, hardly comforted,
responded. General Surovikin, the man thought to be particularly close
to Wagner, issued a plea. "I urge you to stop. The enemy is just waiting
for our internal political situation to worsen. [. . .] Before it's too late,
you need to obey the will and order of the popularly elected President of
the Russian Federation. Stop the columns and return them to their
permanent deployment points." Next came General Alekseyev of the
GRU, one of the officers who helped mastermind the PMC program,
including Wagner's. Prigozhin's actions were a stab in the back, Alekseyev declared. "Only the president has the right to appoint the highest
leadership of the armed forces, and you are trying to encroach on his
power."

Prigozhin was undeterred. On Saturday morning at 1:00 a.m., President Putin was briefed that Prigozhin was in armed rebellion. Six hours later, in the early hours of June 24, Prigozhin announced that his men had arrived in Rostov and that the first MoD plane had been shot down. Befuddled mercenaries grabbed coffees or a pastry from the local café, waiting for orders.

When Pyotr arrived in Rostov, he got the impression that his boss was there to try and negotiate with the MoD and the Kremlin one last time. It soon became clear he wasn't going home anytime soon, though he could never have anticipated the events that day. "I knew Prigozhin was right," Pyotr told me. "We simply wanted to answer for all the 200s [KIAs] that day, to put them in the middle of the square. We simply couldn't believe that the Ministry of Defense, and the government, were willing to kill those defending the motherland." Pyotr steeled himself for whatever would come next. When he walked around Rostov, he found courage in the support locals showed Wagner. Despite Prigozhin's request for Russian citizens to stay at home, curiosity got the best of many residents who went out to take photos and selfies with the Wagnerites. Some thanked Pyotr, telling him and his comrades, "Good job boys," and cheered them on to Moscow.

A few hours later, Deputy Minister of Defense Yunus-bek Yevkurov and General Alekseyev met Prigozhin at the military headquarters in Rostov, which Wagner troops had surrounded then seized. Wagner tanks surrounded other government buildings in Rostov, while mercenaries ran patrol through the downtown. Wagner occupied the city.

Prigozhin sat down with the two generals on a bench in an inner courtyard and told the two officers his men already shot down helicopters. "Shot down?" Yevkurov asked, hands clenching the bench. "Three already," Prigozhin responded. Yevkurov let out a heavy sigh. Prigozhin reiterated that his men would not leave until they "get" Shoigu and Gerasimov.

The talks between the three went nowhere. At 9:30 a.m., the column of Wagner fighters departed for Voronezh, almost certainly with the ultimate destination of Moscow. With mercenaries sprinting up the M4 highway, the Russian government declared a counterterrorism operation for the regions in their path.

In the White House, President Biden and his aides watched in disbelief as footage from television, satellites, and intercepted images beamed in. "For a while we wondered whether Putin's shield of vulnerability had cracked," a national security aide told journalist David Sanger, author of *New Cold Wars*. A discussion broke out whether Putin or Prigozhin would be more brutal, or a bigger threat to the United States. "I'm not sure we had a clear view," another participant admitted to Sanger.

Around 10:00 a.m. on Saturday June 24, Wagner had seized all military sites in Voronezh, only five hundred kilometers from Moscow. Finally, an incensed President Putin delivered an address to the nation:

> We are fighting for the right to remain Russia, this battle requires the unity of all forces, when everything that divides us must be thrown aside. And therefore, actions that split our unity are, in essence, apostasy and a stab in the back of Russia and our people. This is exactly the blow that was dealt in 1917, when our country fought in the First World War, and victory was stolen from it.

Prigozhin was the greatest threat to Putin's twenty-year rule. "Those who organized the rebellion and raised weapons against their comrades," the Russian president added, "have committed a crime and will answer for it [. . .] that which has confronted us is treason." The elite in Moscow watched nervously, most preferring to stay quiet and on the sidelines.

The plan, once in Moscow, was fairly straightforward. According to Pyotr: "We had one task. It was to arrive in Moscow to take the Ministry of Defense from Shoigu. And during the assault on the ministry, we were supposed to eliminate [shoot] him. Prigozhin wanted to take his place."

Few, if any, outsiders knew the targets of this March for Justice, and many assumed that Prigozhin was seeking to overthrow Putin himself. It was imperative that Prigozhin clarify his intentions. In another audio message, he shot back at President Putin's allegations of treason. "The president was deeply mistaken. We are patriots of our Motherland, [. . .] we do not want the country to continue to live in corruption, deceit and bureaucracy. When we fought in Africa, they told us that we needed Africa—and after that they abandoned it because they stole all the money that was supposed to go to help. When they told us that we were at war with Ukraine, we went and fought. But it turned out that ammunition, weapons, all the money that was put toward them were also stolen." Prigozhin's appeals did little to ease Russians' minds and for several hours it appeared the country may descend into civil war.

The column raced on, each step closer to the center of power, the greater the certainty of serious bloodshed. Pyotr saw an aircraft, the fourth, shot down in flames. Prigozhin wasn't lying. "Well, it's come to this," he thought. "The point of no return."

At 4:00 p.m., the column was spotted near Lipetsk, only four hundred kilometers from Moscow. The government blocked Prigozhin's social media channels and media outlets. Officers raided Wagner's offices in St. Petersburg, and, eventually, Prigozhin's home. State media would report fantastical claims about what they had found, including a portrait of beheaded Africans, "a commemorative sledgehammer," hordes of cash, "an arsenal of automatic weapons, crates of gold bullion, a sheaf of false passports and, in one closet, shelf after shelf of unconvincing wigs."

At 8:00 p.m., Russian media announced a breakthrough.

The president of Belarus, Alexander Lukashenko, had been negotiating between Prigozhin and the Russian government throughout the day, and he finally convinced Prigozhin to end his March for Justice. Prigozhin confirmed an agreement had been reached, and he was turning the column around. "They wanted to disband PMC Wagner," he explained to Russia's citizens. "We went out on June 23 for a March for Justice. In one day, we went within 200 km of Moscow. During this time, we did not shed a single drop of our fighters' blood. Now the moment has come when blood could be shed. Therefore [. . .] we turn our columns around and go in the opposite direction to the field camps according to the plan." Unmentioned, of course, were the deaths of at least thirteen Russian servicemen. In the late evening of June 24, Prigozhin, who had remained at the Southern Military District's headquarters, hopped into a black vehicle. A crowd surrounded him as he left, cheering and taking photos with the man who boldly stood up to Moscow.

Pyotr and the other mutineers returned to their camps. They were then transferred to dingy hotels in the southern resort town of Anapa, where, not allowed to leave the premises, they smoked, drank, and mused about their fate. The majority of the mutineers were convict recruits. Whether their amnesty would be honored was an open question.

Within Wagner, the reactions to Prigozhin's March for Justice were mixed. First it was important that "Prigozhin did not organize this mutiny alone," according to Maksim Shugalei, the sociologist with Prigozhin's think tank. Top commanders, including Utkin himself, were almost certainly in the loop in planning the operation, though their locations during the mutiny are unknown. According to Pyotr, Ratibor led the convoy, suggesting the March for Justice was a product not just of Prigozhin's ego, but Wagner's. When the foot soldiers found out what was happening, some, like Pyotr, were eager to participate. Others were surely just following orders.

Many Wagner veterans were home when the mutiny started. Nazar watched the rebellion on TV from Siberia and couldn't believe his eyes. "The whole thing was bizarre," he told me. "It just didn't make sense that Wagner would turn on Moscow." Sasha, who had left Wagner in early February, was incensed. "At first, I didn't quite understand what was going on; there were thoughts that this was a possible maneuver to provoke the enemy, etc. Then, when it turned out that this was a rebellion and especially when our comrades from the Moscow Region began to die, I and some of my colleagues who had brains strongly condemned what was happening, it could be called treason." The ultraconservative and arch-Orthodox Arkady, who served with Wagner in Syria but returned to his Imperial Legion for the full-scale invasion of Ukraine, thought the March for Justice might finally establish "pro-Russian" policies in the Kremlin. "When the rebellion happened," he wrote me, "my first thought was: Finally, something is happening in our politics! The end of the story has not come!"

Others, especially those serving in Africa, were more careful to toe the line between Prigozhin and Putin. In Bangui, Vitaly chose his words with care and, as always, a dollop of sarcasm: "I'm not thinking about anything," he told me that day. "Today is Sunday, I'll drink vodka, play the harmonica, and sing the song 'Don't Be a Fool, America.' This song is by Lyube, Russian president V. V. Putin's favorite band."

When the March for Justice was finally called off, work began on defining just what it was. The Russian government needed to paint Prigozhin as an ungrateful beneficiary of the state's generosity. On June 27, President Putin for the first time acknowledged the Russian government's relationship with Wagner, claiming the PMC was fully funded by the Kremlin. The president further clarified that from May 2022 to May 2023, Wagner received nearly $1 billion from the government. He also said that Prigozhin earned around $900,000,000 supplying food to the military. While the figures could easily have been inflated, they proved that Prigozhin probably made more of his money from catering than he did from his PMC over the years. The dates listed for the figures, May 2022 to May 2023, also coincided with Wagner's intervention in Ukraine. The figures showed how lucrative the war in Ukraine was for security entrepreneurs like Prigozhin but offered little clarification on operations in places like Africa, where Kremlin subsidies were much more difficult to come by.

While the Kremlin's propaganda machine was busy denigrating Prigozhin and Wagner, Putin met his former "chef" and the top commanders. "Well, you finally got your meeting," the president reportedly sneered. While the exact details are unclear, there are reports that Putin suggested Wagner's managing director, Andrei "Sedoi" Troshev, take over leadership. Prigozhin balked at any changes at the top—if he wasn't going to be minister of defense, then at least he would retain his leadership over Wagner. Only Prigozhin thought he would get away with mutiny; many Russia analysts were surprised he got a meeting in the first place and interpreted it as a sign of regime weakness.

Those expecting swift retribution from Putin would be disappointed. In fact, it was Igor "Strelkov" Girkin, the man who started the war in Donbas, who was the first to suffer. Like Prigozhin, Strelkov had been highly critical of the Kremlin's handling of the war in Ukraine—he mostly claimed that the Russian government wasn't doing enough. Even though he had no role in the mutiny, and was in fact no friend of Prigozhin's, Strelkov was arrested and sentenced to four years in prison on charges of "extremism."

Prigozhin, however, was still a free man and his fellow mutineers were also unscathed. One top Wagner commander told Russian media his men were "simply on vacation," and work would start soon in Belarus. Indeed, as part of Prigozhin's agreement with Lukashenko and the Russian government, the Belarusian leader proposed Wagner relocate its headquarters to his country. The PMC's instructors and mercenaries would help train the Belarusian army and, presumably, provide security for Lukashenko. For decades, Lukashenko deftly walked a tightrope between independence and economic reliance on Russia. In hosting Wagner, the Belarusian leader found a rare chance to exert leverage on Russia's domestic affairs. On July 19, the flag in Wagner's old base in Molkino was lowered, and a new one was raised at what appeared to be Wagner's new camp in Tsel, a Belarusian village in the center of the country.

At dusk, amid the constant drone of insects in the cooling Belarusian countryside, Prigozhin stood in front of hundreds of fighters: "Welcome to Belarus!" he shouted. "Ura!" rumbled the chorus. "We fought honorably," he continued. "You have done much for Russia. Now what's occurring on the front is a disgrace, in which we need not participate [. . .] Therefore, the decision has been made that we will spend some time here in Belarus. In that time, I am sure, we will make the Belarusian army the second best in the world [. . .] we will also prepare for new phase in Africa." Prigozhin then turned it over to Utkin, "the commander who gave us the name Wagner."

"This is not the end," Utkin roared, "but only the beginning." And, switching into English, he shouted: "Welcome to Hell!"

★ ★ ★

Wagner's operations in Africa posed a serious problem for the Kremlin. Because the continent was not a major national security priority, Prigozhin enjoyed outsized freedom to pursue projects and operations as he saw fit, particularly in the Central African Republic. Wagner represented the majority of personnel in places like Libya, Sudan, CAR, and Mali. Prigozhin's success was always in part a function of the Russian government's lack of will and capacity to project formal force there.

Yet Prigozhin had helped develop a narrative around Russia as an anti-colonial leader, which became useful for the Kremlin's efforts to show Russians they weren't isolated after the full-scale invasion of Ukraine. Instead, countries like Mali and CAR were seeking Russian assistance in breaking the shackles of Western dominance, at least according to media.

Now, the government had to decide between cutting all investment and pulling Wagner out of Africa, leaving operations in Prigozhin's hands, or cutting Prigozhin out and investing more heavily. The Ministry of Foreign Affairs also had to calm Bamako, Bangui, and Benghazi, assuring leaders who had grown reliant on Wagner's security provision that operations would continue as usual. Prigozhin even made an appearance at the Russia-Africa summit in St. Petersburg, though he could only be photographed with lower-ranking African officials. CAR President Faustin-Archange Touadéra and others were careful not to display overt loyalty to Prigozhin and thus be seen as meddling in Russian domestic affairs.

The mutiny caught Touadéra, Goïta in Mali, and Haftar in Libya completely off guard. In Africa, Prigozhin and his team had used their ambiguous relationship with the Kremlin to their advantage. Wagner positioned itself to clients as a representative of the Russian state. For African governments, it was more prestigious to partner on security issues with a fellow nation-state than a private military company. These governments could tolerate the ambiguity of a state-backed PMC, as long as the sponsor state and the PMC weren't in open conflict. Touadéra, Goïta, and Haftar had little interest in choosing between Putin and Prigozhin.

But the conflicts themselves had not slowed. In Mali, the fight against JNIM and ISIS-GS was only ramping up, and, covertly, plans for the capture of Kidal from Tuareg separatists were underway. In CAR, President Touadéra needed Wagner's support for a July 30 referendum on the constitution that would allow him to run for a third term. That referendum, in fact, embodied the difficulties facing the MoD in subsuming Wagner's operations. As one Wagner source noted:

> The vast majority [of the MoD has] no information about the real structure of Wagner either in Syria or in Africa. The military part is just the tip of the iceberg . . . without economic, humanitarian, and intelligence programs everything will quickly begin to deteriorate . . . the referendum itself is an initiative of the local analytical center of Prigozhin. Who will take this over, the GRU?

Prigozhin understood the Kremlin's desire to project stability and normalcy, so day and night he battled to retain influence over operations. It was probably true that no one could do it better, but there was no lack of other Russian security entrepreneurs willing to fill the gap.

Russian PMCs, like Redut and PMC Convoy, for example, smelled blood in the water. Rumor spread that PMC Redut would take over for Wagner operations in Africa, even though Redut's own commanders were unfamiliar with any of the plans. PMC Convoy, whose head, Konstantin Pikalov, formerly worked for Wagner in Madagascar and CAR, said they might move in. "Nothing's happened yet," one of Convoy's founders told me. "But discussions are underway."

The constitutional referendum in CAR, for which Wagner provided security and logistics, went without a hitch. The political opposition was too weak to contest meaningfully, not for lack of trying from some members of the Constitutional Court. Armed groups were strapped for cash and no longer had support from traditional outside sponsors in Chad and Sudan. After the vote Prigozhin flew down for a visit, part of a whirlwind tour through Bangui, parts of the Central African countryside, and Mali. In the latter, Prigozhin posted his first video address since the rebellion. Just like in Bakhmut, he was in fatigues, bearing a rifle. "We're working," he told the camera. "The temperature is over fifty degrees. Everything as we love it [we are making] Russia even greater on all continents, and Africa [we're making] even more free [. . .] we're destroying ISIS and al-Qaeda." Prigozhin then informed the audience that Wagner was once again recruiting.

There are two theories why Prigozhin was in Africa in the second half of August. The first, posited by journalists, was that his trip was an attempt to woo African governments away from the Kremlin; in other words, to convince Touadéra and Goïta to support Wagner over any MoD replacement. That would have been a tough sell. The second opinion, posited by insiders, seems more likely. The decision to replace Wagner's operations in Africa had already been made in May, when Prigozhin was withdrawing his men from Bakhmut. "Prigozhin," one source posits, "knew that the government's takeover was inevitable. His last-ditch tour through Africa was an effort to convince Putin that he should be the man to run the new government program."

After the Africa tour, Prigozhin flew back to Russia on August 23. In what had become routine, he and Dmitry Utkin boarded his Embraer Legacy 600 jet in Moscow for a quick hop to St. Petersburg. Joining them were Valery Chekalov, a director in many of Prigozhin's companies and the technical owner of Evro-Polis; Yevgeny Makaryan, a former fighter injured in the Battle of Khasham; Sergei Propustin and Alexander Totmin, who had served in Africa; and Nikolai Matusevich, Prigozhin's personal bodyguard. Also on the flight were two pilots and a flight attendant, Kristina Raspopova. At 6:00 p.m., the jet took off from Moscow's Sheremetyevo Airport, bound for St. Petersburg.

Soon after 6:00 p.m., the Embraer jet had reached an altitude of twenty-eight thousand feet over the Tver region northwest of Moscow. Then data transmission stopped. An explosion ripped through the plane. Residents of the small town of Kuzhenkino paused and pointed to a small object tumbling toward the earth, a trail of gray smoke inscribing its terrifying trajectory against a bright blue sky. The jet crashed in a country field. Though it was soon announced that the flight manifest named a one Yevgeny Prigozhin, the heat of the fire made it impossible to recognize victims. DNA evidence was collected from the bodies, though there was little doubt who died.

The next day, Putin offered his condolences. "It's always a tragedy," Russia's leader stated. "And they say that there were also employees of Wagner [on board]. I want to note that these are men who made a serious contribution to our shared struggle against the neo-Nazi regime in Ukraine."

"I've known Prigozhin a long time," the president continued, "since the early 1990s. He was a man with a complicated fate, he made many serious mistakes in life, but he also achieved the results he needed and, when I asked him for it, for the common cause as well."

Whether the Russian government was behind the plane crash or not was immaterial. Every member of Wagner, every Russian citizen, and the rest of the world were convinced the Russian state had assassinated Prigozhin. Putin made little effort to disabuse Russian society that his government was behind the crash. A few weeks later, the president claimed the cause of the explosion was likely a grenade that had exploded in the hands of a drunk passenger.

In Prigozhin's twenty-year career as a government contractor and security entrepreneur, there was a wealth of experience he could have drawn on to better navigate tension with the MoD. From the early years of the war in Donbas, he should have recalled that the Kremlin's tolerance for wayward, ultranationalists went only so far. It was Utkin's men, after all, who were responsible for assassinating at least one of the pro-Russian militia leaders in Donbas, and for reeling in unruly Cossacks militias as well.

In his April 21 message, Prigozhin himself admitted his force could be a threat in Russian domestic politics. If Prigozhin was still unsure of the fate that awaited him, he could have looked to Syria, where the Syrian PMC his men initially partnered with, the Desert Hawks of the Jaber brothers, had also grown too powerful. Not soon after egotistical ravings about controlling Latakia province, Jaber was forced to flee Syria, his private force was disbanded.

As one of the most successful implementers within Putin's system, Prigozhin should have known the deal. His success in Africa would result in a takeover. Such an arrangement could have easily resulted in a large payout, and even a formal position in the government. As one person familiar with the matter noted, "If he didn't pull that mutiny, he could've lived out several decades as the Kremlin's guy in Africa."

Instead, on August 29, Wagner's boss was buried in his hometown of St. Petersburg. The Kremlin worked hard to downsize in death a man who had been larger-than-life, though they couldn't prevent small vigils taking place across the country. The funeral itself was a closed, quiet affair. Details on the event had been kept deliberately vague to prevent a public outpouring. In the end, only twenty or thirty relatives and friends were allowed to attend, while the police and national guard stood outside. The funeral for the world's most infamous warlord, a private individual who took on a global superpower, a NATO-backed military, and finally, his own government, lasted just forty minutes. The small group of family and friends said their goodbyes and laid red flowers on the fresh grave. After that, they left.

Conclusion

"We tell ourselves stories in order to live."

—Joan Didion, *The White Album*

"But the claim that story brings you to world dominance seems by now so banal that it's common wisdom."

—Peter Brooks, *Seduced by Story: The Use and Abuse of Narrative*

In February 2023, I was in Bria, a diamond-trading town in the Central African Republic's northeast. Given the many occupations Bria had experienced, the town was relatively calm. In June 2021, after François Bozizé's CPC alliance tried to take Bangui, Wagner's counteroffensive rolled in. The following months were tense: random ID checks among a population that rarely had IDs and night raids against suspected armed group members.

I had always wanted to visit Bria, the most important town in a region many Central Africans associate with violence and rebellion. And like other journeys to destinations long imagined, my arrival was imbued with a certain irreality, an overexposed quality to the light that rendered surroundings artificial. Just outside the bustling market, a pickup truck parked beside me, a large red skull painted over green camouflage. Men hopped out in balaclavas and dark sunglasses—the entire scene felt ripped out of some comic book: bad guys of unexplained origin operating in a generic poor country at war.

The scene was very real, however. The next day, Sudanese Arab mercenaries hired by Noureddine Adam, the FPRC leader, attacked a CAR army outpost a hundred kilometers away. Wagner helicopters flew low into Bria, buzzing the town as a show of force. One helicopter made a steep vertical climb, stalled at the apex, and went into free fall. At the last second, the pilot righted the chopper and whizzed over our heads. My Central African friends held their hands above their eyes to shield the morning sun's intense glare. They smiled and laughed as the pilot traced figure eights. We were being treated to an entertaining, albeit slightly intimidating, airshow.

"I think they've done a good job," said my friend next to me. His only criticism was Wagner's recruitment of ex-combatants into their ranks. Meanwhile, Peul in Bria, who suffered from locals' belief that they supported armed groups, were asking Russian mercenaries to stop Central African soldiers from stealing their cattle.

From Bria I flew to Birao, the capital of CAR's most northeast province of Vakaga, on the border with Sudan's Darfur. Two months earlier, there had been a significant armed group mobilization, which included men in the CPC, Sudanese militias, Chadian rebel groups, independent mercenaries, and a new CAR armed group, Coalition Siriri (which means "peace" in Sango).

Uninterested in fighting a rebel offensive on the border alone, the CAR government gathered a delegation that included Hassan Bouba and Wagner advisors. They met with representatives of Sudan's Hemedti and his Rapid Support Forces in Birao. Despite official statements surrounding the meeting, the primary goal was to dismantle armed group training camps. Three days later, Hemedti announced the "closure" of Sudan's border with CAR. The RSF moved more troops to the Sudanese side of the border town to block the rebel offensive.

Coalition Siriri's leader confirmed to me on the phone that he had been caught up in a "geopolitical game" in Sudan. His faction of the rebel offensive was indirectly backed by Sudan's Armed Forces (SAF), led by Abdel Fattah al-Burhan, while Hemedti's Rapid Support Forces backed the CAR government. When Hemedti accused SAF of sponsoring rebellion in CAR, it became clear the RSF and SAF themselves were heading for war. On April 15, the RSF and SAF clashed at bases across the country, including Khartoum. Once more, a militia sought to overthrow the state that created it. And like Haftar in his assault on Tripoli, Hemedti had convinced the UAE that he could take Khartoum with ease. When it proved difficult, the UAE doubled down.

Though Coalition Siriri disbanded, the outbreak of violence between the RSF and SAF in Khartoum inevitably ricocheted back to the CAR border. In Am Dafok, Djazouli Ahmet, the local RSF commander and arms smuggler, received permission from his father-in-law, the sultan of Birao, to move his men into CAR territory. Wagner contractors who, like the Sultan, had long-standing relations with both the RSF and Bangui, then escorted Djazouli to Birao. After a meeting, the RSF commander started receiving ammunition and provisions at his camp in CAR—transported by Wagner but probably financed by the UAE—before eventually joining the fight in Darfur.

It was clear, however, that there was no infrastructure in northeast CAR to support serious supply lines to Darfur, especially in the rainy season. So the UAE helped Hemedti secure a critical supply route to the north, in Chad. No rebel groups in southern Libya or Darfur would attack Chad, the Emiratis promised leadership in N'Djamena, if they could build an airstrip in the country to supply RSF trucks across the border. Emirati officials paid the rebel group FACT to stay put, using Haftar's 128 Brigade as an intermediary. An airport was built to deliver "humanitarian supplies" to Darfur. Heavy weapons flowed through Chad, while ammunition and men descended south from Haftar-controlled Libya.

Wagner's role in the Sudanese civil war was relatively minimal compared to these other actors. Supply lines through Birao were ad hoc, grafted onto long-standing smuggling routes and reliant on established local arms dealers like Djazouli. International media, however, was laser-focused on covering Wagner's relatively small support to the RSF, in part because Wagner's name was already so well known. This was certainly convenient to Abu Dhabi, but also the U.S., which needed the UAE to maintain relations with Israel, especially after the October 7, 2023, Hamas attack.

Soon, Western outlets published claims that Wagner had made $2.5 billion smuggling gold from Sudan, which financed Russia's war in Ukraine. Few analysts seemed willing to check the math, since those estimates would have made Prigozhin's network one of the largest gold mining companies in the world. Indeed, with the exception of Ndassima in CAR, Prigozhin's men made relatively little effort to industrialize their assets. Even if they had, the sum would have paled in comparison to the $1 billion the EU paid Russia each month for oil and gas. The EU funding Russia's war in Ukraine, though, was far less interesting.

The profit Prigozhin's men did turn from their various ventures in CAR and Sudan probably took several years to do so. Graft existed at all levels of the system. Employees stole from Prigozhin and Prigozhin stole from the Russian government. So much of Wagner's business activity existed in the informal sector, and Prigozhin's men preferred to extract rents or flip the concessions governments leased them. On the ground, Wagner mercenaries taxed artisanal miners who worked the pits each day, or periodically raided them for whatever was at hand. Their behavior mirrored the armed groups they ousted, local officials armed groups ousted before them, and the colonial officers those local officials had replaced.

Foreign intervenors often think of themselves as separate from the local conflict. But once an outside force intervenes, they become a local actor. This is true for U.S. forces in Afghanistan, aid workers in the Democratic Republic of Congo, and Wagner throughout Africa.

Intervenors are constrained by the cultures, terrain, and political environments in which they operate. Nowhere is this more evident than in human rights abuses. Russian mercenaries committed abuses in every theater, but the scale, scope, and type of abuse varied by country. The massacre in Mali's Moura, for example, would have been impossible in Libya. Over time, Wagner's employment of violence tended to reflect patterns that preexisted their arrival. This is not to absolve Wagner of guilt. Patterns may have stayed the same, but Prigozhin's men were often force multipliers; they increased the capacity of governments to commit abuses against their citizens. The rise of Hemedti's RSF in Sudan, accused of ethnic cleansing in Darfur, could not have occurred without the support of networks like Prigozhin's. We shouldn't, however, let the EU, which funded the RSF to stop migration to Europe, or the international community, which legitimized Hemedti in peace negotiations, off the hook.

The alliances at work in Sudan's civil war offer a glimpse into the next decades of conflict. Militia, corporations that act like states, and states that act like corporations (the UAE and Rwanda, for example) work together in ways unimaginable a few decades ago. In Libya militias are the state, whether it's an uneasy alliance of armed groups controlling Tripoli, or a more centralized coalition of armed forces in Benghazi. Both sides and their foreign backers hire mercenaries: from Russia, America, Chad, Sudan, Syria, and elsewhere.

For now, these powerful actors aspire to seize the reins of the state, or a greater role within it. Even in countries where the state has long been absent, or arguably never existed, most security entrepreneurs still believe in its values: that a central government *should* hold a monopoly over the legitimate use of force within a defined territory. Few see militia-rule as preferable to state-rule and states still prefer to deal with states. Even while Wagner provided support to the RSF, the Russian government called for an end to hostilities and hosted SAF representatives.

The norms of the nation-state are deeply entrenched, and states are fighting back against their nonstate rivals. SAF has nearly pushed the

RSF out of Khartoum, sparking new negotiations with Moscow on a naval port. Sudan's territorial integrity is still at stake, however, as the RSF effectively controls Darfur and could threaten secession. The most vivid example of state revenge, of course, came out of burning wreckage on a small field outside Kuzhenkino.

Yet Prigozhin's legacy survives the flames. The tactics employed by Wagner on the front in Ukraine—small, nimble squadrons, the use of prisoners, the execution of deserters—have been adopted by the MoD, a phenomenon military expert Michael Kofman calls the "Wagnerization of the Russian army." Much to Prigozhin's chagrin, the quasi-PMC model, volunteer battalions often funded by private businessmen, was in place when he was alive. Some would even argue, a year later, that Prigozhin got the last laugh, as Putin fired Shoigu and other MoD insiders he had disparaged. The greatest testament to Wagner's success, though, is that the Russian state kept its operations around the globe, albeit in new forms.

In Libya, Wagner underwent a rebranding and its mercenaries signed a new contract with Africa Corps, under the command of the deputy defense minister, Colonel General Yunus-bek Yevkurov. In Mali, despite the critical role the MoD played while Prigozhin was alive, a rebranding to Africa Corps has yet to take place. Formally and confusingly, Lotus, who took part in the counteroffensive in CAR, is, as of this writing, considered the head of Wagner in Mali. In November 2023, the Malian army, backed by Wagner, took the strategically important town of Kidal from Tuareg separatists. Nonetheless, Russian military planners are taking a page out of Prigozhin's book and staying flexible. It is unclear if their intervention against jihadist armed groups will prove a success.

Wagner was kept in CAR too, but for different reasons. While the country was a serious project for Prigozhin at an individual and organizational level, it was never important to the Russian government. The MoD wanted to focus on far more prestigious projects in the Sahel instead. Of course, some leadership changes had to be made. Vitaly Perfilev, the man I often met at the Ledger, disappeared. Some say he was killed, but a return to Russia seems more likely. His partner Dmitry Syty stayed on to manage CAR's business interests, which the MoD had little interest in taking over. Sensing Russian retreat, Touadéra's government hosted representatives from Bancroft Global Development, an American PMC with a presence in Libya, Somalia, and the UAE. Wagner was furious and several Western journalists and humanitarians were detained as a result.

Back in the Sahel, victory in Kidal led to Africa Corps' further expansion. Before his death, Prigozhin had set his sights on Burkina Faso. Captain Ibrahim Traoré, wary of Russians' penetration of CAR's economy, eschewed Wagner's services and shored up his forces through militia recruitment. Africa Corps, however, was an official MoD entity that implied a state-to-state partnership. The new structure paved the way for Russian instructors.

The law of large numbers, of course, hides some of the more interesting individual trajectories. Some Wagner mercenaries have experienced picaresque adventures that would make any fascist jealous. Vlad, the Russian convict with a swastika tattoo I interviewed in Ukrainian detention, is now fighting with a Russian neo-Nazi battalion—on behalf of Kyiv. Igor Mangushev, who worked on Radio Lengo Songo, never lived to see the rebellion. He had returned to Ukraine for the full-scale invasion and filmed himself holding what he claimed to be the skull of an Azovstal defender. Mangushev, a friend of his told me, had contacted Prigozhin to gauge interest in working together yet again, this time fielding a drone unit under the Wagner banner. A few months later, he was shot in the head at a Russian checkpoint far from the front lines. He was driving, his friend said, to a karaoke bar—Mangushev was a big karaoke fan—when he was stopped by a Russian unit. An argument ensued and Mangushev was beaten up. When the Russian soldiers discovered who he was, they killed him to avoid punishment from Magushev's friends in high places. Despite their on-again-off-again relationship, Prigozhin launched an investigation. One man was found and Wagner "solved the issue."

In general, however, those mercenaries who wanted to keep fighting in Ukraine signed up with Lotus, under the Russian National Guard, or Ratibor, who curiously joined Chechen strongman Ramzan Kadyrov's Akhmat Battalion. Those who wanted nothing to do with the Russian government after the mutiny and Prigozhin's death could "fuck off to Belarus," as one source put it succinctly. There they would form a small Belarusian PMC to train Minsk's army. Those who preferred the relative safety, compared to Ukraine, abroad could sign up for Africa Corps.

The thousands of men who passed through Wagner or other Russian PMCs join the thousands more Serbians, Syrians, Central Africans, Sudanese, and others willing to go to war for a paycheck. Not just Russia is taking advantage. Turkey's SADAT is already in the business of shipping Syrians to various conflicts, while the UAE is mulling its own foreign legion. Western PMCs like Bancroft aren't far behind. The West was happy to leverage Wagner as shorthand for all the evils of a war economy. But the reality is that the world is filled with Prigozhins, from nation-states selling weapons systems all the way down to the humbler arms smugglers like Djazouli, who took advantage of his connections and civil war in Darfur to raise his status within the community.

On March 17, 2024, Niger's National Council for the Safeguard of the Homeland (CNSP) suspended its military agreement with the United States after a visit by senior U.S. officials to the capital, Niamey. Niger hosted around one thousand U.S. troops and a drone base. The country was a key partner on counterterrorism, but relations deteriorated after Niger's presidential guard removed Mohamed Bazoum in a coup. The U.S. delegation insisted Niger not work with Russia. Ironically, their attempt to counter Russian influence only pushed the CNSP to seek ties with Moscow. A month later, roughly one hundred Russian trainers, many veterans of the Mali campaign, arrived in Niger and moved into a military base where American soldiers were still stationed. SADAT and its Syrian mercenaries touched down soon after.

The threat of Wagner was useful to Washington, until it overplayed its card. In an interview with the *Washington Post* after American troop withdrawal, Niger's prime minister stated that U.S. Assistant Secretary of State for African Affairs Molly Phee urged him during the March visit to refrain from engaging with Iran and Russia in ways objectionable to Washington.

"When she finished, I said, Madame, I am going to summarize in two points what you have said. First, you have come here to threaten us in our country. That is unacceptable. And you have come here to tell us with whom we can have relationships, which is also unacceptable. And you have done it all with a condescending tone and a lack of respect."

"The Americans stayed on our soil," the prime minister later recounted, "doing nothing while the terrorists killed people and burned towns. It is not a sign of friendship to come on our soil but let the terrorists attack us. We have seen what the United States will do to defend its allies, because we have seen Ukraine and Israel."

The Russians had no plans to enter Niger. Yet the West's fear of their arrival made it a self-fulfilling prophecy. Ironically, this is perhaps Wagner's most important legacy: the story it told about itself, and the story we told about it. And yet thousands of lives were wasted in the ruins of Bakhmut, in the deserts of Syria, Libya, northern Mali, and in the jungles of the Central Africa to fuel one man's drive for wealth and acceptance, before he too ultimately succumbed to the powers he unleashed. The conflicts in which these lives were lost continue, unabated, after his death.

ACKNOWLEDGMENTS

"The ugly fact is books are made out of books," Cormac McCarthy once told the *New York Times*, and this one is no exception. The Wagner Group operated in some of the world's most complex conflicts, and this work relied on the incredible research of the many scholars and authors cited. Detailing the history of Wagner Group would have been impossible, too, without the brave interviewees and sources, on all sides, who contributed their stories, impressions, and beliefs to me and others. This book owes a great debt to the many journalists in Russia, Ukraine, Syria, Libya, Sudan, Central African Republic, Mali, and elsewhere who took serious risks and, in some cases, lost their lives, bringing these stories to light. They continue to work and deserve far more resources and support than they receive.

My thinking on Russian mercenaries has evolved over time, and it will continue to evolve well after this book is published. I've relied on long conversations with experts and scholars in a wide variety of fields. Jack Margolin, Candace Rondeaux, Sorcha MacLeod, Sean McFate, Alec Bertina, Lilia Yapparova, Ilya Barabanov, Marat Gabidullin, and several sources unnamed have shaped my thinking of the phenomenon. Jade McGlynn, Anna Arutunyan, Mark Galeotti, and Tatiana Stanovaya have been instrumental in my analysis on Russian politics. Hanna Notte and Kirill Semenov offered key insights on Russia's role in Syria. Raga Makawi and Kholood Khair provided generous guidance on the Sudan chapters, while Jalel Harchaoui and Wolfram Lacher spent hours explaining the intricacies of Libyan politics. Adam Sandor and Alexander Thurston shared their expertise on CAR and the Sahel and offered comments on several chapters.

I could not have traveled to the conflict zones described in this book without the help of my local fixers over the years. Through great effort Marian in Ukraine and my friends in Libya took me where I needed to go. My friends in Mali got me into the country and many more friends around the world—most of whom I've never met—then got me out. I am especially indebted to my friends in the Central African Republic, a country I fell in love with after my first visit in 2019, who have hosted me from Bangui, to Baoro, Bria, and Birao.

Joel Rosenthal and Paul Golob were the first to think a book possible. And my agent, Michael Signorelli, and my editor, Morgan Jones, took a chance on me before Wagner made international headlines. Without their advice on countless drafts, this project would have never materialized.

Finally, I have been blessed in life to have had the constant support of my parents, John and Mary, and my siblings: Liz, Julia, and Duncan. Their encouragement, whether toward sobriety or a career change, set me up for success. My wife, Sothir, has been by my side throughout this journey. She has not only championed my efforts to work and travel in the places I love, but gotten me out of several jams, too. For that and much more, I am eternally grateful. Thank you.

NOTES

INTRODUCTION

xiii **SERGEANT-MAJOR: That's just for show:** Schiller, Friedrich. *The Robbers; Wallenstein.* Translated by F. J. (Francis John) Lamport (New York: Penguin Books, 1979).

xiii **left his country years ago to find work:** Interview with Ukrainian soldier. Kyiv, Ukraine. May 1, 2023.

xiv **His Slobozhan speech is an expressive:** For an excellent overview of Ukraine's language politics, see: Bilaniuk, Laada. *Contested Tongues: Language Politics and Cultural Correction in Ukraine* (Ithaca, NY: Cornell University Press, 2005).

xiv **"PMC Wagner":** In Russian *Chastnaya Voennaya Kompaniya Vagner* (ChVK Wagner). In English, from which the term originated, ChVK is usually translated to private military company (PMC).

xv **said he was from Kievan Rus:** Here I use the Russian spelling to align to a Russian nationalist speaking to Bogdan.

xv *zeky:* Russian slang, short for *zaklyuchyonnii* or "prisoner."

xvi **private warfare is back, albeit in new ways:** The former American contractor Sean McFate has written an excellent history of mercenaries. See: McFate, Sean. *The Modern Mercenary: Private Armies and What They Mean for World Order* (New York: Oxford University Press, 2014).

xvi **"an honest, albeit bloody trade":** Ibid., 27.

xvi **"the career of a soldier had offered them":** Wedgwood, C. V. (Cicely Veronica). *The Thirty Years War* (New York: New York Review Books, 2005), 485.

xvii **"who were reluctant to surrender them":** Tilly, Charles. *Coercion, Capital, and European States, AD 990–1990* (B. Blackwell, 1990).

xvii **"the state made war":** Ibid.

xviii **path to global prosperity:** Lipset, Seymour Martin. "Some Social Requisites of Democracy: Economic Development and Political Legitimacy." *The American Political Science Review* 53, no. 1 (1959): 69–105.

xviii **narrative of progress:** Przeworski, Adam, and Fernando Limongi. "Modernization: Theories and Facts." *World Politics* 49, no. 2 (1997): 155–83.

xviii **"withdrawing services from the country's peripheries":** See: Craze, Joshua. "Rule by Militia." *The Boston Review*, June 26, 2024.

xviii **"dispossession, and looting":** Ibid.

xviii **or United Nations peacekeepers, could not:** Rubin, Elizabeth. "An Army of One's Own: A People Still Besieged, in a City Not yet Saved." *Harper's Magazine*, Feb. 1, 1997.

xix **a small footprint:** Scahill, Jeremy. *Blackwater: The Rise of the World's Most Powerful Mercenary Army* (New York: Nation Books, 2007), 51.

xix **"like venture capitalists":** Ibid., 51.

xix **Iraq and Afghanistan:** Peltz, Robert D. "Blackwater Rising: The Legal Issues Raised by the Unprecedented Privatization of U.S. Military Functions." *University of Miami Law Review* 76 (2021).

xix **to keep costs low:** Franklin, Jonathan. "US Contractor Recruits Guards for Iraq in Chile." *Guardian*, March 5, 2004.

xix **networks for future contracts:** See Scahill, Jeremy.

xix **"Total Force":** Scahill, Jeremy, 57.

xix **"involvement of the nation":** Singer, Peter W. "The Dark Truth About Blackwater." *Brookings*, Oct. 30, 2007.

xix **report deaths of contractors:** "Risks of Afghan War Shift from Soldiers to Contractors." *NBC News*, Feb. 12, 2012.

xix **killed than U.S. troops:** Ioanes, Ellen. "More US Contractors Have Died in Afghanistan than US Troops—but the Pentagon Doesn't Keep Track." *Business Insider*, Dec. 10, 2019.

xix **"conduct autonomous military campaigns":** McFate, Sean, 13

xx **"could see right through me":** Interview with an associate of Yevgeny Prigozhin. January 2024.

xxi **"into bloody conflict":** Gibbons-Neff, Thomas. "How a 4-Hour Battle Between Russian Mercenaries and U.S. Commandos Unfolded in Syria." *New York Times*, May 24, 2018.

xxi **"respect for human rights":** "Wagner Group, Yevgeniy Prigozhin, and Russia's Disinformation in Africa." United States Department of State, May 24, 2022.

xxi **"scramble for Africa":** Hicks, Marcus, et al. "Great-Power Competition Is Coming to Africa." *Foreign Affairs*, March 4, 2021.

xxii **"against the civilian population"**: "Macron Warns of 'Predatory' Russian Mercenaries in Mali." *France 24*, Feb. 17, 2022.

xxiii **Frederick the Great:** Burns, Alexander S. "What Frederick the Great's Army Can Tell Us About Russia's Private Military Company." *War on the Rocks*, March 27, 2023.

xxiii **feudal Japan:** Editorial Board. "How to Tame the Russian Mercenaries Who Are Destabilizing Africa." *Washington Post*, July 17, 2023.

xxiii **"stability or security"**: Machiavelli, Niccolo. *The Prince* (London: Penguin Books, 1999).

xxiii **"consequences of their own decisions"**: Derluguian, Georgi M. *Bourdieu's Secret Admirer in the Caucasus: A World-System Biography* (Chicago: University of Chicago Press, 2005).

xxiv **"labels of 'corporation' and 'state'"**: Rogers, Douglas. *The Depths of Russia: Oil, Power, and Culture after Socialism* (Ithaca, NY: Cornell University Press, 2015).

xxiv **"Putin's Friends and Associates"**: Stanovaya, Tatiana. "Unconsolidated: The Five Russian Elites Shaping Putin's Transition." Carnegie Endowment for International Peace, Feb. 11, 2020.

xxiv **effective management:** Ibid.

xxiv **"do not make big mistakes"**: Ibid.

xxv **smartest guy in the room:** Interview with former colleague of Prigozhin. 2024.

CHAPTER 1: SOLDIERS

1 **consensus on global issues:** Laub, Zachary. "The Group of Eight (G8) Industrialized Nations." Council on Foreign Relations, March 3, 2014.

3 **turnips and baby zucchini:** "Abominable Showman: A Profile of Wagner's Yevgeny Prigozhin." *Economist*, June 12, 2023.

4 **raspberry mille-feuille for dessert:** Zhegulev, Ilya. "Расследование: как личный кулинар Путина накормит армию за 92 млрд рублей." *Forbes.ru*, March 18, 2013.

4 **reunification with East Germany:** For a definitive history of NATO expansion, see: Sarotte, M. E. *Not One Inch: America, Russia, and the Making of Post-Cold War Stalemate* (New Haven, CT: Yale University Press, 2021).

5 **pushed to join NATO:** Ibid., 220.

5   question of whether to "when": Ibid., 184.

5   "between NATO and the Russian Federation": Ibid., 271.

5   "in the post–Cold War order": Bechev, Dimitar. *Rival Power: Russia's Influence in Southeast Europe* (New Haven, CT: Yale University Press, 2017), 24.

6   bridge between the West and Serbia: Ibid., 37.

6   clearly the junior partner: Ibid., 37.

6   "systematic campaign of violence": Sarotte, M. E., 305.

7   Chechnya in the future: Ibid., 316.

7   "1999 Kosovo campaign": Stent, Angela. *Putin's World: Russia against the West and with the Rest*. (New York: Twelve, 2019), 124.

7   U.S. military bases in Central Asia: Hill, Fiona. "Putin and Bush in Common Cause? Russia's View of the Terrorist Threat After September 11." Brookings, June 1, 2002.

7   "deep and complex": Stent. *Putin's World*, 265.

7   "could fuel extremism and terrorism": Ibid., 265.

8   feared a thin line: Ibid., 40.

8   "governor of Donetsk Oblast": Plokhy, Serhii. *The Russo-Ukrainian War: The Return of History* (New York: W. W. Norton & Company, 2023).

8   price of natural gas: Ibid.

8   democratic backsliding: Whitmore, Brian. "Expect No Showdowns at G8 Summit." Radio Free Europe/Radio Liberty, Feb. 2, 2012.

8   boycott the summit altogether: Ibid.

9   "assistance from the [IMF]": Ibid.

9   "would do the same thing": U.S. Department of State. The Office of Electronic Information, Bureau of Public Affairs. President Bush and Russian President Putin Participate in Press Availability. https://2001 -2009.state.gov/p/eur/rls/rm/69059.htm.

9   "situation in the world today": U.S. Department of State. The Office of Electronic Information, Bureau of Public Affairs. U.S. Recognizes Kosovo as Independent State. Feb. 18, 2008, https://2001-2009.state.gov /secretary/rm/2008/02/100973.htm.

9   "on the head someday": "Putin Warns West over Kosovo Support." *Chicago Tribune*, Feb. 24, 2008.

10 trusted with a second term: Arutunyan, Anna. *Hybrid Warriors: Proxies, Freelancers and Moscow's Struggle for Ukraine* (London: Hurst and Company, 2022), 55.

11 **Ukraine's Carpathian Mountains:** Interview with Marian. 2024.

11 **accelerating events:** Arel, Dominique, and Jesse Driscoll. *Ukraine's Unnamed War: Before the Russian Invasion of 2022* (Cambridge University Press, 2023), 10.

11 **nine policemen, were killed:** Ibid., 86.

12 **killing thirty-nine in one hour:** Ibid., 89.

12 **the east back to the west:** Ibid., 1.

12 **Defense Minister Sergei Shoigu:** Galeotti, Mark. *Putin's Wars: From Chechnya to Ukraine* (Osprey Publishing, 2022), 170.

13 **raised the Russian flag:** Ibid., 172.

13 **"no-fly zone was created":** A translation of General Valery Gerasimov's article can be found here: https://www.armyupress.army.mil /portals/7/military-review/archives/english/militaryreview_20160228 _art008.pdf.

14 **"loyalty to one's ancestors":** Interviews with Alexander Kravchenko. 2023.

14 **during the late Soviet nationalist revivals:** For an excellent history of Cossack organizations following Soviet collapse, see: Hryb, Olexander. *Understanding Contemporary Ukrainian and Russian Nationalism: The Post-Soviet Cossack Revival and Ukraine's National Security* (Ibidem-Verlag, 2020).

14 **"gave him the opportunity":** Александр Кравченко—русский доброволец. Воспоминания о Стрелкове. Часть 1. 2024. YouTube, https://www.youtube.com/watch?v=AatKS6n6ATI.

15 **"Russians would help us in Serbia":** Interview with Hadži Bratislav Živković. 2023.

16 **Girkin began raising a militia:** Arutunyan, Anna, 120–24.

16 **"persuading":** Ibid., 72.

17 **(RIM) was in Crimea:** Interview with Stanislav Vorobyev. 2024.

17 **"suburban building in St. Petersburg":** See: https://mappingmilitants .org/profiles/russian-imperial-movement.

18 **Russian imperialist newspaper:** Dolgov, Anna. "Russia's Igor Strelkov: I Am Responsible for War in Eastern Ukraine." *Moscow Times*, Nov. 21, 2014.

18 **against insurgents:** "Ukraine Says Donetsk 'anti-Terror Operation' under Way." BBC News, Apr. 15, 2014.

18 **"particularly like Yanukovych, either":** Interview with Luhansk resident. 2023.

19 "destroying innocent people": Interview with "Boyar." 2023.

20 for religious reasons: Interview with "Arkady." 2023.

21 "country's central authorities": "Address by President of the Russian Federation." President of Russia, March 18, 2014.

21 engage in sedition: Arel, Dominique, and Jesse Driscoll offer a comprehensive analysis on the logic of sedition in Crimea and eastern Ukraine.

22 "organizational core of the unit": Wagner Leaks, Dossier Center. Indexing provided by C4ADS.

22 to tell things how they are: Telegram post, @boris_rozhin, July 9, 2023. https://t.me/boris_rozhin/91688.

23 he won his first medals: "Вагнера ищет боевая подруга." Газета.Ru, https://www.gazeta.ru/social/2016/12/16/10431467.shtml.

23 "career of a military officer": Ibid.

23 close to the border with Ukraine: Ministry of Defense source, Dossier Center. 2023.

24 "not a particularly important role": Ibid.

24 "opportunity to join [him]": Interview with "Andrei." 2023.

24 knowledgeable commander: Interview with Marat Gabidullin. 2024.

24 "Rusich battalion for a brief period": Rusich spokesman. 2024. See also: Rondeaux, Candace; Margolin, Jack; Imhof, Oliver. "The Abu Dhabi Express." New America, Nov. 2021.

24 Ministry of Internal Affairs: "Они сражались за Пальмиру (фото)." fontanka.ru—новости Санкт-Петербурга, 29 Mar. 2016.

24 houses and targets to rob: Zakharov, Andrei, et al. "Chef and Chief." Proekt Media. July 12, 2023.

24 "girlfriends invited him to": Ibid.

25 robbed her: "За что в 1981 году в СССР судили Евгения Пригожина, которого теперь весь мир знает как «повара Путина». Публикуем текст судебного документа." Meduza, June 15, 2021.

25 Energetikov Avenue: Zakharov, Andrei, et al. "Chef and Chief." Proekt Media. July 12, 2023.

25 New Island: Ibid.

25 "And he was good at it": Walker, Shaun, and Pjotr Sauer. "Yevgeny Prigozhin: The Hotdog Seller Who Rose to the Top of Putin's War Machine." Guardian, Aug. 23, 2023.

26 "fucked them up one more time": Zakharov, Andrei, et al. "Chef and Chief." Proekt Media. July 12, 2023.

26 thrill of the chase: Walker, Shaun, and Pjotr Sauer. "Yevgeny Prigozhin: The Hotdog Seller Who Rose to the Top of Putin's War Machine." *Guardian*, Aug. 23, 2023.

26 the Old Customs House: Внимание к Мелочам: Ресторатор Тони Гир Рассказал, Как Пригожин Создал «Старую Таможню»—Аргументы Недели. https://argumenti.ru/society/2022/12/802433.

26 gambling industry: Margolin, Jack. *The Wagner Group: Inside Russia's Mercenary Army* (Reaktion Books, 2024).

26 "bringing the plates myself": Walker, Shaun, and Pjotr Sauer. "Yevgeny Prigozhin: The Hotdog Seller Who Rose to the Top of Putin's War Machine." *Guardian*, Aug. 23, 2023.

26 connections were invaluable: Barabanov, Ilya, and Denis Korotkov. *Nash biznes—smert'* (Meduza Publishing, 2024).

26 "my mum could hardly count it all": Walker, Shaun, and Pjotr Sauer. "Yevgeny Prigozhin: The Hotdog Seller Who Rose to the Top of Putin's War Machine." *Guardian*, Aug. 23, 2023.

26 passed it to Putin: Margolin, Jack. *The Wagner Group*.

26 for the schools and military: Walker, Shaun, and Pjotr Sauer. "Yevgeny Prigozhin: The Hotdog Seller Who Rose to the Top of Putin's War Machine." *Guardian*, Aug. 23, 2023.

27 to the private sector: Maglov, Mikhail et al. "Часть 2. Котлетки псов войны." Настоящее Время, Feb. 20, 2019.

27 "Concord Food Combine": Maglov, Mikhail, et al. "Часть 1. Земля, вода и небо Евгения Пригожина." Настоящее Время, Feb. 20, 2019.

28 roughly $10,000,000 at the time: Ibid.

28 advertisement on social media: Interview with Alexandra Garmazhapova. 2023.

28 blogs, social media: Garmazhapova, Alexandra. "Где живут тролли. И кто их кормит. Специальный репортаж из офиса, в котором вешают лапшу в три смены." Новая газета. Sep. 7, 2013.

29 G-20 Summit: The G-20 is a forum for the world's largest economies to discuss economic cooperation and other issues.

29 that vilified the protestors: Girin, Nikita, and Diana Khachatryan. "Анатомия про тесто. Повар правительства Евгений Пригожин обслуживает чиновников и одновременно имеет под рукой «специальную службу», которая организует бот-атаки и снимает пропагандистское кино." Новая газета, Apr. 8, 2012.

29 positive coverage: See: Barabanov, Ilya, and Denis Korotkov. *Nash biznes—smert'* (Meduza Publishing, 2024).

30 "everything will work fucking great": Zakharov, Andrei, et al. "Chef and Chief." *Proekt Media*, Jul. 12, 2023.

30 land at Luhansk airport: Wagner Leaks, Dossier Center. Indexing provided by C4ADS.

31 at that point in the war: "Why the Battle for Luhansk Airport Is Just as Important as the Battle for Donetsk Airport." *Euromaidan Press*, Feb. 10, 2018.

31 "pour into the regional capital": See: https://boosty.to/astramilitarum /posts/b673e6e9-11a8-4440-9003-39e5922cfe01

31 lost thirty soldiers and three tanks: Ibid.

31 least for that day, was over: Ibid.

32 to train his "volunteers": Walker, Shaun, and Pjotr Sauer. "Yevgeny Prigozhin: The Hotdog Seller Who Rose to the Top of Putin's War Machine." *Guardian*, Aug. 23, 2023.

32 fought in Bosnia and Kosovo: Interview with "Branko." 2024.

33 paramilitary veteran: Ristic, Marija. "Serb Fighters' Mercenary Path from Ukraine to Syria." *Balkan Insight*, Apr. 22, 2016.

33 mysteriously in a bomb blast: Ibid.

34 weapons and grenade launchers: Gusel'nikov, Andrey. "Bednyy Betman." *URA. RU*, Jan. 3, 2015.

34 was killed: "В Луганске убит обвиняемый в пытках командир ополченцев «Бэтмен»." РБК, Jan. 2, 2015.

34 his own wedding: Kirillov, Dmitriy. "«Батя» не доехал до свадьбы." Газета.*Ru*, June 27, 2024.

35 "allowed to open fire": Interview with "Jan." 2023.

35 around January 22: Telegram post, @grey_zone, January 19, 2021. https://t.me/grey_zone/6961.

35 "retreat with injuries": Interview with "Arkady." 2023.

36 "are going to shoot me soon": PMC "Wagner" Commander Utkin Conversation with Deputy Troshev. YouTube. https://www.youtube .com/watch?v=wsXTQIReegM.

36 upward of eighty casualties: Margolin, Jack.

36 that was anything but: Luhn, Alec, and Oksana Grytsenko. "Ukrainian Soldiers Share Horrors of Debaltseve Battle after Stinging Defeat." *Guardian*, Feb. 18, 2015.

37 **and salaries were irregular:** See: Gabidullin, Marat. *Moi Marat* (Michel Lafon. 2022), 39–49.

37 **shot him:** Interview with Marat Gabidullin. 2023.

37 **"five hundred to seven hundred men":** Wagner Leaks, Dossier Center. Indexing provided by C4ADS.

37 **alcohol and firearms increased:** Gabidullin, Marat. *Moi Marat,* 51–61.

38 **"into line":** Wagner Leaks, Dossier Center. Indexing provided by C4ADS.

38 **"pepper them with fire":** Bellingcat Investigation. "MH17—Russian GRU Commander 'Orion' Identified as Oleg Ivannikov." *Bellingcat,* May 25, 2018.

CHAPTER 2: OIL MEN

42 **ways to profit from it:** Interview with Marat Gabidullin. 2023.

42 **opposition to take up arms:** For a history of the Syrian revolution and the Assad family, see: Dagher, Sam. *Assad or We Burn the Country: How One Family's Lust for Power Destroyed Syria* (New York: Little, Brown and Company, 2019).

42 **split along community lines:** Dagher, Sam. *Assad or We Burn the Country.*

42 **naval base at Tartus:** Interview with Kirill Semenov. 2023.

42 **al-Qaeda operatives from prison:** Dagher, Sam. *Assad or We Burn the Country.*

43 **embassies in revenge:** Dagher, Sam. *Assad or We Burn the Country.*

43 **"Popular Resistance Committees":** Dagher, Sam. *Assad or We Burn the Country.*

43 **"profit for themselves":** Solomon, Christopher. "The Syrian Desert Hawks: Flying No More." *Clingendael,* Feb. 2020.

43 **national security contacts:** Ibid.

43 **Jaber brothers with an opportunity:** Ibid.

43 **1996 Criminal Code:** Professor Kimberly Marten was one of the first to write about the relationship between Russian PMCs and the state. See: Marten, Kimberly. "Russia's Use of Semi-state Security Forces: The Case of the Wagner Group." *Post-Soviet Affairs* 35 (2019): 181–204.

44 convoys in Iraq and Afghanistan: Candace Rondeaux's mapping of the Russian PMC space remains the best. See: Rondeaux, Candace. "Decoding the Wagner Group: Analyzing the Role of Private Security Contractors in Russian Proxy Warfare." *New America*, Nov. 7, 2019.

44 under the guise of tourism: Interview with Russian PMC employee. 2023.

44 FSB brokered the deal: See Ukrainian intelligence report: https://uacas.org/?article=149. Also, Martemyanov, Maksim. "Казаки по вызову: кубанские наемники в сирийской пустыне." *GQ Россия*, July 28, 2014.

44 several contractors in Nigeria: Barabanov, Ilya, and Denis Korotkov. *Nash biznes—smert'* (Meduza Publishing, 2024).

44 was already underway: See Dossier Center's May 2022 evidence submission to UK Parliament. https://committees.parliament.uk/writtenevidence/108385/html/.

44 it hadn't worked out: Interview with "Andrei." 2023.

44 weapons to the test: Bouckaert, Peter. "Attacks on Ghouta." Human Rights Watch, Sept. 2013.

45 *muzhiky*: The term *muzhik* has many connotations in Russian. The term originally denoted a Russian (male) peasant. Now, it can also be used to describe "a man's man," but also simply "fellow," "chap," or "dude."

45 fired into the sand: Martem'yanov, Maksim. "Казаки по вызову: кубанские наемники в сирийской пустыне." *GQ Россия*, July 28, 2014. Marat notes there was a shooting range on the beach.

45 from any refusenik: See Ukrainian intelligence report: https://uacas.org/?article=149l

45 ISIS ambush: While the exact composition of the attacking forces has not been determined, Syrian experts believe, given the time and location, the force was likely ISIS.

45 returning fire: See Ukrainian intelligence report: https://uacas.org/?article=149.

46 the battlefield: Ibid.

46 wouldn't be pleased, either: Ibid.

47 following the events in Ukraine: Interview with Kirill Semenov. 2023.

47 leaders in the MoD: Ministry of Defense source, Dossier Center. 2023.

47 down later that month: Gabidullin, Marat. *Moi Marat*, 63–69.

47 "activities in eastern Ukraine": Interview with Marat Gabidullin. 2024.

48 plan yet how to hide casualties: Interview with Marat Gabidullin. 2024.

48 offensive on rebel-held Latakia: For Marat's full account of the Latakia campaign, see: Gabidullin, Marat. *Moi Marat*, 73–141.

49 report to Russian military headquarters: Interview with Marat Gabidullin. 2024.

49 higher salaries than the regular army: Solomon, Christopher. "The Syrian Desert Hawks: Flying No More." *Clingendael*, Feb. 2020.

50 Hawks were poor soldiers: Gabidullin, Marat. *Moi Marat*, 73–141.

50 outskirts of Kinsabba: For Marat's account of Kinsabba, see: Gabidullin, Marat. *Moi Marat*, 143–83.

51 "held death in contempt": The Palmyra campaign can be found in: Gabidullin, Marat. *Moi Marat*, 183–233.

52 120 wounded: Wagner Leaks, Dossier Center. Indexing provided by C4ADS.

52 "from the highest levels": Interview with Marat Gabidullin. 2024.

53 Moscow shared with the GRU: Wagner Leaks, Dossier Center. Indexing provided by C4ADS.

53 recaptured Palmyra: Sly, Liz. "Hezbollah, Russia and the U.S. Help Syria Retake Palmyra." *Washington Post*, May 24, 2023.

53 the main threat: Kofman, Michael. "Syria and the Russian Armed Forces." Foreign Policy Research Institute, Sep. 2020.

53 Jaber told *Der Spiegel*: Schaap, Fritz. "Assad Power Slips in Syria as Warlords Grow More Powerful." *Der Spiegel*, Mar. 8, 2017.

53 motorcade at gunpoint: Solomon, Christopher. "The Syrian Desert Hawks: Flying No More." *Clingendael*, Feb. 2020.

54 oil fields' profit: " 'Фонтанка': 'повар Путина' получит 25% сирийской нефти и газа." Радио Свобода, June 27, 2017.

54 production, and drilling: "Немного бизнеса в сирийской войне (фото, видео)." *fontanka.ru*, June 26, 2017.

54 named Evro-Polis's General Director: Ibid.

54 Badia region: Solomon, Christopher. "The Syrian Desert Hawks: Flying No More." *Clingendael*, Feb. 2020.

54 diagnosed with cancer: Gabidullin, Marat. *Moi pozyvnoi "Martin."* (ISIA Media Verlag, 2023), 238.

54 preparing for a fight: Ibid., 239.

55 carefully thought-out plans: Ibid., 240.

55 PMC at that time: Wagner Leaks, Dossier Center. Indexing provided by C4ADS.

55 "for our Russian mother": Interview with "Arkady." 2023.

56 "understand it that way": Interview with "Arkady." 2023.

56 "Hayan and Jazel": Wagner Leaks, Dossier Center. Indexing provided by C4ADS.

56 three hundred fighters helped recapture Palmyra: Ibid.

56 ISIS positions in Palmyra: Sly, Liz. "Hezbollah, Russia and the U.S. Help Syria Retake Palmyra." *Washington Post*, May 24, 2023.

57 including leader Aleksei Milchakov: Rusich spokesman. 2024.

57 other far-right paraphernalia: "Фашист-живодер из Петербурга приехал воевать за ополченцев ЛНР." *MKRU*, July 4, 2014.

57 Ukrainian corpses: Kozhurin, Dmitry. "Who Are the Neo-Nazis Fighting for Russia in Ukraine?" Radio Free Europe/Radio Liberty, May 27, 2022.

57 storming enemy positions: Interview with Marat Gabidullin. 2023. See also: https://informnapalm.org/en/list-of-the-karpaty-company-task -force-who-of-the-donbas-militants-recruited-to-the-russian-wagner -pmc-photo/.

57 cheaper to pay: Gabidullin, Marat. *Moi pozyvnoi "Martin."* 243.

57 *mukhabarat*: Ibid.

57 Wagner's lines: Testimony from "Arkady" and Marat. 2023.

58 that stayed on base: Ibid.

58 family from Lebanon: Rondeaux, Candace. "Inquiry into the Murder of Hamdi Bouta and Wagner Group Operations at the Al-Shaer Gas Plant, Homs, Syria 2017." *New America*, June 8, 2020.

58 ties to Rusich: Ibid.

59 response from the other side: Wagner Leaks, Dossier Center. Indexing provided by C4ADS.

59 oil and gas fields as possible: Kofman, Michael. 2023.

59 town of Khasham: Telegram post, @grey-zone, February 7, 2023. https://t.me/grey_zone/17071.

59 seizing Conoco: Interview with Marat Gabidullin. 2023.

59 450 million cubic feet of gas per day: Abdulrahim, Raja. "U.S.-Backed Forces Seize Syrian Gas Plant from Islamic State." *Wall Street*

Journal, Sep. 25, 2017. See also Conoco's 2001 Annual Report: https://www.sec.gov/Archives/edgar/vprr/0203/02030714.pdf.

60 **revealed Number 1's order:** For Marat's full account of the Battle of Khasham, see: Gabidullin, Marat. *Moi pozyvnoi "Martin."* 251–62.

60 **around al-Khasham:** Ibid.

61 **.50-caliber machine guns on the roof:** Maurer, Kevin. "Special Forces Soldiers Reveal First Details of Battle with Russian Mercenaries in Syria." *The War Horse,* May 11, 2023.

62 **"across the black sand":** Ibid.

62 **Russian Air Force:** Ibid.

62 **had them painted:** Stein, Aaron. *US War against ISIS: How America and Its Allies Defeated the Caliphate* (Bloomsbury, 2022).

63 **B-1B bombers from Saudi Arabia:** Kofman, Michael. 2023.

63 **"destroy the entirety of Syria":** Romanovskyy, Kirill, "Eight Years with Wagner."

63 **the early morning:** Gabidullin, Marat. *Moi pozyvnoi "Martin."* 262–68.

63 **more mundane reasons:** Ibid.

64 **once again incensed:** Interview with Marat Gabidullin. 2023.

65 **"where they have oil":** "Syria Says U.S. Oil Firm Signed Deal with Kurdish-Led Rebels." Reuters, 2 Aug. 2020.

66 **private security firm:** Atwood, Kylie, and Ryan Browne. "Former Army Delta Force Officer, US Ambassador Sign Secretive Contract to Develop Syrian Oil Fields." CNN, Aug. 5, 2020.

66 **"U.S. political and social issues":** See https://www.justice.gov/file/1035477/download.

66 **generate advertising revenue:** Interview with Andrei Zakharov. 2023.

67 **"said and wrote about him":** Ibid.

67 **"work for one reader alone":** Chikishev, Nikolai. "Prigozhin's Mutiny Shatters Illusion of Powerful Media Empire." Carnegie Endowment for International Peace, Aug. 14, 2023.

CHAPTER 3: DIPLOMATS

74 **opportunity to mine gold:** Interview with Mikhail Potepkin. 2023.

70 **around Port Sudan:** "Professor kislykh schey." Dossier Center, Nov. 27, 2020.

70   indicted by Robert Mueller's team: "Золото в обмен на наемников: как «повар Путина» добывает для России «ключ от Африки»." *The Bell*, June 4, 2018.

70   "politicians is quite small": Interview with Alexandra Garmazhapova. 2023.

71   play nice with Western diplomats: For an excellent analysis of Omar al-Bashir's regime and the role of peace negotiations in fueling conflict, see: Srinivasan, Sharath. *When Peace Kills Politics: International Intervention and Unending Wars in the Sudans* (Oxford University Press, 2021).

72   effectively fueled conflict in Darfur: Ibid.

72   political strategist: Malik, Nesrine. "Sudan's Outsider: How a Paramilitary Leader Fell out with the Army and Plunged the Country into War." *Guardian*, Apr. 20, 2023.

73   "importance of gold": Interview with Kholood Khair. 2023.

73   cheaper rates: Interview with Russian PMC source close to events. 2023.

73   construction contracts for the Russian military: "Золото в обмен на наемников: как «повар Путина» добывает для России «ключ от Африки»." *The Bell*, June 4, 2018.

74   Meroe Gold: Leaked documents provided by C4ADS.

74   vehicles and equipment: Ibid.

74   reviewed contracts: Ibid.

74   mine gold in 2016: Russian PMC insider. 2024.

75   provided by Concord: "Золото в обмен на наемников: как «повар Путина» добывает для России «ключ от Африки»." *The Bell*, June 4, 2018.

75   "cool to work for them": Interview with "Nazar." 2023.

76   AFRIC: "Treasury Escalates Sanctions Against the Russian Government's Attempts to Influence U.S. Elections." U.S. Department of the Treasury, June 24, 2024.

76   twenty African countries in total: Badanin, Roman, et al. "Shev i povar." *Proekt media*, March 13, 2019.

77   "influence in the world": Ibid.

77   agreed to send a team: Schwirtz, Michael, and Gaelle Borgia. "How Russia Meddles Abroad for Profit: Cash, Trolls and a Cult Leader." *New York Times*, Nov. 11, 2019.

78 on live television: Sokolyanskaya, Kseniya. "Съеденные бумаги, выборы на Мадагаскаре и тюремный срок в Ливии. Кто такой Максим Шугалей и что его связывает с Пригожиным." Настоящее Время, June 16, 2021.

78 favorable coverage of the incumbent: Schwirtz, Michael, and Gaelle Borgia. "How Russia Meddles Abroad for Profit: Cash, Trolls and a Cult Leader." *New York Times*, Nov. 11, 2019.

78 misspelling his name: Ibid.

78 overstating invoices: Ibid.

78 decision-making process: Interview with Maksim Shugaley. 2023.

78 bodyguard for the campaign trail: "Putin Chef's Kisses of Death: Russia's Shadow Army's State-Run Structure Exposed." *Bellingcat*, Aug. 14, 2020.

78 Andry Rajoelina: Ibid.

78 Ferrum Mining: Badanin, Roman et al. "Shev i povar." *Proekt media*, Mar. 13, 2019.

79 Russians for assistance: Interview with Dmitry Syty. 2024.

79 CAR's ambassador to Russia: Margolin, Jack. *The Wagner Group: Inside Russia's Mercenary Army* (Reaktion Books, 2024).

79 Touadéra's administration: "Убийство журналистов было только началом." *Dossier Center*, June 18, 2023.

79 Ilyushin-76: https://dossier.center/wp-content/uploads/2019/07/B.18-With-Watermark.pdf

80 security services: Ibid.

80 Somalia the previous year: "How Russia Moved into Central Africa." *Reuters*, Oct. 17, 2018.

81 Vakaga province: Maglov, Mikhail et al., "Часть 4. Тайное завоевание Африки." Настоящее Время, Feb. 20, 2019.

81 French Foreign Legion: "Как кыргызстанец оказался среди наемников в Африке: версия знакомого." Радио Азаттык, March 8, 2019.

81 to marry: Ibid.

81 could speak French: Ibid.

81 they found a drone: Maglov, Mikhail et al., "Часть 4. Тайное завоевание Африки." Настоящее Время, Feb. 20, 2019.

82 COSI: Interview with Lobaye Invest employee. 2023.

82 "Influence Group": Interview with Marat Gabidullin. 2023.

82 **was in charge:** Ibid.

82 **seven sites:** Ward, Clarissa et al., "Putin's Private Army Is Trying to Increase Russia's Influence in Africa." CNN, Aug. 2019.

82 **$500 million:** See http://www.axmininc.com/images/Axmin_NI_43 _101.pdf.

82 **two hundred military instructors:** Wagner Leaks, Dossier Center. Indexing provided by C4ADS.

83 **forced labor and porterage:** The anthropologist Louisa Lombard has written seminal texts on CAR society. Lombard, Louisa. *Hunting Game: Raiding Politics in the Central African Republic* (Cambridge University Press, 2020).

83 **sixty thousand African forced laborers:** For a history of the Congo-Océan, see: Daughton, J. P. (James Patrick). *In the Forest of No Joy: The Congo-Océan Railroad and the Tragedy of French Colonialism* (W. W. Norton & Company, 2021).

83 **"first high school":** Lombard, Louisa. *Hunting Game.*

84 **FPRC:** "Central African Republic: A Conflict Mapping." *IPIS,* August 2018.

84 **"threats of a coup":** Hoefer, Adrian. "Central African Republic: Ground Zero for Russian Influence in Central Africa." Atlantic Council, Oct. 22, 2020.

85 **Hassan Bouba:** Interview with armed group source. 2023.

85 **Chadian intelligence:** Interview with Baba Laddé. 2023.

85 **special advisor:** "République centrafricaine : Un ministre inculpé pour atrocités." Human Rights Watch, Nov. 24, 2021.

85 **nonsecurity portfolio:** Faucon, Benoit, and Gabriele Steinhauser. "The Elusive Figure Running Wagner's Embattled Empire of Gold and Diamonds." *Wall Street Journal,* Sep. 21, 2023.

85 **meat-processing facility:** Interview with armed group source. 2023.

86 **Bangassou:** Interview with armed group source. 2023.

86 **northeast of the country:** "Убийство журналистов было только началом." Dossier Center, June 18, 2023.

86 **viewed peace in CAR:** Interview with Khartoum Agreement participant. 2023.

86 **started in May:** Russian participant in Khartoum Agreement. 2023.

87 **raids on migrants:** "Умер создатель ЧВК «ЕНОТ» Игорь Мангушев. Несколько дней назад его ранили выстрелом в голову." *Meduza.*

87 **support from the FSB:** Friend of Igor Mangushev. 2023.

87 **news he believed in:** Interview with Russian journalist. 2023.

87 **touched down in CAR:** Vasil'yev, Viktor. "Что делал в Африке погибший в Донбассе капитан Мангушев (позывной Берег)." *Regnum*, Feb. 9, 2023.

87 **Economic Community of Central African States:** Interview with armed group source. 2023.

88 **inclusive narrative:** Russian participant in Khartoum Agreement. 2023.

88 **"blessing":** Ibid.

88 **paid the rebel leaders:** Armed group participant in Khartoum Agreement. 2023.

88 **perceived closeness to the UAE:** Russian participant in Khartoum Agreement. 2023.

88 **Ngrébada agreed to pay:** Armed group participant in Khartoum Agreement. 2023.

89 **identity interests:** Russian participant in Khartoum Agreement. 2023.

89 **"hijack the anti-Balaka":** Russian participant in Khartoum Agreement. 2023.

89 **"some of his own funds":** Ibid.

89 **"stability in their country":** "Central African Republic: UN Chief Hails Signing of New Peace Agreement." https://www.un.org /peacebuilding/news/central-african-republic-un-chief-hails-signing -new-peace-agreement.

90 **to work in their territories:** Armed group participant in Khartoum Agreement. 2023.

90 **wanted free circulation:** Armed group participant in Khartoum Agreement. 2023.

90 **"political marketplace":** De Waal, Alex. *The Real Politics of the Horn of Africa: Money, War and the Business of Power* (Polity, 2015).

91 **"But I will negotiate":** Ibid., 3.

91 **a few days earlier:** Ibid., 4.

91 **bring peace for years:** Russian participant in Khartoum Agreement. 2023.

91 **"Deputy Defense Minister Ruslan Tsalikov":** Russian participant in Khartoum Agreement. 2023.

91 **"armed groups that are to blame":** Interview with Georges. 2019.

CHAPTER 4: MERCENARIES

94   "and economic methods": "«Публичные казни мародеров и другие зрелищные мероприятия»: советы людей Пригожина свергнутому диктатору." МБХ медиа, April 25, 2019.

94   with "Russia": Ibid.

94   "there's a lot of misunderstanding": Interview with Mikhail Potepkin. 2023.

94   and Darfuri politician: Berridge, Willow, et al. *Sudan's Unfinished Democracy: The Promise and Betrayal of a People's Revolution* (Oxford University Press, 2022).

95   "slums outside the capital": Interview with "Nazar." 2023.

96   "mosque, hospital, and kindergarten": "«Публичные казни мародеров и другие зрелищные мероприятия»: советы людей Пригожина свергнутому диктатору." МБХ медиа, April, 25, 2019.

96   "looters": Lister, Tim; Shukla, Sebastian; Elbagir, Nima. "Fake News and Public Executions." CNN, Apr. 25, 2019.

96   broached the idea of Bashir's ouster: Berridge, Willow, et al. *Sudan's Unfinished Democracy.*

96   yielded little: Margolin, Jack. *The Wagner Group: Inside Russia's Mercenary Army* (Reaktion Books, 2024).

97   "never appear one leader's lackey": Russian PMC source. 2024.

97   gold business with the RSF leader: Russian source close to events. 2024.

97   "and helicopter engines": Margolin, Jack. *The Wagner Group.*

97   "immigration, and import activities": Margolin, Jack. *The Wagner Group.*

98   Great Toyota War: Ball, Sam. "Coup Leader? CIA Asset? Mystery Surrounds Libya's Rogue General Haftar." France 24, May 19, 2014.

98   opposition in Chad: Ibid.

98   France deployed special forces: "Anger on Libyan Streets over French Military Action." *Al Jazeera*, July 21, 2016.

99   deal between Russia and Egypt: Interview with Jalel Harchaoui. 2024.

99   equipment was discussed: "Egypt Acts as Middleman for Russia-Libya Arms Deal." *Al-Monitor*, Feb. 19, 2015.

99   attack helicopters: "UAE Weapon Deliveries to Haftar 'Escalated' Since Arms Embargo." *New Arab*, Sept. 30, 2020.

99 ordered another eleven: Ibid.

99 "the first Russian PMC": "«Мы поднимем имидж страны»: основатель первой российской частной военной компании дал интервью RT." *RT*, Jan. 25, 2018.

99 "personal protection": Ibid.

99 convoys in Iraq: See RSB website: https://rsb-group.org/phoenix-iraq

99 "king of beasts": "«Мы поднимем имидж страны»: основатель первой российской частной военной компании дал интервью RT." *RT*, Jan. 25, 2018.

100 Sergei Shoigu's brainchild: Interview with source close to events. 2024.

100 an offer he couldn't refuse: Ibid.

100 "we will work more in Libya": Interview with source close to events. 2024.

100 fair price, paid in cash: Ibid.

100 Stanislav Petlinsky brokered the deal: Dobrokhotov, Roman, et al., "A Most Wanted Man: Fugitive Wirecard COO Jan Marsalek Exposed as Decade-Long GRU Spy." *Insider*, Mar. 1, 2024.

100 Austrian national and GRU asset: Ibid.

101 "hand with the money in it?": Interview with source close to events. 2024.

101 Prigozhin would supply the men: Rondeaux, Candace; Margolin, Jack; Imhof, Oliver. "The Abu Dhabi Express." New America, Nov. 2021.

102 oil production under his control: Lachner, Wolfram. "Libya's Conflicts Enter a Dangerous New Phase." *Stiftung Wissenschaft und Politik (SWP)*, Feb. 22, 2019.

102 left Saudi Arabia with more funding: "Timeline: Haftar's Months-Long Offensive to Seize Tripoli." *Al Jazeera*, Feb. 19, 2020.

102 appeared on the battlefield: Eltagouri, Yousuf. "Haftar's Final Play." Foreign Policy Research Institute, Apr. 19, 2019.

102 undermining the GRU: Interview with source close to events. 2024.

103 "intercept ships at sea": "Erik Prince Accused of Helping Rebel Libyan General." *Financial Times*, https://www.ft.com/content/661e941b-4c56-4f58-b545-104ffdf67863.

103 Bulgarian and Serbian companies: Dragojlo, Sasa. "Serviced in Serbia: The Lethal Crop Duster Destined for War in Libya." *Balkan Insight*, May 20, 2021.

103 **"criminals really, on the other side"**: Interview with Christiaan Durrant. 2024.

104 **"mercenaries were in the country"**: Interview with Heithem. 2022.

105 directly from the United States: "US Authorizes Financial Support for the Free Syrian Army." *Al-Monitor*, July 27, 2012.

105 **United Kingdom**: Curtis, Mark. "How Britain Engaged in a Covert Operation to Overthrow Assad." *Middle East Eye*, April 27, 2018.

105 **free up GNA personnel**: Pack, Jason, and Wolfgang Pusztai. "Turning the Tide: How Turkey Won the War for Tripoli." Middle East Institute, Nov. 2020.

105 **fought with al-Hamzat militia**: Interview with "Ahmed." 2023. Interviews and research conducted with Syria expert Safa Faki.

105 **"sold off on the black market"**: Interview with Syrian fighter. 2023. Interviews and research conducted with Syria expert Safa Faki.

106 **"maybe going to Raqqa"**: Interview with "Basil." 2024. Interviews and research conducted with Syria expert Safa Faki.

107 **hasty retreat from Tripoli**: "Hundreds More Russian Mercenaries Flee Western Libya: GNA Forces." *Al Jazeera*, May 25, 2020.

108 **"society is not structured that way"**: Interview with Abdul. 2022.

109 **motivation to seize the capital**: Barabanov, Ilya, and Denis Korotkov. *Nash biznes—smert'* (Meduza Publishing, 2024), 190.

110 **"resting on our laurels"**: Russian participant in Khartoum Agreement. 2023.

110 **authorities that benefit them the most**: Plichta, Marcel; Ingasso, Vianney; Lechner, John. "Wagner Is Only One Piece in Central African Republic's Messy Puzzle." *World Politics Review*, Jan. 31, 2023.

110 **enhance their domestic political and economic position**: In other words, extraversion. See: Bayart, Jean-François. *The State in Africa: The Politics of the Belly*, 2nd ed. (Polity, 2009).

111 **an internal investigation found**: Wagner Leaks, Dossier Center. Indexing provided by C4ADS.

111 **large amounts of alcohol**: Ibid.

112 **"fake news"**: Interview with Maka Gbossokotto. 2020.

113 **peddling fake accounts**: See https://about.fb.com/news/2020/12/removing-coordinated-inauthentic-behavior-france-russia/.

113 **through norms and values**: Zakharov, Andrei, et al. "Chef and Chief." *Proekt Media*. July 12, 2023.

113 **"soccer, and samba":** Interview with "Jean-Paul." 2020.

114 **one hundred children were massacred:** "Central African Empire Accused of Killing Students." *New York Times*, May 15, 1979.

114 **diamonds during his reign:** "The Diamond Scandal That Helped Bring Down France's Giscard." *AFP*, Dec. 3, 2020.

114 **from exile in late 2019:** "Former CAR President François Bozizé Back from Six-Year Exile, Says Party." France 24, Dec. 16, 2019.

114 **international warrant for his arrest:** "Bozizé Returns to Central African Republic." Human Rights Watch, Dec. 23, 2019.

114 **ruled against his candidacy:** "C.A.R.'s Ex-President François Bozizé Barred from Dec. Polls." *Africanews*, Dec. 3, 2020.

114 **to overthrow Touadéra:** Interview with armed group leader. 2023.

115 **allocation of ministerial posts:** Interview with armed group leader. 2023.

115 **dealing with drones:** Friend of Igor Mangushev. 2024.

116 **"We promised the president we would protect him":** Interview with Vitaly Perfilev. 2023.

116 **oversee the defense of Bangui:** Interview with Marat Gabidullin. 2023.

116 **"attacking towns along the way":** Interview with UPC fighter. 2023.

116 **"something would be done":** Interview with armed group leader. 2023.

116 **Bimbo in the south:** "First Post-Election Attacks on Bangui." *ReliefWeb*, Jan. 14, 2021.

117 **pushed back the ill-equipped assault:** Olivier, Mathieu. "Centrafrique-Russie : qui est Vitali Perfilev, le patron de Wagner à Bangui ?" JeuneAfrique.com, April 1, 2022.

117 **40 percent:** Lechner, John, and Alexandra Lamarche. "Outside Powers and Making the Conflict in the Central African Republic Worse." *Foreign Policy*, Jan. 22, 2021.

117 **hometown of Bossongoa:** Interview with "Jacque." 2022. Conducted in collaboration with Barbara Debout.

119 **pulled into Boyo:** "Architects of Terror." *The Sentry*, June 2023.

120 **"told us to kill all the men":** Ibid.

120 **"harsh but effective military force":** Interview with former Russian military officer. 2023.

120 **"no sentimentality":** Ibid.

120 **"settle in the villages":** "Architects of Terror." *The Sentry*, June 2023.

121   "border with Cameroon": Margolin, Jack. *The Wagner Group.*

121   present around Bambari: Ibid.

122   "there's security": Interview with "Omar." 2022.

122   "they are not part of armed groups": Interview with pro-government commander. 2023.

124   "learned through experience": Interview with Vitaly Perfilev. 2023.

124    $35,000,000 per year: "Affaire de 400 millions de Wagner, le ministre des finances, Hervé Ndoba, dans le collimateur." *Corbeau News*, April 25, 2023.

125   preferential mining allowance: "Treasury Sanctions Illicit Gold Companies Funding Wagner Forces and Wagner Group Facilitator." U.S. Department of the Treasury, June 27, 2023.

125   reaching those levels: "Russian Mercenaries Exploit African Country as They Fight in Ukraine." NBC News, June 1, 2023.

125    $200,000 of lumber: Interview with Western official. 2023.

125   "with Russian technology": Cohen, Roger, and Mauricio Lima. "Putin Wants Fealty, and He's Found It in Africa." *New York Times*, Dec. 24, 2022.

125   "Russians will get out of Africa": Maclean, Ruth, et al. "Russian Official in Africa Wounded by Package Bomb, Moscow Says." *New York Times*, Dec. 16, 2022.

CHAPTER 5: LIBERATORS

129   "zombie host for Wagner": Loyd, Anthony. "Diamond-Rich African Country Is a Zombie Host for Wagner." *Times*, May 19, 2023.

129   "wandering European enters at his peril": Achebe, Chinua. "An Image of Africa: Racism in Conrad's 'Heart of Darkness.'" *Massachusetts Review* 57, no. 1 (2016): 14–27.

129   "submitting to the control of logic": Woolf, Virginia. *Collected Essays*, 1st American ed. (Harcourt, Brace and World, 1967).

130   territorial integrity of Ukraine: "Treasury Sanctions Companies and Individuals Advancing Russian Malign Activities in Africa." U.S. Department of the Treasury, June 24, 2024.

130   "2016 U.S. presidential election": "Treasury Escalates Sanctions Against the Russian Government's Attempts to Influence U.S. Elections." U.S. Department of the Treasury, June 24, 2024.

130 **malign operations in Africa:** Ibid.

130 **claim to shaping world order:** For an authoritative account on the (mis)use of history in post-Soviet Russia, see: McGlynn, Jade. *Memory Makers: The Politics of the Past in Putin's Russia* (Bloomsbury Publishing Plc, 2023).

131 **a Western proxy:** Ibid.

131 *extraversion:* Bayart, Jean-François. *The State in Africa: The Politics of the Belly,* 2nd ed. (Polity, 2009).

132 **$20,000 per month:** Source close to events. 2023.

132 **just beginning to tackle:** See: Perera, Suda. "Methodology of the Excluded: Conspiracy as Discourse in the Eastern DRC." *Peacebuilding*: 1–16.

133 **techniques of governance:** Harrison, Graham. "Wagner in Africa: Political Excess and the African Condition." *ROAPE*, July 13, 2023.

133 **diamond fields:** Shukla, Sebastian, and Tim Lister. "Murdered Journalists Were Tracked by Police with Shadowy Russian Links, Evidence Shows." CNN, Jan. 10, 2019.

134 **an assassination plot:** Ibid.

134 **ties to Russian trainers:** Ibid.

134 **ideology: action movies:** Barshad, Amos. "How Russian Action Movies Are Selling War." *New York Times*, Oct. 12, 2022.

134 **"was an unknown entity":** Interview with Maksim Shugalei. 2023.

134 **recruit a Tuareg militia:** "Saif al-Islam Makes New Appearance." *Libya Times*, July 29, 2018.

135 **Russian film industry:** "Впервые в мире художественная документалистика: продюсер «Трииксмедиа» раскрыл секреты съемок «Шугалея»" *Argumenti*, March 2, 2020.

135 **"first to arrive to fight Gaddafi":** Interview with Kirill Semenov. 2023.

135 **Gazprom and Tatneft:** Ibid.

137 **economic and political marginalization:** See Crisis Group: https://www.crisisgroup.org/africa/east-and-southern-africa/mozambique

137 **"decrease his dependence":** Russian source close to events. 2023.

138 **"Everyone and their uncle":** South African PMC source. 2023.

138 **"a major state backing them":** Ibid.

138 **touched down in Maputo:** "Russian Think Tank Publishes Illegal Pro-Frelimo Opinion Poll." *Zitamar News*, Oct. 10, 2019.

138 **beheadings of Wagner:** Sauer, Pjotr. "7 Kremlin-Linked Mercenaries Killed in Mozambique in October—Military Sources." *Moscow Times,* Oct. 31, 2019.

139 **"first President Modibo Keita":** Thurston, Alexander. *Jihadists of North Africa and the Sahel: Local Politics and Rebel Groups* (Cambridge University Press, 2020), 106.

140 **hereditary government offices:** Ibid., 152.

140 **"strategic engagement":** Ibid., 118.

140 **MNLA's popularity:** Ibid., 90.

140 **acceptable to the West:** See Thurston on "off-ramps," 140.

140 **politically relevant:** Ibid., 103.

141 **"coup within a coup":** "After Two Coups, Mali Needs Regional Support to Bolster Democracy." United States Institute of Peace, December 2021.

141 **perhaps eighty-five soldiers:** "Mali." United States Department of State, https://www.state.gov/reports/country-reports-on-terrorism -2019/mali/.

142 **Guinea and Mali:** Russian PMC source. 2023.

143 **"conflict of interest between the two":** Russian source in Mali. 2023.

143 **"would be a government initiative":** Ibid.

144 **$10 million per month:** https://www.state.gov/potential-deployment -of-the-wagner-group-in-mali/.

144 **"went to Russia's account":** Russian source in Mali. 2023.

145 **Sergei Laktionov:** Roger, Bejamin. "Wagner's Mercenary Gold Rush in Mali." *Africa Report,* July 7, 2023.

145 **mining portfolio:** Ibid.

145 **"were al-Qaeda and ISIS":** Interview with "Nazar." 2023.

145 **in the Mopti region:** "Au Mali, premiers accrochages entre Wagner et djihadistes." *Le Figaro,* Jan. 5, 2022.

146 **under the control of JNIM:** "Mali: Massacre by Army, Foreign Soldiers." Human Rights Watch, April 5, 2022.

146 **"were taken out and shot":** Ibid.

146 **"point blank":** Ibid.

147 **source of government revenue:** Roger, Bejamin. "Wagner's Mercenary Gold Rush in Mali." *Africa Report,* July 7, 2023.

147 **safety and stability:** Interview with Gao resident. 2023.

147 **"it's bad now":** Interview with local official. 2023.

148   "animals in the bush to hunt": Interview with *dozo* leader. 2023.

148   killed their parents and children: Interview with local official. 2023.

150   French military base: Risemberg, Annie. "France Blames Russian Mercenaries in Mali for False Claims About Mass Graves." *Voice of America*, Apr. 22, 2022.

CHAPTER 6: HEROES

152   "product of the Soviet era": "Article by Vladimir Putin 'On the Historical Unity of Russians and Ukrainians.'" President of Russia, July 12, 2021, http://en.kremlin.ru/events/president/news/66181.

153   "so too is the Russian Federation which he leads": Interview with Stanislav Vorobyev. 2023.

153   as a security issue: McGlynn, Jade. *Memory Makers: The Politics of the Past in Putin's Russia* (Bloomsbury Publishing Plc, 2023), 17.

153   and war reenactments: Ibid.,128–55.

154   themselves in Russian history: Zygar, Mikhail. *War and Punishment: Putin, Zelensky, and the Path to Russia's Invasion of Ukraine* (New York: Scribner, 2023), 352.

154   Russia's glorious past: Ibid.

154   "very narrow circle": Ibid., 357.

154   for just a few meetings: Ibid., 352.

154   Sergei Kiriyenko: Yapparova, Lilia. "Грубо говоря, мы начали войну Как отправка ЧВК Вагнера на фронт помогла Пригожину наладить отношения с Путиным—и что такое «собянинский полк». Расследование «Медузы» о наемниках на войне в Украине." *Meduza*, July 13, 2022.

155   GRU General Vladimir Alekseyev: "Best of Enemies: Wagner Chief Prigozhin's Feud with Defense Minister to Blow Up in His Face." *Insider*, May 12, 2023.

155   manage the recruitment drive: Ibid.

155   Prigozhin furious: Ibid.

155   absence to address it: Interview with "Adam." 2023.

155   "like its own family": Interview with Redut commander. 2023.

156   backtracked on his threats: "Best of Enemies: Wagner Chief Prigozhin's Feud with Defense Minister to Blow Up in His Face." *Insider*, May 12, 2023.

156 **Beijing Olympics:** Zygar, Mikhail. *War and Punishment*, 364.

156 **on the phone:** "Best of Enemies: Wagner Chief Prigozhin's Feud with Defense Minister to Blow up in His Face." *Insider*, May 12, 2023.

156 **he told Ukraine's citizens:** Marson, James. "Ukraine's Leader Zelensky Is 'Target Number One' for Putin." *Wall Street Journal*, Feb. 25, 2022.

156 **looking for the president:** Rana, Manveen. "Volodymyr Zelensky: Russian Mercenaries Ordered to Kill Ukraine's President." *Times*, July 8, 2023.

157 **"lay down arms and go home":** "Address by the President of the Russian Federation." President of Russia, Feb. 24, 2022.

000 **center and asylum shelter:** "United States Designates Russian Imperial Movement and Leaders as Global Terrorists." U.S. Department of State, April 7, 2020.

158 **Yunus-bek Yevkurov:** "Best of Enemies: Wagner Chief Prigozhin's Feud with Defense Minister to Blow Up in His Face." *Insider*, May 12, 2023.

158 **Wagner was in the fight:** Ibid.

158 **"Wagner is in Ukraine":** Prigozhin associate. 2024.

158 **"higher priority for Prigozhin":** Russian source in Mali. 2024.

158 **"Africa was never raised":** Ibid.

159 **humanitarian corridor to Russia:** Interview with Viktoriya. 2022.

159 **lost up to sixty men:** Yapparova, Lilia. "Грубо говоря, мы начали войну Как отправка ЧВК Вагнера на фронт помогла Пригожину наладить отношения с Путиным—и что такое «собянинский полк». Расследование «Медузы» о наемниках на войне в Украине." *Meduza*, July 13, 2022.

159 **"with its 170-year history":** Interview with "Boyar." 2023.

159 **"toward Popasna":** Margolin, Jack. *The Wagner Group: Inside Russia's Mercenary Army* (Reaktion Books, 2024).

160 **"it was great news":** "Герой России, командир ЧВК "Вагнер" Ратибор вспоминает, как с отрядом вступали в спецоперацию." *LiveJournal*. June 24, 2023. https://deda14.livejournal.com/1558532.html.

160 **"a distance of ten feet":** Interview with Boyar. 2023.

160 **"Orchestra Awaits You":** "Оркестр W ждет тебя В российских городах появились билборды с призывом «трудоустроиться» в ЧВК и стать наемником. Издание «Верстка» рассказало истории вербовщиков, которые стоят за этим." *Meduza*, July 20, 2022.

161   **systems of governance:** Schwirtz, Michael. "Vory v Zakone Has Hallowed Place in Russian Criminal Lore." *New York Times*, July 29, 2008.

161   **were switched off:** Savel'yev, Sergei. "Данные о вербовке заключённых для войны в Украине (сентябрь 2022)." *Gulagu.net*, Nov. 15, 2022.

161   **were acting differently:** Interview with Russian PoW. 2023.

161   **"prisoner-to-soldier program":** Telegram post, @poisk_in_ua, December 12, 2022. https://t.me/poisk_in_ua/9191.

162   **assault on Vuhledar:** *Ugledar* in Russian.

162   **southwest of Donetsk:** Telegram post, @teamnavalny, September 14, 2022. https://t.me/teamnavalny/13903.

162   **for convict recruitment:** Interview with Mark Galeotti. 2023.

162   **formed seven years earlier:** Statiev, Alex. "Penal Units in the Red Army." *Europe-Asia Studies* 62, no. 5 (2010): 721–47.

162   **penal battalions:** Ibid.

162   **"crimes with their blood":** Ibid.

162   **"execute any soldier":** Ibid.

162   **Vladimir Vysotsky:** Ibid.

163   **Overcrowding is widespread:** "Russia behind Bars: The Peculiarities of the Russian Prison System." OSW Centre for Eastern Studies, Feb. 7, 2019.

163   **advocate Marina Litvinovich:** "«Ты зверь, тебя не жалко» Как сотрудники ФСИН оправдывают пытки в российских колониях и тюрьмах." *Lenta*, Oct. 11, 2021.

163   **named Vlad told me:** Interview with Russian PoW. 2023.

163   **"motherland with blood":** Telegram post, @poisk_in_ua, December 12, 2022. https://t.me/poisk_in_ua/9191.

163   **"considered deserters and shot":** Telegram post, @teamnavalny, September 14, 2022. https://t.me/teamnavalny/13903.

163   **forty-eight thousand to forty-nine thousand convicts to fight in Ukraine:** Interview with Olga Romanova. 2023.

164   **"Of course, you have to go":** Interview with Russian PoW. 2023.

164   **"used to a regimented schedule":** Reuters interviews with Russian prisoners. Special thanks to Felix Light for sharing research notes. See also: Lebedev, Filipp, and Felix Light. "Wagner's convicts tell of horrors of Ukraine War." *Reuters*, Mar. 16, 2023. https://www.reuters.com /investigates/special-report/ukraine-crisis-russia-wagner/

"what an idiot I was": Ibid.

164 "of them figured things out": Interview with Dmitry. 2023. See also: Lebedev, Filipp, and Felix Light. "Wagner's convicts tell of horrors of Ukraine War." *Reuters*, Mar. 16, 2023. https://www.reuters.com/investigates/special-report/ukraine-crisis-russia-wagner/

165 tell right away were "200": "200" or "Cargo 200" (gruz dvesti, or dvukhsotnye) was a Soviet military term for the transportation of military fatalities. The term is still used by soldiers throughout the former Soviet Union.

165 storming Lysychansk and Severodonetsk: Barabanov, Il'ya. "Назвать тебя нечем, кроме одного слова'. Как война в Украине поссорила Пригожина и Герасимова и вскрыла конфликты среди российских силовиков." BBC News Русская служба, Dec. 27, 2022.

165 entirety of the Luhansk region: Ibid.

165 whole of Donbas: "Битва за Бахмут: хронология одного из самых кровопролитных сражений войны в Украине." ГОЛОС АМЕРИКИ, May 23, 2023.

165 part of the assault detachments: Interview with "Sasha." 2023.

165 "them into hell right away": Interview with former Wagner fighter. 2023.

167 "crawling out of the trenches": Interview with Ukrainian soldier, Sam. 2023.

168 "Thirty minutes later, another wave": Interview with Ukrainian soldier, Salam. 2023.

169 the city's trolley depot: Interview with Azov commander, "Erik." 2023.

169 eighty pro-Russian militants out of the city: "Эрнест Громов, позывной Эрик, экс-разведчик полка "Азов": Спокойствие наказывает людей, к войне надо относиться серьезно!" *Will Live!*, March 11, 2020.

169 army until 1995: Fokht, Elizaveta, and Anastasia Lotareva. " 'Тот, кто нам тело отдаст, по-любому будет виновный'. История жизни и смерти Евгения Нужина, забитого кувалдой." BBC News Русская служба, Nov. 17, 2022.

169 twenty-four years: "Что-То Не То Скажешь и Тебя Обнулят, Так Двоих Расстреляли"—Полонений Російський Зек "Вагнеровець." https://www.youtube.com/watch?v=t4dJRPHuzFg.

169 slapped onto his stint: Ibid.

170 "small amount of the time": "'Тот, кто нам тело отдаст, по-любому будет виновный'. История жизни и смерти Евгения Нужина, забитого кувалдой." BBC News Русская служба, Nov. 17, 2022.

170 "I have relatives here": "Что-То Не То Скажешь и Тебя Обнулят, Так Двоих Расстреляли"—Полонений Російський Зек "Вагнеровець." https://www.youtube.com/watch?v=t4dJRPHuzFg.

170 nostalgic for life in the Soviet Union: "'Тот, кто нам тело отдаст, по-любому будст виновный'. История жизни и смерти Евгепия Нужина, забитого кувалдой." BBC News Русская служба, Nov. 27, 2022.

170 "fight against the Russians": Кутепов, Слава. "«Так животных не убивают, как эти нелюди». Что известно о казни экс-бойца ЧВК Вагнера Евгения Нужина." *RTVI*, Nov. 23, 2022.

170 prison system to Ukraine: Interview with Mark Galeotti. 2023.

171 "betrayed consciously": Faulconbridge, Guy. "Video Shows Sledge-hammer Execution of Russian Mercenary." Reuters, Nov. 13, 2022.

171 bloody sledgehammer to the EU Parliament: Sota (@Sota_Vision), X, Nov. 23, 2022, https://x.com/Sota_Vision/status/1595652215934418944.

172 terrorist organization: "Russia's Wagner Group Says Sending Blood-Stained Sledgehammer to EU Parliament." *Moscow Times*, Nov. 24, 2022.

172 gifting a sledgehammer: "Лидер «Справедливой России» Миронов получил кувалду в подарок от Пригожина." Газета.*Ru*, Jan. 20, 2023.

172 legalizing Wagner in Russia: "Russian Politician Poses with Sledge-hammer in Tribute to Wagner Mercenaries." Reuters, Jan. 20, 2023.

172 recruiting convicts on its own: "Минобороны России—вслед за ЧВК Вагнера—начало вербовать заключенных на войну с Украиной Из них создают спецотряд «Шторм», куда войдут осужденные сотрудники силовых ведомств." *Meduza*, Oct. 11, 2022.

172 "a higher chance of survival": Ibid.

172 denied the allegations: Sharp, Alexandra. "Gruesome Videos Put Russia's Brutality Back in the Spotlight." *Foreign Policy*, April 12, 2023.

173 children on orders: Pennington, Sarah, and Josh Dean. "Two Russians Claiming to Be Former Wagner Commanders Admit Killing Children and Civilians in Ukraine." CNN, April 18, 2023.

173 **from his service in March:** Kottasová, Ivana, et al. "A Wagner Soldier Returned Home after Fighting for Russia. Days Later He Was a Murder Suspect." CNN, March 31, 2023.

173 **knife around town:** Ibid.

173 **eighty-five-year-old woman:** "В Кировской области арестовали экс-бойца 'Вагнера' за убийство пенсионерки." РИА Новости, March 31, 2023.

173 **Giorgiy Siukaev:** Interview with Alik Puhati. 2023. See also: Sauer, Pjotr. "Murder, 'Alcohol and Prostitutes': Wagner Convicts Pardoned by Putin Return to Terrorise Home Towns." *Guardian*, April 22, 2023.

173 **murder of a beloved local:** Sauer, Pjotr. "Murder, 'Alcohol and Prostitutes': Wagner Convicts Pardoned by Putin Return to Terrorise Home Towns." *Guardian*, April 22, 2023.

174 **"rude" to passersby:** "ЧВК «Вагнер» опубликовала «справку» об убийстве в Цхинвали." Эхо Кавказа, April 19, 2023.

174 **"stealing bicycles":** "Пригожин сообщил об истечении контрактов с ЧВК «Вагнер» у 26 тыс. бывших заключенных." Коммерсантъ, May 2, 2023.

174 **prior to the military operation in Ukraine:** Ibid.

174 **new lease on life:** See: Lebedev, Filipp, and Felix Light. "Wagner's Convicts Tell of Horrors of Ukraine War." Reuters, March 16, 2023.

174 **"delivered on all his promises":** Ibid.

174 **twenty thousand men to their deaths:** See: "Russia's Meat Grinder Soldiers—50,000 Confirmed Dead." BBC, April 17, 2024.

CHAPTER 7: TRAITORS

176 **for assault and robbery:** Interview with "Pyotr." 2023.

177 **for Bakhmut itself:** "The Battle for Ukraine's Bakhmut: A Timeline." *Al Jazeera*, May 20, 2023.

177 **own enlistment of prisoners:** "Минобороны России—вслед за ЧВК Вагнера—начало вербовать заключенных на войну с Украиной Из них создают спецотряд «Шторм», куда войдут осужденные сотрудники силовых ведомств." *Meduza*, Oct. 11, 2022.

177 **"volunteer from prison":** Ibid.

177 **"list of what was needed":** Telegram post, @Prigozhin_hat, February 16, 2023. https://t.me/Prigozhin_hat/2660.

178 **"bypassing Shoigu"**: Lee, Rob. 2023. Twitter, https://twitter.com/RALee85/status/1613204188368097282.

178 **"management of Russian forces"**: "Ukraine War: Sergei Surovikin Removed as Commander of Ukraine Invasion Force." BBC, Jan. 11, 2023.

179 **"tip of the spear biting"**: Telegram post, @Prigozhin_hat, March 10, 2023. https://t.me/Prigozhin_hat/2823.

180 **Alexander Khodakovsky**: See: "«Боеприпасов просто стали давать как всем»: Ходаковский прокомментировал ситуацию с боеприпасами для ЧВК Вагнер." *Dzen.ru,* Feb. 22, 2023. https://dzen.ru/a/Y_W1qyCGcVQwO9uh?experiment=931375.

180 **"Wagner control 70% of Bakhmut"**: "Пригожин написал открытое письмо Шойгу—Новости—город Рязань на городском сайте RZN. info." RZN.info, March 20, 2023.

181 **"future fate of this ammunition"**: Telegram post, @Prigozhin_hat, March 29, 2023. https://t.me/Prigozhin_hat/2959.

181 **"everyone needs a private army"**: Telegram post, @Prigozhin_hat, April 21, 2023. https://t.me/Prigozhin_hat/3154.

181 **"[and] no doctors"**: Telegram post, @brussinf, April 21, 2023. https://t.me/brussinf/5885. See also: Fokht, Elizaveta, and Il'ya Barabanov. "'Поток' под Бахмутом. Что известно о ЧВК, связанных с 'Газпромом.'" BBC News Русская служба, May 16, 2023.

182 **"mess of a PMC they've created"**: Ibid.

182 **Wagner's flanks**: Ibid.

182 **to continue fighting**: Ibid.

182 **an audience of one**: Interview with Andrei Zakharov. 2023.

183 **"ultimately his downfall"**: Associate of Yevgeny Prigozhin. 2024.

183 **"mahogany offices"**: See: https://www.youtube.com/watch?v=j-bALDPCp4w

183 **ten thousand men had died fighting**: "Yevgeny Prigozhin: Wagner Group Boss Says He Will Pull Fighters out of Bakhmut." BBC, May 5, 2023.

183 **"reckless behavior"**: Interview with "Sasha." 2023.

183 **leaving Bakhmut on May 10**: Telegram post, @Prigozhin_hat, May 5, 2023. https://t.me/Prigozhin_hat/3252.

184 **"politically speaking"**: Interview with Stanislav Vorobyev. 2023.

184 **idiot decisions of their commanders**: "Prigozhin Claims 'Deception' and 'Threats' from Defense Ministry." *Moscow Times,* May 9, 2023.

184   **"Ministry of Intrigue"**: Telegram Post, @Prigozhin_hat, May 9, 2023. https://t.me/Prigozhin_hat/3280.

184   **"a complete asshole"**: "Пригожин записал видео к 9 мая—про «победу дедов» и какого-то «счастливого дедушку», который может оказаться «законченным мудаком» Попробуйте угадать, кого он имел в виду. Вот главное из этого видео." *Meduza*, May 9, 2023.

185   **the necropolis below**: See https://x.com/Jack_Mrgln/status /1660725557460615168

185   **official MoD project**: Source close to events. 2024.

185   **pass along Americans warnings**: "Евгений Пригожин о трагедии 8 февраля 2018 в Хишаме." https://vk.com/@bolshayaigra_war -evgenii-prigozhin-o-tragedii-8-fevralya-2018-v-hishame.

186   **sign a contract with the Ministry of Defense**: Faulconbridge, Guy. "Prigozhin Says Wagner Will Not Sign Contracts with Russia Defence Minister." Reuters, June 11, 2023.

186   **"from under Shoigu's thumb"**: Former Prigozhin associate. 2024.

186   **tanks, and armored vehicles**: Pancevski, Bojan. "Wagner's Prigozhin Planned to Capture Military Leaders." *Wall Street Journal*, June 28, 2023.

186   **across the border of Luhansk**: Ibid.

186   **two days before it was to take place**: Ibid.

187   **"together with the whole NATO block"**: "Wagner Chief Says Russian Invasion of Ukraine Unjustified." *Moscow Times*, June 23, 2023.

187   **Putin's close inner circle**: Sauer, Pjotr. "Wagner Chief Accuses Moscow of Lying to Public about Ukraine." *Guardian*, June 23, 2023.

187   **"they wanted more"**: "Wagner Chief Says Russian Invasion of Ukraine Unjustified." *Moscow Times*, June 23, 2023.

187   **there were many losses**: Telegram post, @Prigozhin_hat, June 23, 2023. https://t.me/Prigozhin_hat/3797.

188   **"then return to the front"**: Telegram post, @Prigozhin_hat, June 23, 2023. https://t.me/Prigozhin_hat/3799.

188   **"March for Justice"**: Telegram post, @Prigozhin_hat, June 23, 2023. https://t.me/Prigozhin_hat/3803.

188   **"permanent deployment points"**: «Пока не поздно, нужно остановить колонны и подчиниться воле президента». Генерал

Суровикин призвал бойцов ЧВК Вагнера «решить вопросы мирным путем».” *Meduza*, June 24, 2023.

189 **clenching the bench:** Meduza. “Пригожин встретился в Ростове-на-Дону с замминистра обороны и замглавы Генштаба.” YouTube, June 24, 2023, https://www.youtube.com/watch?v=YBoYuGxp4Tc

190 **regions in their path:** “В Москве, а также в Московской и Воронежской областях ввели режим «контртеррористической операции» Теперь силовики смогут законно читать вашу переписку и входить в любые помещения без решения суда.” *Meduza*, Jun 24, 2023.

190 **“not sure we had a clear view”:** Sanger, David E. *New Cold Wars: China's Rise, Russia's Invasion, and America's Struggle to Defend the West* (New York: Crown, 2024).

190 **“victory was stolen from it”:** For a full play-by-play, see Meduza's Telegram channel: https://t.me/meduzalive.

190 **“has confronted us is treason”:** Ibid.

191 **“were also stolen”:** Ibid.

191 **“shelf of unconvincing wigs”:** Millar, Paul. “How Russian State Media Is Tearing Down Prigozhin's Reputation as a 'Man of the People.'” France 24, Jul. 7, 2023.

191 **convinced Prigozhin to end:** Telegram post, @meduzalive, June 24, 2023. https://t.me/meduzalive/86607.

192 **according to the plan:** Telegram post, @meduzalive, June 24, 2023. https://t.me/meduzalive/86612.

192 **thirteen Russian servicemen:** See also: Pigni, Giovanni. “'Half Patriot, Half Traitor': Wagner Fighters Reflect on Botched Rebellion with Resentment, Uncertainty.” *Moscow Times*, July 9, 2023.

192 **“was bizarre”:** Interview with “Nazar.” 2023.

193 **“end of the story has not come!”:** Interview with “Arkady.” 2023.

193 **“Putin's favorite band”:** Correspondence with Vitaly Perfilev. 2023.

193 **$1 billion from the government:** “Путин сообщил о госфинансировании ЧВК 'Вагнер' на сумму 86 млрд рублей.” Радио Свобода, June 27, 2023.

193 **“finally got your meeting”:** “Путин рассказал «Ъ» подробности встречи с бойцами ЧВК «Вагнер».” Коммерсантъ, July 13, 2023.

194 **four years in prison:** “Prominent Russian nationalist who insulted Putin jailed for four years.” *Reuters,* Jan. 25, 2024.

195 **"for new phase in Africa"**: Telegram post, @Prigozhin_hat, July 19, 2023. https://t.me/Prigozhin_hat/3819.

195 **would continue as usual:** "Wagner Will Continue Mali, C. Africa Operations—Lavrov." *Moscow Times*, June 26, 2023.

196 **Russian domestic affairs:** "Prigozhin: Wagner Boss Spotted in Russia during Africa Summit." BBC, July 28, 2023.

196 **"take this over, the GRU?":** Wagner associate. 2023.

197 **"Nothing's happened yet":** Interview with PMC Convoy representative. 2023.

197 **"destroying ISIS and al-Qaeda":** Telegram post, @Prigozhin_hat, August 21, 2023. https://t.me/Prigozhin_hat/3828.

197 **support Wagner over any MoD replacement:** See, for example, "Putin Moves to Seize Control of Wagner's Global Empire." *Wall Street Journal*, June 28, 2023.

197 **"new government program":** Source close to events. 2024.

198 **Kristina Raspopova:** "Who Was on the Plane That Crashed, Presumably Killing Yevgeny Prigozhin?" *Al Jazeera*, Aug. 24, 2023.

198 **region northwest of Moscow:** "Wagner Chief Prigozhin Was on Plane That Crashed in Russia, Aviation Agency Says." CNN, Aug. 23, 2023.

198 **"for the common cause as well":** AKI press news. "Путин высказался о возможной гибели Пригожина." YouTube, Aug. 24, 2023, https://www.youtube.com/watch?v=RyizUcUFpD4.

200 **lasted just forty minutes:** For details on Prigozhin's funeral, see Barabanov, Ilya, and Denis Korotkov. *Nash biznes—smert'*. Meduza Publishing, 2024.

200 **red flowers on the fresh grave:** Ibid.

CONCLUSION

201 **armed group members:** "L'emprise des mercenaires russes Wagner en Centrafrique." RFI, Feb. 6, 2022.

202 **"closure":** zain. "ميدتى: قفلنا الحدود مع افريقيا الوسطى ءادر للفتنة." 3 Jan. 2023.

203 **"geopolitical game":** Interview with Coalition Siriri representative. 2023.

203 **move his men into CAR territory:** Interview with source close to events. 2023.

203 **Haftar's 128 Brigade as an intermediary:** Interview with source close to events. 2024.

204 **each month for oil and gas:** McWilliams, Ben et al. "The European Union–Russia Energy Divorce." *Bruegel*, Feb. 22, 2024.

204 **local officials had replaced:** See Schouten, Peer. *Roadblock Politics: The Origins of Violence in Central Africa* (Cambridge University Press, 2022).

204 **separate from the local conflict:** See Lombard, Louisa. *State of Rebellion: Violence and Intervention in the Central African Republic* (Zed Books Ltd, 2016).

205 **ethnic cleansing in Darfur:** Gallopin, Jean-Baptiste. " 'The Massalit Will Not Come Home.' " Human Rights Watch, May 2024.

205 **funded the RSF to stop migration to Europe:** Bando, Suliman. "Border from Hell: How the EU's Migration Partnership Legitimizes Sudan's Militia State." *Enough*, April 2017.

206 **"Wagnerization of the Russian army":** Kofman, Michael. 2024.

207 **Bancroft Global Development:** Fernand Koena, Jean. "US Firm Bancroft Eyes Wagner Group's Influence in CAR." *DW*, Jan. 4, 2024.

207 **skull of an Azovstal defender:** Kirby, Paul. "Notorious Russian Nationalist Igor Mangushev Shot Dead in Ukraine." BBC, Feb. 8, 2023.

207 **Wagner "solved the issue":** Friend of Igor Mangushev. 2024.

209 **objectionable to Washington:** Chason, Rachel. "U.S. Threats Led to Rupture of Vital Military Ties, Nigerien Leader Says." *Washington Post*, May 14, 2024.

209 **"lack of respect":** Ibid.

209 **"Ukraine and Israel":** Ibid.

IMAGE CREDITS

INDEX

A NOTE ON THE AUTHOR

JOHN LECHNER is a journalist and an independent researcher and consultant to NGOs and other institutions working in Africa. He holds a master's degree in foreign service from Georgetown University. He speaks Russian, French, Turkish, Georgian, Chechen, Sango, and more. His reporting has been featured in outlets such as the *New York Times*, the *Atlantic*, the *Washington Post*, and the BBC and published in *Foreign Policy*, *Lawfare*, and *War on the Rocks*, among others. A native of Boston, Massachusetts, he lives in Washington, D.C.